A TIME TO STAND

A TIME TO STAND

by WALTER LORD

BONANZA BOOKS
New York

This 1987 edition is published by Bonanza Books, distributed
by Crown Publishers, Inc., 225 Park Avenue South, New
York, New York 10003, by arrangement with Harper & Row
Publishers, Inc.

Manufactured in the United States of America

Library of Congress Cataloging-in-Publication Data

Lord, Walter, 1917–
    A time to stand.

    Bibliography: p.
    Includes index.
    1. Alamo (San Antonio, Tex.)—Siege, 1836.   I. Title.
F390.L66   1987   976.4′03   87-9237
ISBN 0-517-64299-9

h g f e d c b a

To SIMMIE FREEMAN

A group of illustrations follows page 112.
Maps are on pages 69, 103, 157, and 185.

CONTENTS

Foreword   11

1. "To . . . All Americans in the World"   13

2. "I Am Determined to Provide for You a Home"   19

3. "Come Forward and Assist Your Brethren"   41

4. "The Supreme Government Is Supremely Indignant"   62

5. "We Will Rather Die in These Ditches Than
   Give It Up"   75

6. "The Enemy Are in View"   92

7. "I Answered Them with a Cannon Shot"   100

8. "I Don't Like to Be Penned Up"   114

9. "30 Men Has Thrown Themselves into Bears"   123

10. "I Will Report the Result of My Mission"   132

11. "Take Care of My Little Boy"   141

12. "Great God, Sue, the Mexicans Are
    inside Our Walls!"   154

13. "It Was But a Small Affair"   167

14. "Remember the Alamo!"   180

Riddles of the Alamo   198

The Men Who Fell at the Alamo   213

Acknowledgments   220

Sources   227

Index   247

7

*"Thermopylae had her messenger of defeat
—the Alamo had none."*

General Thomas Jefferson Green, 1841

Foreword

These men were all kinds.

They were farmers, clerks, doctors, lawyers. There was a blacksmith . . . a hatter . . . a house painter . . . a jockey . . . a shoemaker . . . a Baptist preacher. Very few were the frontier type, although one was indeed the greatest bear hunter in all the West.

They came from Boston, Natchez, New York, Charleston, Philadelphia. From Illinois . . . New Jersey . . . Tennessee . . . eighteen states altogether. A few were from across the ocean, but only two or three had been in Texas as long as six years.

As a group, they had little in common—yet everything. For they were all Americans, sharing together a fierce love of liberty and a deep belief that the time had come to take their stand to keep it.

CHAPTER ONE

"To . . . All Americans in the World"

In the bare headquarters room of an improvised fort called the Alamo, Lieutenant Colonel William Barret Travis picked up his pen and began to write. Travis was a rebel, commanding some 150 other rebels, in the insurgent Mexican territory of Texas. He was hundreds of miles from the United States border—two weeks from New Orleans, a month from Washington—but it never occurred to him that his words were of limited application. With bold, unhesitating strokes, he addressed his message "To the People of Texas & all Americans in the world."

Outside, his men went about their duties. It was late afternoon, and some were already cooking supper in the large open space that formed the heart of the Alamo compound. Others hoisted the fort's best gun, a fine 18-pounder, onto a new mounting. Hot work, for it was surprisingly warm for this time of the year—February 24, 1836.

Still other men crouched behind the walls and barricades, squinting across the flat Texas landscape toward the hills to the north and east, some shanties to the south, or the little town of San Antonio de Bexar directly to the west. Here they could see a red banner flapping from the top of the town's church tower. And occasionally they also saw tiny figures moving about in the distance—soldiers of His Excellency General Antonio López de Santa Anna, President of the Republic of Mexico.

It was growing dark now—a good time for a courier to slip out unseen. Travis scribbled on, filling the page with dashes and hasty abbreviations, somehow in keeping with his quick, abrupt way of doing things. But there was always time to underline—once, three times a single phrase—and this too seemed in character, for he had a great flair for theatrics. Briefly, he explained his situation:

> Fellow citizens & compatriots—I am besieged, by a thousand or more of the Mexicans under Santa Anna —I have sustained a continual Bombardment & cannonade for 24 hours & have not lost a man—The enemy has demanded a surrender at discretion, otherwise, the garrison are to be put to the sword, if the fort is taken—I have answered the demand with a cannon shot, & our flag still waves proudly from the walls—I shall never surrender or retreat. Then, I call on you in the name of Liberty, of patriotism & everything dear to the American character, to come to our aid, with all dispatch—The enemy is receiving reinforcements daily & will no doubt increase to three or four thousand in four or five days. If this call is neglected, I am determined to sustain myself as long as possible & die like a soldier who never forgets what is due to his own honor & that of his country— Victory or Death.

A pause; then a short, moralizing postscript: "P.S. The Lord is on our side—When the enemy appeared in sight we had not three bushels of corn—We have since found in deserted houses 80 or 90 bushels and got into the walls 20 or 30 heads of Beeves."

No time for more. Now to get it out. A tricky assignment, which Travis gave to 30-year-old Captain Albert Martin. He came from Gonzales, the first stop some seventy miles away, and knew the country like a book.

The Alamo gate flew open, and before the startled Mexicans could move, the young Captain galloped off into the dusk. First south along the irrigation ditch . . . then left, onto the Gonzales road. Up the hill, by the white stone walls of the powder house, and out into the country.

Across the dry, little Salado Creek he raced, and on over the bare, winter landscape. No more houses now, just the scrubby mesquite trees, the occasional live oaks, the endless, rolling prairie. The only sound: his horse's hoofs, pounding through the silent, empty night.

All next day, the 25th, Martin rode on. Behind him he could hear the distant rumble of a heavy cannonade. They must be attacking, he thought, and rode harder. It was late afternoon when he passed Bateman's—his first house the whole day—and headed down into the flatland, or bottom, of the Guadalupe River. He splashed across the ford, up the bank, and onto a straggling little street of one-story frame houses. He had reached Gonzales at last.

"Hurry on all the men you can," Martin wrote on the back of Travis' dispatch. Young Launcelot Smithers, who would relay the message on, didn't need to be told. He had arrived from the Alamo himself the day before, bringing a brief estimate of the Mexican strength. Now he was rested, ready to ride to San Felipe, next stop to the east.

Smithers galloped off into the night. Ninety miles. The weather had shifted; a hard, icy wind now blasted his ears—one of the famous "northers" which Texans already boasted about with a streak of perverse pride.

It was early Saturday, the 27th, when Smithers finally reached San Felipe. He pounded down the main street—an uneven double row of houses, stores and saloons. This was the metropolis of Texas—the center of business and political life— and the news put the place in an uproar. At 11 A.M. the citizens held an emergency meeting and spent the next hour debating and shouting interminable resolutions. Smithers himself, a simple man, seemed closer to the heart of the matter. Adding his own postscript to Travis' dispatch, he scrawled, "I hope that Every one will Randeves at Gonzales as soon poseble as the Brave Soldiers are suffering. do not neglect the powder. is very scarce and should not be delad one moment."

More couriers sped the news on. Fanning out over the faint trails and roads, they headed north for the ambitiously christened new capital, Washington-on-the-Brazos . . . east for the lively gambling town of Nacogdoches . . . south for Columbia and the thriving Gulf settlements.

In ever widening circles, hurry and confusion, alarm and excitement. When the courier stopped by Dr. P. W. Rose's place at Stafford's Point, Mrs. Rose read Travis' message aloud to the children, and 11-year-old Dilue burst into a flood of tears. She recalled the time Travis had stopped at their place and sent her a little comb afterward.

No time for weeping, she was told; she spent the rest of the day melting lead in a pot, dipping it up with a spoon, molding homemade bullets. The older men in the family rushed to get ready for the army, and Mrs. Rose sat up all night sewing two striped hickory shirts—her idea of what a good militiaman should wear.

Now the news was at Columbia, thirty miles further south. Here the courier's horse broke down. No men around, so 15-year-old Guy Bryan jumped into his saddle and carried the word on to Brazoria and the Gulf. He reached Velasco late at night—probably March 4—feeling every inch a hero as he gave the message to the men at the little trading post.

Here the coastal schooners took over—spreading the story
to the bustling cotton ports that dotted the Gulf Coast—
Galveston . . . Mobile . . . Pensacola . . . and, of course,
New Orleans.

It was early in the morning of March 16 when Captain
Flaherty's boat brought first word to New Orleans, but by
that afternoon it was all over town. Crowds milled around
the *True American's* bulletin board, where Travis' dispatch
was posted. That night there was talk of little else at Hewlitt's
Coffee House. "This town is like a barracks," a New Orleans
businessman wrote a friend back East.

River steamers soon relayed the news up the Mississippi
. . . rickety little railways carried it inland . . . coastal pack-
ets headed for the Atlantic ports. Everywhere the reaction
was the same—intense excitement, indignation meetings, angry
editorials.

New York heard when the steamboat *Columbia* arrived
from Charleston on March 30. By afternoon the *Evening
Post* was hawking the story. "LATE FROM TEXAS," ran
that journalistic innovation, the headline.

At 4 o'clock that afternoon the Providence steamer pulled
out, and next day—only five weeks after Travis wrote his
message—even faraway Boston knew. Again, excitement
erupted everywhere—at the auction sales of coffee and spices,
at the tables of the Tremont House, in the lobby of the
Lion Theatre, where a new producer named W. Barrymore
was putting on *Little Goodie Two Shoes*.

Washington learned the same day, and here, as always, the
subject took on political overtones unknown to the rest of
the country. What would this do, asked the hangers-on at
Brown's Indian Queen Hotel, to the rumored negotiations
for the purchase of Texas from Mexico? A new Mexican
Minister, Señor Don Manuel Eduardo de Gorostiza, had just
been presented to President Andrew Jackson—how would

he take the news? The Whig paper *National Intelligencer*, against all such foreign adventures, happily prophesied an end to the scheme. But others saw it differently—these men in the Alamo were fellow Americans; they must be helped.

Whatever the reaction, the whole country was shaken. William Barret Travis knew what he was doing when he addressed his words to "all Americans in the world."

But how did he know? Travis was, after all, writing from a remote garrison in a distant land belonging to another country. And he himself carried no weight. Nobody even knew how to spell his name—the New York *American* called him "Travers" and the New Orleans *Bee* "Fravers." What made this unknown man in a faraway fort intuitively realize that his message was immensely important to all Americans everywhere? The answer lay in the years just past—a brief, turbulent period that shaped not only the future of Texas, but that of America itself for centuries to come.

"I Am Determined to Provide for You a Home"

CHAPTER TWO

America was already called the land of opportunity, yet it must have seemed anything but that to John Hubbard Forsyth of Avon, New York, on December 25, 1828. For him, nothing had ever gone quite right. His father had given him the best schooling—far better than most upstate farm boys got—yet he never made much use of it. Later, he studied medicine but didn't do anything with that either. And now, his wife had died on Christmas Day.

There are times when every man longs for a fresh start, and at this point John Forsyth decided to move. He packed his gear . . . left his baby son with his father . . . and headed west.

There were thousands like him—all trying to take advantage of something that had never happened before. For centuries men yearning to better their lot could do little about it: few opportunities, poor transportation kept them glued to one place. Even the opening of the New World didn't help much—travel remained as primitive and difficult as ever. Now suddenly all this was changing. Alongside the newspaper ads for candle tallow, sealskin caps and powder horns, strange new notices began to appear for things called boiler tubing,

flywheels and steam presses. New inventions, new machinery
—that whole complex miracle called the industrial revolution
was bursting into focus, changing the ways of centuries . . .
waking people up . . . getting them on the move.

"This is the age of locomotion," marveled the Baltimore
American. "For one person that traveled a hundred years
ago, there are now not a hundred, but a thousand." And it
was true. Passengers swarmed over the flimsy new railroads
that fanned out from the Eastern cities. Thousands more
jammed the steamboats that puffed along the rivers and the
coast—by 1830 seven lines served New York alone.

Time ceased to be an insoluble problem. The Boston-Phila-
delphia mail now took only thirty-six hours—against twenty-
one days a few decades ago. The New York *Commercial
Advertiser* found a Boston man who made a business trip to
Manhattan and back in less than thirty-three hours.

Along with the commercial travelers went a growing tide
of people with no set goal in mind. Discontented, disappointed,
or merely restless, they regarded the railroads and steamboats
as heaven-sent blessings that would let them escape from
their rut. Often they went first to the big cities—New York
grew 30 per cent between 1830 and 1835—but sooner or later,
they usually drifted west. Here, in the new towns springing
up—or along the vast, untouched frontier—hope and opportunity loomed brightest of all.

John Forsyth, crushed by his wife's death on Christmas
Day, was just such a man. So was John Flanders of Salisbury,
Massachusetts. Working in the family business, he had fought
with his father over foreclosing a mortgage. Young Flanders
lost . . . the situation was impossible . . . he cleared out.

Nor did it need a great family crisis to put a man on the
road. When Dr. Amos Pollard felt his New York practice
lagging, he simply took down his shingle and left. Dolphin
Floyd, a carefree North Carolina country boy, found farm

life unbearably dull. Gaily telling his family he was off to marry "some old rich widow," he sauntered westward and never returned.

Usually these men had no particular destination in view—just something better than they left behind. Young Daniel Cloud, a struggling Kentucky attorney, headed for Illinois where he heard there were more clients. But he found the weather too cold, the fees too low, and the "Yankee lawyers" too active. He pushed on to Missouri—and found the same story. Moving on to the rich Red River Valley of Arkansas, he finally discovered the life that suited him. He felt he could stay here forever.

For others it wasn't so simple. By 1830 far more people were on the move than the bustling but simple towns of the West could absorb. The Alexandria *Gazette* warned that the tide of immigrants to the Southwest was far too great and rapid. The New Orleans *Bee* lamented that the city was glutted with lawyers, doctors and accountants.

Yet New Orleans remained an irresistible lure. The city was no longer the easygoing Creole town of ten years earlier —the steamboat had changed all that. Now the waterfront was always jammed with steamers from St. Louis, Cairo, Louisville, a dozen other river ports. And as gateway to the interior, the harbor teemed with great sailing ships from all over the world. The shops bulged with New Bedford sperm candles, Richmond tobacco, New York lace goods, Swiss muslins, French cologne water, Naples umbrellas. The population was soaring toward 60,000, the sixth largest city in America.

It was almost inevitable that Dolphin Floyd, the gay Carolina farm boy, should drift here. Likewise Amos Pollard, the wandering New York physician; and John Flanders, still smoldering over the fight with his father back in Massachusetts. Mingling with them in the crowded arcades and coffee-houses were others with even less roots—men like dark, brawny Robert Cunningham, who left a secure Indiana home to float down the river on flatboats.

Together, they helped compose the busy, cosmopolitan world of New Orleans; yet basically, they were still drifting, and the fresh start remained as far away as ever. For only shrewd insiders were getting rich in this lively city, where the banks were chartering railroads and the railroads were chartering banks. The unknown and the unlucky continued to roam, searching for chances that never came. Even the great open land farther west was no longer a way out. The federal government, harassed by its own financial troubles, had stopped selling homesteads on credit.

Then suddenly word spread of still another opportunity— a new hope brighter than all the rest—a promised land just over the horizon: the Mexican province of Texas. It was said that the young republic was practically giving the place away—immense tracts for as little as four cents an acre. Perhaps here was that fresh start after all.

Hoping to develop her vast stretches of empty territory, Mexico had embarked on an ambitious program of colonization. Under laws of 1824 and 1825 foreigners were invited to settle in Texas and live for ten years free of taxes and duties. Every family got 4,428 acres of land for a nominal payment of $30—padded perhaps to $200 by the time Mexican bureaucracy had taken its bite. In return, the colonists had only to take the Mexican oath of allegiance and promise to be at least nominal Catholics. The whole program was put in the hands of contractors, called *empresarios*, who received huge grants of land in return for establishing colonies and bringing in settlers.

Led by Stephen F. Austin, a tactful administrative genius who had received his grant even before the general law, the *empresarios* went to work. Newspaper notices appeared, describing the wonderful sites available. McKean's bookstore in New Orleans blossomed with maps, showing the best routes. Guidebooks sang of the future: "No sturdy forest here for months defies the axe, but smiling prairies invite the plough. Here no humble prices reduce the stimulus to labor, but the reward of industry is so ample as to furnish the· greatest incentive."

Dolphin Floyd, Dr. Pollard, all the others quickly succumbed. The "Texas fever," as it was called, swept New Orleans and spread across the South. In Tennessee, a 26-year-old blacksmith named Almeron Dickinson told his bride to start packing. In Kentucky, Green B. Jameson, a lawyer with a mechanical bent, gathered his things too. Throughout the Mississippi Valley men scrawled "G.T.T." (Gone To Texas) on their cabin doors and headed for the border.

Soon the whole country knew. On a remote Missouri farm, Andrew Kent explained it all to his wife Elizabeth and began laying plans. Hiram Williamson, a footloose Philadelphia bachelor, decided there was room for him too. In Athens, Georgia, a wild 18-year-old named William Malone went on a drinking spree . . . couldn't face his martinet father . . . set off the following day. In Illinois, young Jonathan Lindley also got ready to go. His father had heard that the Mexican government gave families an extra 160 acres for every child—and the Lindleys had eleven.

Land was the magnet, but most of these people weren't just speculators hoping to turn a quick profit. Lewis Duel was a Manhattan plasterer . . . Marcus Sewell an English shoemaker . . . William Jackson a landlocked sailor.

They were, in fact, all types. Henry Warnell was as raucous a character as roamed the frontier. A freckled, red-headed little jockey, he drank hard, talked fast, and chewed mountainous wads of tobacco. Sometime in the early '30's he turned up in Arkansas . . . married (or didn't marry) a girl in Sevier County . . . found himself a father . . . decided it was time to move on to Texas.

Micajah Autry was the opposite. An adoring husband, he wrote poetry, sketched pictures and played the violin beautifully. But somehow he could never make any money. Born well-to-do in North Carolina, he tried his hand at "literary pursuits," teaching and the law. In 1831 he brought his family and slaves to Jackson, Tennessee, where he practiced a little, then opened a store. Of course it failed. Deciding Texas might be the answer, he headed west once more, planning to send for his family later. He was one of the last to come, but a letter to his wife Martha conveyed a thought that might well have been written by any of them: "I am determined to provide for you a home or perish."

One and all, they poured across the Sabine River and into the promised land. Some with great fanfare—like Sam Houston, the brilliant ex-governor of Tennessee. Houston had resigned in disgrace after mysteriously parting from his bride . . . brooded for a while among the Cherokee Indians . . . finally decided that Texas held the key "to grace his name for after ages to admire." But most came unnoticed, quietly putting up with immense hardships for this great new chance. It was August, 1830 when Jacob Darst piled his wife and two children on an oxcart and creaked away from his Missouri farm. Crawling over the faintest trails, lurching along dry stream bottoms, they took nearly six grinding, painful months to reach the Texas border.

But it was worth it. For once, the glib promoters were not exaggerating. Texas proved to be an eye-opening, breathtaking sight.

"It does not appear to me possible that there can be a land more lovely," wrote William Dewees, one of the first arrivals. "No language can convey anything adequate to the

emotion felt by the visitor," echoed David Edward, another
early traveler.

And indeed it did defy language, judging from the efforts
of Mary Austin Holley, whose handbook became almost a
bible: "One feels that Omnipotence has here consecrated in
the bosom of Nature and under Heaven's wide canopy, a
glorious temple in which to receive praise and adoration of
the grateful beholder."

The sheer abundance of everything staggered the imagination. No drought or falling water table had yet taken its toll.
The prairie was an endless sea of waving grass and wild
flowers—dahlias, geraniums, primroses, carpets of violets. The
fresh green river bottoms were thick with bee trees, all drip-
ping honey. Deep, limpid pools lay covered with lilies. The
streams were full of fish, and game was everywhere—bear,
deer, rabbits, turkeys, prairie chickens. Mustangs and buffalo
roamed at will—there for the taking.

It was enough to give birth to a Texas penchant for super-
latives that was destined to endure. Travelers described sugar
cane that grew twenty-five feet in a single season . . . pump-
kins as large as a man could lift . . . a sweet potato so big
that a whole family dined on it, and there was enough left
over to feed the pigs.

Exaggerated or not, the reaction was immensely significant.
It meant that at last these restless people had found what
they wanted. Old sorrows were forgotten in the discovery
of this great new land, and from the very beginning, they
were determined never to lose it again. "We're here all united
together," wrote William Dewees, "bound together by an
indissoluble tie. As the past has been full of bitterness, we
of course look forward to future happiness. . . ."

Some moved in among the Mexicans, settling in the sleepy
mission towns, the lazy Gulf ports, and especially the old

provincial capital of San Antonio de Bexar. Often known simply as Bexar, the town had been an important center in the days of Spanish rule. But with Mexico's independence, it became merely a neglected outpost and soon crumbled into decay. In ten short years, half the population left.

Yet, the place still had undeniable charm. During the hot, sunny day, brightly dressed Mexicans lolled against the flat-roofed adobe houses that lined the narrow streets. Others bathed in the sparkling little San Antonio River on the eastern edge of town, or gossiped in the two central squares whose names, Main Plaza and Military Plaza, carried a trace of past grandeur. In the evening, fires glowed in every yard, and guitar music drifted from half-closed doorways. Nobody worked very hard in San Antonio—just enough to stay comfortable.

It was hard for an American not to fall under the spell of this pleasant life. Nat Lewis, a shrewd young man from Falmouth, Massachusetts, opened a store on Main Plaza; by 1832 nearly everybody owed him money. John W. Smith, a versatile Missourian, became the town's leading carpenter, engineer, entrepreneur and boardinghouse keeper.

But of them all, Jim Bowie was the one who really stood out. To the settlers in Texas, this tall, sandy-haired man was a living legend. He had grown up in the tough sugar cane country of Louisiana. He had roped and ridden alligators. He had fought in that most famous of all frontier brawls, the Sand Bar Fight, where his big knife killed Major Morris Wright in one fierce thrust. He had used it in other fights too, so it was said, and although the details were hazy, nobody cared to take issue with him. He had made vast fortunes— $65,000 slave trading with the pirate Jean Lafitte . . . $20,000 on Arkansas land titles that already smelled of fraud . . . huge speculations in Texas; by now he was said to own a million acres. He had gone to San Antonio in 1828, turned

Catholic, become a Mexican citizen and married the richest girl in town—blond 19-year-old María Ursula de Veramendi. He had made still more money, survived countless adventures —like the fabulous Indian fight near the San Saba mine, where he and ten friends fought off 164 Indians for two days.

A typical performance, for Bowie was the toughest of fighters. But never in a rough-and-tumble way. On the contrary, he was smooth, polished, rarely raised his voice. But this very coolness somehow made him seem, when aroused, all the more lethal.

Such moments were rare, for Bowie was quite used to getting his way. Once, returning on an exhausted horse from deep inside Mexico, he fell in with Sam Houston. Bowie's greeting was brief and to the point: "Houston, I want your horse."

"You can't have him. I have only one and I need him."

"I'm going to take him," said Bowie, and left the room for a moment.

"Do you think it right," Houston asked a friend, "for me to give up my horse to Bowie?"

"Perhaps," answered the friend quietly, "it might be proper under the circumstances."

"Damn him, let him take the horse."

Yet Houston liked the man. Unlike Austin, who always sniffed at Bowie as an impossible adventurer, Houston saw in him the admirable qualities of a born leader, a good friend.

And Bowie was all this. Generous, even extravagant, he gave much to his friends and expected much in return. Once in San Antonio Bowie got into a fracas and asked a companion why he didn't offer better support. "Why, Jim," the man said, "you were in the wrong."

"Don't you suppose I know that? That's just why I needed a friend."

Underneath this hard, uncompromising approach ran a streak of curious gentleness. To people in distress he was instantly helpful. Once he intervened in a marriage ceremony to save a girl from a well-known charlatan. On another occasion he brought order to a rowdy congregation so that a frightened young Bible student might be heard. And in his relations with women he was positively courtly.

Perhaps it was this gentleness that made his marriage such a success. He was the most devoted of husbands, and Ursula a perfect wife. As the daughter of Vice Governor Juan Martín Veramendi, a proud aristocrat of pure Spanish blood, she might have been impossibly sheltered and aloof. Actually, she was wise, tactful and immensely helpful in Bowie's myriad business deals. She seemed especially useful in fending off various Mexicans who had given Bowie unsecured funds for investment. She would write him tactfully that "here they have another way of thinking." But whatever the problem, she would always close her letters: "Receive thou the heart of thy wife."

All this ended in 1833. When cholera broke out that summer, Bowie packed Ursula and their two children off to the safer climate of the Veramendi summer home at Monclova. Then he took off himself on a business trip East. He was in Mississippi when he got the shattering news—the cholera had swept Monclova too; Ursula, the children, her father and mother were all dead.

Bowie couldn't get over it. For months he grieved in Louisiana, then returned to San Antonio, where he tried to pick up the strings again. More dealing, but his heart was no longer in it. He lived a lonely life in the big empty Veramendi house on Soledad Street, surrounded by odds and ends of the past—Ursula's black dress, Ursula's apron. People noticed that he was drinking more than before.

Bowie's career was of course anything but typical. Few other Americans, even in San Antonio, mixed as deeply in

Mexican affairs. Most of the new arrivals took the opposite course—they stayed clear of the Mexicans completely. Instead, they formed new towns of their own, or settled in the American-dominated communities flourishing in eastern Texas. John McGregor, a jaunty Scot devoted to his bagpipes, moved to Nacogdoches near the Louisiana line. This was the convivial center for gamblers, smugglers and other shadowy figures who found it convenient to operate near an international border.

The more ambitious flocked to San Felipe, center of Stephen Austin's colony. Here Green B. Jameson set up a legal practice in 1830. He soon found he had anything but the town to himself. The place swarmed with lawyers, surveyors and investors of every sort. Everyone had a scheme to make money. Small deals involving a calf or two; big deals that made men giddy—like the huge land speculations of Samuel Swarthout, Collector of the Port of New York, who preferred Eastern life but had local lieutenants. They all played the game—Houston himself was Swarthout's man.

But the real strength of Texas lay not in the nimble minds of San Felipe; far more important were the sturdy families beating back the wilderness in little American settlements like Columbia, Brazoria, Gonzales. These people too loved their deals and swaps, but basically they had come to work, to farm, to build a new life in a new country.

It was not easy. One night at Gonzales Mrs. Isaac Baker barely escaped from a wildcat that sprang out from the dark and mauled her dog to death. Far worse, it might have been Indians—whooping and howling, stealing the horses, raiding the crops. When a party of Comanches murdered a French trader near Gonzales, the men of the town decided to act. Next day, Jacob Darst, Wash Cottle, Jesse McCoy and Almeron Dickinson helped avenge the killing with a raid on the Indian camp. No wonder these men found themselves gradually drawn together by tighter bonds than they ever dreamed possible.

Life was a challenge even when nothing was happening. The crude log cabins, with their puncheon floors and glassless windows, were anything but comfortable. Homemade stools and plank tables graced the rooms; gourds were used for glass and china. Clothes were buckskin or homespun, and had to be, for it was astronomically expensive to bring anything in. If Almeron Dickinson paid only four cents a pound for pork, he had to spend five dollars for a razor and two dollars for even a pencil.

It was hard on the women especially. The very roughness of the life gave a man satisfaction—hunting, fishing, riding the prairies, even the occasional "shooting scrapes." But the women put in long, lonely hours of drudgery—pounding corn into meal, spinning cotton, pouring soap, molding candles in cane stalks. There was more than a little truth in pioneer Noah Smithwick's observation that "Texas was heaven for men and dogs; hell for women and oxen."

But the good part made up for everything: the land . . . the spirit of sharing . . . decent neighbors . . . even a government that let a man alone. "A live mastodon would not have been a greater curiosity than a tax collector," remarked John J. Linn, another early arrival.

There seemed no limit to the Mexicans' easygoing tolerance. "So reasonable are all the parties in Mexico of the dependence on public sentiment," explained Woodman's *Guide to Texas Immigrants*, "that none have even ventured to attempt any change in the fundamental principles of government. Neither do the feuds of the different parties in Mexico reach Texas, or have any influence over the minds of the people there. The colony is too far off to feel the throes of political convulsion in Mexico."

It wasn't quite that simple. Mexico had gone through many political upheavals since the Colonization Law of 1825—and the government was indeed preoccupied with troubles closer to home—but down underneath was a growing, deep-rooted fear of "Anglo-American" expansion in Texas.

There was much to worry about. By 1830, Americans made up over 75 per cent of the population. American syndicates illegally controlled huge blocks of territory. American traders engaged in wholesale smuggling. American planters disregarded the government's stand against slavery. American settlers refused to pay taxes—only 1,665 pesos collected in two years. American families ignored the religious requirement; many openly called themselves "Muldoon Catholics" in honor of a genial San Felipe padre who didn't care what they did. To top it all, the American government itself was offering to buy the province, and each overture somehow conveyed the impression that if Mexico didn't sell, she would lose Texas anyhow.

And underlying everything was the difference in background and temperament. It hadn't mattered in the early days, but as the Mexicans realized they were losing control, the idea became an obsession. They bitterly pictured a host of Viking invaders, "possessed of that roving spirit that moved the barbarous hordes of a former age in a far remote north."

The first distant rumblings came in February, 1830, when the influential Mexican Minister of Relations, Lucas Alamán, blurted out his pent-up feelings on the subject. Action quickly followed. Under a new law that April, no foreigner could settle in Mexican territory bordering the country he came from—a clear slap at American immigrants. In addition, the law suspended all unfilled colonization contracts . . . ended the colonists' monopoly on coastal shipping . . . banned future slavery . . . required all foreigners to have passports issued by the Mexican Consulate at their place of residence.

Most trying of all, the colonists lost the duty exemption which Mexico had given them on essential goods and materials.

Things moved slowly in Mexico, but by 1831 General Manuel Mier y Teran was stationing troops all over Texas to see that the law was enforced. He jailed two minor officials . . . dissolved the council or *ayuntamiento* at the town of Liberty . . . closed all the ports except Anáhuac.

The Texans were indignant. They believed they were guaranteed self-government under the Mexican Constitution of 1824. Now it was being scrapped in favor of "centralism." They thought there was a tacit understanding about little things like smuggling and slavery—and suddenly this easy tolerance was gone. They felt cheated and deceived. Protest meetings were held; incidents erupted. A growing number of American settlers were sure that Mexico had finally shown her colors. The only course was for Texas to break free. Of this group, none was more vocal than William Barret Travis.

In many ways Travis was typical of these men who had come to Texas for a fresh start in life. Like so many others he came from the South—born 1809 near Red Bank, South Carolina. When he was nine, his family joined the great trek west, finally settling in southern Alabama. Here Travis grew up—a tall, raw-boned young man. He studied law in nearby Claiborne, taught school on the side to earn his way. This proved unexpectedly rewarding: in 1828 he married one of his pupils, Rosanna Cato, daughter of a prosperous farmer. They soon had a son, another child on the way. With a promising legal practice, Travis seemed heading for a smooth, if uneventful life.

Then came the crushing blow. The marriage blew up early in 1831. No one ever knew why, but Travis certainly considered Rosanna unfaithful. Loose tongues said he even killed the other man. In any case, he stormed away and headed west alone.

He turned up in Texas in May, 1831. Applying for his headright, Travis quickly fell in with the Texans' knack of burying the past. He listed himself as "single," later as "widower." He settled first in the little port of Anáhuac, then moved to San Felipe, where he plunged into the town's wildly varied legal practice. He wrote wills . . . recovered a stolen rifle . . . fought the sale of a blind horse. He took on anything and accepted any fee—once a yoke of oxen.

Socially, he was now very much a bachelor at loose ends. He lived out of a satchel at Peyton's boardinghouse, inveigling Mrs. Hamm to mend his shirts. He drank a little and gambled a lot—faro, monte, brag, poker—usually losing more than he won. He liked racy clothes; his white hat and red pantaloons were quite a sight in this buckskin community. And of course he had girls—casual affairs noted briefly in Spanish in the diary he meticulously kept. He liked wild evenings, and the dance after Christmas, 1833 must have been terrific. In his diary next day, all he could say was, "Hell among the women about party."

But that very night he fell in love again. She was Rebecca Cummings, a lively, capable girl who managed her brother John's inn at Mill Creek. Travis pursued her with schoolboy ardor. He bought her a brooch, took a lock of her hair. He gave her brother tobacco and legal advice. He explained about Rosanna and his plans for divorce. And she said she was willing to wait.

Meanwhile his practice prospered. No more stolen rifles and blind horses, he was now deep in land. By May, 1834 he needed a law clerk. And still the clients came: "Williamson retains me to represent the Alabama Company . . . retained by Hoxie to defend title . . . retained by Major Reynolds to defend eleven-league claim." Yet true to the Texas tradition, he could never resist even the smallest deal: one day he carefully wrote in his diary, "Gave a bad dollar for 50¢."

Typical, yet in many ways so different. Despite those gay evenings, Travis usually seemed formal and proper; it was no coincidence that his name was used as reference for a girls' boarding school. He was quite religious; he actively tried to persuade clergymen to come to Texas. He was intellectual—read Herodotus, Disraeli, Addison, Steele, Scott, even owned bookplates. He was farsighted: one of the first to back a steamboat for Austin's colony. He was moody, touchy, easily offended, given to long spells of reverie that once led a friend to write, "I almost think sometimes that was you with me, you could enjoy some pleasure."

Above all, he was ambitious. Intensely self-centered, by the time he was twenty-three he had already written his autobiography. He liked to dramatize himself and had a deep, almost mystical sense of mission. Perhaps the most significant line in his whole diary came the day after mud and high water kept him from visiting Rebecca: "*The first time I ever turned back in my life.*"

Such a man might never be popular—yet still be born to lead. Sheer ability and determination can do a lot; and Travis had plenty of both.

From the start his heart was with the American colonists in the growing friction with Mexico. By May, 1832, he felt it was time to act. When Colonel John Bradburn, the Mexican commander at Anáhuac, began using high-handed tactics to stop smuggling, Travis and his friend Patrick Jack warned Bradburn that a hundred angry colonists had risen in arms. The Colonel stayed up all night waiting for the onslaught, and it didn't help when he learned it was all a practical joke. He arrested both Travis and Jack.

Now the colonists really rose. Hundreds of them marched on Bradburn, demanding that the prisoners be released. They found Travis and Jack pinioned to the ground, with Bradburn threatening to kill them both if anyone fired a shot. It was a moment made for Travis. Dramatically he called on his friends to fire: he would rather die a thousand deaths than permit this oppressor to remain unpunished.

The colonists laid siege instead, and soon groups were rising all over eastern Texas. Ultimately the storm blew over. Bradburn was replaced, Travis and Jack were released, and an uneasy truce restored. Peace seemed insured by news of another revolution in Mexico—the fierce Presidente Bustamente was out, and the new strong man was General Santa Anna, a professed liberal who seemed sympathetic to the Texans. As a sign of good faith, customs duties were lifted for another two years.

Travis was not impressed, but a far more important Texan saw reason to hope. Stephen Austin, the original *empresario*, had always believed in co-operating with the government. In every way he tried to be a loyal Mexican citizen. Now he urged caution and patience with all his strength. The real source of Texas' troubles, he felt, lay in the poor local administration from distant Coahuila. The two provinces were run as one, but Texas had always been promised separate statehood as soon as it had enough people. Surely this new liberal government would agree that the time was ripe. He would go to Mexico City himself and persuade them to act. So, with a petition for statehood and a proposed constitution in his pocket, Austin hopefully set off for Mexico in the summer of 1833.

Travis remained unconvinced. By now he was a confirmed member of the so-called "War party," the group that saw no solution except rebellion and independence. By 1834 he was urging the Texans to set up their own government, whatever the Mexicans said. They would never get anywhere by waiting for Mexico to act.

And it certainly looked that way. Once entrenched, Santa Anna had turned into just another anti-American dictator.

Austin, after getting the run-around for months, was now in
jail in Mexico City. Yet times were certainly better than the
stormy days of Bradburn, and in the end the Texans decided
to wait a little longer. The "Peace party"—the group trying
to get along with Mexico—was in the saddle, and Travis had
to back down.

But trouble again erupted early in 1835. Santa Anna was
now more hostile than ever. He reopened the Customs House
at Anáhuac. He again slapped duties on the colonists. He sent
a new man, Captain Antonio Tenorio, to Anáhuac to see that
the Texans paid up.

Travis for once was quiet—jolted by an unexpected development that unnerved even this intensely determined man.
Rosanna had suddenly turned up from Alabama. She was in
Brazoria demanding that Travis either rejoin her or give her
a divorce. It was an easy choice to make. He probably would
have divorced her long ago, except that he was so absorbed
in all these great deeds and ambitious projects. He quickly
gave Rosanna her freedom but kept his little son Charles with
him in Texas. He hardly knew the boy, but he dreamed of
great things for him; he would give him fame and fortune
someday.

Now he could concentrate on Texas. Conditions were worse
than ever. The local legislature at Monclova was gone—closed
down by Santa Anna after it tried to raise money by selling
four hundred leagues of Texas land to hungry U.S. speculators. Most Texans were opposed to this step too—and no one
liked being governed from Monclova—but Santa Anna's solution left them even worse off. They now had no government
at all, and their representatives were under arrest.

Along the coast Mexican garrisons stepped up their campaign to stop smuggling and collect customs duties. At
Galveston they seized the Texas schooner *Martha*, loaded with

supplies for the colonists. A message taken from a careless Mexican courier hinted that even more troops were on the way. Angrily the settlers burned some lumber ordered by Captain Tenorio at Anáhuac.

Travis had a better idea. Late in June he raised a company of twenty-five men and marched on Tenorio's headquarters. He dramatically gave the Mexicans fifteen minutes to surrender or be "put to the sword." Tenorio quickly capitulated. He was then packed off to San Felipe, where he philosophically resigned himself to a pleasant evening at the Americans' Fourth of July Ball.

The colonists couldn't adjust that easily. They were shocked at Travis' audacity. This wasn't merely a case of smuggling, dodging customs collectors, or playing a practical joke on Colonel Bradburn. This was throwing out the garrison commander. Practically open rebellion. Few were ready to go that far.

Apologies . . . regrets . . . stern words for Travis. Repudiated, he lapsed into one of his moody spells. He published a note in the *Texas Republican* asking people to "reserve judgment." He morosely wrote a friend that he felt ashamed.

At this point, Santa Anna overplayed his hand. Deeming Travis' setback a sign of weakness, he decided that this was the time to finish off his enemies. During August he poured more troops into Texas and told his brother-in-law, General Martín Perfecto de Cós, to take personal command. Cós ordered the arrest of Travis and several other Texas troublemakers.

The Mexican leaders completely misinterpreted the situation. The Texans' real goal was to build a secure future without outside interference. They rebuked Travis because he seemed to be inviting a fight. Now they saw an infinitely greater threat—martial law, military occupation, the arrest of good friends. Almost overnight the pendulum swung the other way, and the people of Texas turned violently against Santa Anna.

Committees of Safety sprang up in every town. The highly influential *Telegraph and Texas Register* hammered away for liberty and freedom. Travis discarded his moody gloom; his letters now sang of "the hour that will try men's souls." Then on September 1 came an electrifying development—Stephen Austin suddenly reappeared from Mexico.

Next week a thousand people jammed the banquet given in his honor at Brazoria. The room fell silent as the trusted leader rose to speak. He had always preached moderation; after a year in Mexican jails, how did he feel?

He left little doubt. Santa Anna was destroying the people's rights; a General Consultation must be held—clearly a call for a provisional government. And on the question of Mexican troops in Texas, Austin was even more specific. The people had a strong moral sense that "would not unite with any armed force sent against this country; on the contrary, it would resist and repel it, and ought to do so. . . ."

A week later General Cós landed at Copano with 400 men. "WAR is our only recourse," thundered a broadside from Austin. Unfazed, Cós headed for San Antonio. Here the garrison commander Colonel Ugartechea had his hands full, confiscating weapons . . . searching houses . . . disbanding suspicious groups that re-formed as fast as he broke them up.

Word had just come of a serious problem at Gonzales. The colonists there were shining up a cannon—an old 6-pounder given them years ago to ward off Indians. Ugartechea quickly sent Lieutenant Castañeda with perhaps 100 men to take it away. Castañeda reached Gonzales on September 29, found the cannon was now well hidden. But in very plain sight was a group of armed men—Albert Martin, Almeron Dickinson,

Jacob Darst, eighteen altogether. They taunted him about the gun and told him to "come and take it."

Parleys . . . indecision . . . shoot or hold fire? While the two sides dickered, the Gonzales Committee of Safety frantically issued a call for help. Volunteers rushed to the scene, and the little force mushroomed to 150 on September 30 . . . 167 on October 1.

That night the Texans silently slipped across the Guadalupe; and in the fog-shrouded dawn of October 2, they groped toward the Mexican camp. They were sure Castañeda planned to attack this day; they might as well hit him first. Quietly, very quietly, they edged through the fog. With them was the cannon, dug up from the peach orchard where Albert Martin had buried it.

Someone tripped . . . a rifle went off . . . shouts of alarm in the Mexican camp. The Texans halted uncertainly, and at this moment the fog lifted, showing the two sides facing each other about three hundred yards apart. It was almost like a stage curtain going up, but the audience numbered only one: 16-year-old Johnny Gaston, who gaped with excitement, high in the branches of a live-oak tree.

Now more parleys. Again the Mexicans demanded the cannon; again the taunting reply, "Come and take it."

Suddenly a rattle of muskets—no one really knew who fired first. Next the cannon roared, spouting a shower of nails and old horseshoes at the Mexicans. A few scattered shots in reply, then Castañeda's men broke for the road back to San Antonio.

Ironically, William Barret Travis wasn't on hand for this climactic moment. Great men catch colds too, and he was at San Felipe, in bed with a bad sore throat.

But the revolution had begun. The men of Gonzales celebrated all night long. Then another victory—on October 9 Captain Collinsworth captured Goliad, two cannon and hundreds of muskets. More celebrating. Finally on October 13 the little "army"—now 500 strong—set out from Gonzales to throw General Cós out of Texas. Their leader was Stephen Austin. Their artillery was the old 6-pounder, mounted on two slices of tree trunk and drawn by oxen. Their banner— a white cloth decorated with black paint. At the top was a lone star . . . then a cannon barrel . . . and underneath, the neatly lettered words: "COME AND TAKE IT."

In San Antonio, General Cós grimly waited. The Texans would arrive soon, but he would be ready. He built barricades in the streets, stationed sharpshooters in the houses, even installed a small cannon on the church tower that commanded the area. Then he moved more guns and his own headquarters to a position that especially attracted him—an abandoned old mission with tough stone walls across the river just east of town. Occasionally used as a barracks, the mission had once sheltered a Spanish colonial company from Alamo de Parras in Mexico. The name carried over, and by now everyone called the place the Alamo.

CHAPTER THREE *"Come Forward and Assist Your Brethren"*

"Get up if possible a committee in your city," ran the scribbled appeal from Nacogdoches in the Philadelphia *Gazette* of October 24. "Call on those friends of liberty who aided the Poles and the Greeks, and they will I trust hold out their help to their suffering countrymen. Furnish us cannon and ball, rifles, muskets, powder, blankets. Lose no time. . . ."

The earthy Sam Houston was more specific. In a fervent letter planted in the Natchitoches, Louisiana, *Red River Herald*, he urged: "Let each man come with a good rifle and 100 rounds of ammunition—and come soon."

Planning his new law practice in the rich Red River country, Daniel Cloud heard the call for help. He had hoped to stay here—at last the fees were fat and the dockets large—but this changed everything: "The cause of philanthropy, of humanity, of liberty and human happiness throughout the world calls loudly on every man who can, to aid Texas."

Others felt the same. In Natchitoches crowds packed the Red River Exchange the night Houston's message appeared. Cheering wildly, they passed a resolution to send the Texans "all possible assistance in their struggle for liberty." In far-off Boston the *Morning Post* thundered, "BOSTONIANS! You who have so liberally contributed to the aid of the *Poles*, the *Greeks*, and others who have been fighting for liberty, come forward and assist your brethren. . . ." In Pennsylvania, farmer George Dedrick wrote his wife that he was off "to volenteer in ade of the caus of libertey."

"Liberty"—that was the word. It was no idle catch phrase then. It had yet to lose its shine through misuse and overuse. Far from it—the very sound stirred Americans to the depths of their souls. In 1835—barely fifty years after Yorktown— there were many people still alive who knew the exhilarating call of freedom. Even some who had fought for it in battle. And many had a father, or uncle, or brother who had been at Breed's Hill, Cowpens, Valley Forge. For these people, liberty—anybody's liberty—had very real meaning. It was something to fight and die for.

To this legacy of their fathers these Americans added a touch of their own—a romantic rediscovery of heroic Sparta . . . glorious Athens . . . the chivalry of gallant knights. For this was the great romantic revival—the age of Byron and Scott. It was no coincidence that Travis borrowed three Scott novels in one winter . . . or that the New York *Commercial Advertiser* featured the new Dearborn edition of Byron.

So when the Greeks rose against the Turkish Sultan—and the Poles against the Czar—Americans too thrilled at freedom's banner "torn but flying." They poured out money and supplies, and shed their tears when Byron died in Greece. In Congress, Sam Houston made his maiden speech on behalf of Greek independence.

Scott clothed such deeds with a special kind of glory—the romance and pageantry of medieval times. Carried away by the vogue for his rich, rolling prose, the press saw the Greeks, the Poles, and now the Texans, as more than brave men fighting for liberty—they were also "chivalrous" and "knightly." Those who rallied to their cause need have no fears, whatever the outcome:

> One crowded hour of glorious life
> Is worth an age without a name.

Most thrilling of all, these Texans were Americans. The Greeks and Poles might be just as gallant, but they were far away. The men and women across the Sabine were friends and relatives. They came from no hallowed plain of Marathon —they were from Boston, Charleston, Natchez, the farm down the road. As the citizens' resolution at Natchitoches, Louisiana, so fervently put it, the Texans were "bone of our bone and flesh of our flesh."

It was hard to resist such a cause—especially when seasoned with the promise of land. After all, even a chivalrous warrior expects his rations; even the noblest patriot will take his veteran's benefits. Sam Houston understood perfectly, and his first appeal for help—carried all over the country—devoted as much space to real estate as to the rights of Texas: "If volunteers from the U.S. will join their brethren in this section, they will receive liberal bounties of land. We have millions of acres of our best lands unchosen and unappropriated."

Daniel Cloud got the point. Writing home from the Texas border, he neatly phrased the feelings of a man basically moved by idealism, but who also saw the practical side of the matter: "If we succeed, a fertile region and a grateful people will be for us our home and secure to us our reward. If we fail, death in defense of so just and so good a cause need not excite a shudder or a tear."

It worked the other way too. Hundreds of men simply going to Texas for a fresh start saw their quest somehow ennobled by this battle for liberty. What began as a practical venture turned into a great crusade. When Micajah Autry set out from Tennessee in the fall of 1835, he had no interest in anybody's revolution. "Childress thinks the fighting will be over before we get there," he hopefully wrote his wife from Memphis on December 7, 1835. A month on the road and he was writing differently: "I go the whole Hog in the cause of Texas. I expect to help them gain their independence and also to form their civil government, for it is worth risking many lives for."

It was rarely all black and white. Some men were driven by dazzling Byronic visions, yet were not blind to the rich land that might be waiting. Others were initially interested in land, but soon inspired by dreams of a noble cause. Whichever they were—and whatever the mixture of motives—the brew was strong indeed. The combination of idealism and self-interest somehow made men all the more ardent, all the more spirited, all the more determined.

A frenzy of "Texas meetings" swept the land. Philadelphia mobs burned Santa Anna in effigy. Bostonians jammed the Concert Hall to hear Major General John S. Tyler pour his wrath on Mexican tyrants. In Mobile crowds packed the courthouse on October 20, demanding Texas independence. They set up a Committee of Twenty to organize help, and in the parliamentary fashion of the day, they ordered that a "copy of the proceedings" be taken to Texas by one of their leaders—a dark, dashing South Carolina aristocrat named James Butler Bonham. Passionately for the cause, filled with a glowing sense of *noblesse oblige*, Bonham was a man not likely to let them down.

Money poured out. At Mobile's Shakespeare Theater, a rally quickly produced $1,500. . . . The citizens of Macon, Georgia, collected $3,150. . . . Henry Hill of Nashville gave $5,000. . . . Natchez theatergoers raised $396.50 at a symbolically appropriate benefit performance of *Damon & Pythias.*

New York outdid itself. First a big meeting at Stoneall's Tavern. Next, a benefit performance of *The Tragedy of Venice Preserved*. Then, on November 12 a rally at Tammany Hall, where over two thousand people roared their "loyalty" to Texas. Soon it was necessary to set up a receiving station at McDonald & Arnold's warehouse on Front Street for the avalanche of stores and contributions that rolled in.

"Texas, Texas," sighed the Philadelphia *Courier*'s New York correspondent. "Crowded meetings, and gun-powder speeches, calling down vengeance upon the oppressors of the Texonians, is the order of the day.

"This going abroad patrioting is bad business," the writer added mysteriously. "I speak with some experience."

He must have been a Whig. For, apart from a handful of Abolitionists, only the Whig press remained cool. "Their quarrel is altogether a private affair," insisted the Baltimore *Chronicle*. "We have a right to sympathize, but more than that we cannot do," warned the New York *Commercial Advertiser*, pointing to the U.S. treaty of friendship with Mexico.

The New Orleans *Commercial Bulletin* had the answer to that: "Let the government of our country bow to the supremacy of law. As individuals, we do not, or cannot feel ourselves bound by cold and heartless rules; and when the cry of the oppressed reaches our shores, we long to buckle on our armour, and shoulder to shoulder, contend with freemen against their cruel oppressors."

All New Orleans agreed. The whole place was in an uproar. Excited groups swirled about the lobby of Richardson's Hotel, planning great things for Texas. On the waterfront, gangs of slaves sweated in the hot autumn sun, loading cannon and kegs of powder on the schooner *Columbus*. Cheering crowds jammed the rally at Banks Arcade. Another throng at the Arcadia Coffee House pledged $10,000 within minutes. At this point Adolphus Sterne, a visiting Texas leader from

Nacogdoches, shouted that the cause needed not only dollars but men. He had just bought fifty rifles—the first fifty volunteers could have them.

Hundreds of men surged forward . . . clawing, wrestling, stampeding for the guns. Ready-made gray uniforms appeared from nowhere, and almost magically, the New Orleans "Greys" were born. In fact, it turned out there were two separate sets of "Greys," for in the confusion, two different men assumed command and signed up volunteers. Little matter, Texas could use both groups.

The appeals, the rallies, the spirit in the air did their work. All over the country men swarmed toward Texas, usually carrying the prescribed "good rifle and 100 rounds of ammunition."

David Cummings of Lewistown, Pennsylvania, did even better than that. His father, a prosperous Harrisburg canal man who proudly claimed friendship with Sam Houston, bought a box of rifles from the state arsenal and sent them along with the boy.

In their enthusiasm, men simply jettisoned whatever they had been planning to do. William Irvine Lewis, a 23-year-old Philadelphian, was visiting a friend in North Carolina when he heard the call. He abandoned all thoughts of returning home, joined the march for the Sabine. Robert Musselman of Ohio had just finished a hitch against the Seminoles in Florida. His father had died, and certainly he should be getting home. Not at all; he too headed for Texas.

Some traveled alone, riding along the rocky trails that led over the Blue Ridge and down into the Mississippi Valley— like James M. Rose, the hot-tempered, sandy-haired nephew of Ex-President Madison. Others came in twos and threes— like John Purdy Reynolds and his friend William McDowell of Mifflin County, Pennsylvania. They had always done things together: first, the move to help found a new Mifflin in Tennessee; now this, the most exciting dream of all.

But more and more they came in whole battalions—sometimes garishly dressed, usually boisterous, always with stars in their eyes. Major Ward's Georgia battalion . . . Captain Duval's Kentucky Mustangs . . . Captain Shackleford's Red Rovers of Alabama . . . Captain Burke's Mobile Greys, largely organized by James Bonham.

The North was active too. Around the end of November, a large company of Germans piled aboard a Pittsburgh steamboat and set off down the Ohio. In Boston, Lieutenant Wheelock herded his "Dragoons" aboard the steamer for New York, where they transferred to the ship for Texas.

They were not all perfect. As the brig *Matawamkeag* headed south with 210 volunteers from New York, their commander Colonel E. H. Stanley had a bright idea. Taking seventeen of his men in a long boat, he raided a Bahama plantation, was caught in the act by the English brig *Serpent*. Months would pass before these patriots escaped from the toils of British justice.

No such pitfall awaited Captain Breece's "first" company of New Orleans Greys. Leaving the other contingent of Greys still waiting for a ship, Breece's men marched for the border. Legend later turned them into aristocrats—the flower of local society. Actually they were anything but that; few had even been in Louisiana longer than six months. Spirited and restless, they perfectly reflected the shifting currents that made their city the most cosmopolitan center in America.

These New Orleans volunteers were English, German, Scottish, Irish, Americans from north and south. Men like Henry Courtman, a lively young German . . . John J. Baugh, an idealistic if somewhat officious Virginian . . . or Stephen Denison, an amiable Irishman who had roamed from Galway to

Louisiana, trying his hand at glazing, painting, anything. By now a number of those traveling to Texas alone had been swept up in this congenial company, and they happily mixed with the rest—William Linn of Boston . . . Robert Mussel-man of Ohio . . . Robert B. Moore, a 55-year-old private from Virginia who was easily the senior member of the group.

Emotionally, some threw themselves on the ground and kissed the sacred soil when they crossed the Sabine into Texas. A pretty girl greeted them with a handsome banner. It was fittingly romantic: azure blue, fringed with gold. Bold black letters proclaimed "FIRST COMPANY OF TEXAN VOLUNTEERS! FROM NEW-ORLEANS." And in the center a flying eagle bore the proud legend "GOD & LIBERTY."

Giddy with joy the Greys marched on to St. Augustine, where a crowd of colonists noisily greeted them. The town's drummer thumped out a salute, but it was much too mild for these carefree men. Showing him how to do it, the Greys' own drummer broke into the furious beat of "Beer in the Mug." Henry Courtman, Stephen Denison, all the rest yelled with joy.

At Nacogdoches Adolphus Sterne happily welcomed them. He was the one who had started everything by offering the fifty rifles; he was ready with hospitality now. And when he heard that there were German boys in the company, he came up with something extra. "Bob," he called to his Negro, "four of the long slender ones out of the stand in the corner. Do you understand?"

The bare thought of Rhine wine was too much for Henry Courtman. He shouted that he would give his last drop of blood for the new republic.

"Halt, my countrymen," cried Sterne, introducing the Greys to their first taste of Texas politics. "Do you want to stir up the whole of Mexico against us—even the Liberal party? No, another time."

There was good reason for caution. The Texans were still split on whether to seek complete independence or simply their true rights under the 1824 Mexican Constitution. At the moment, they only knew they would have to fight, whatever their choice.

The Greys stood firm, arguing hotly against halfway measures. They hadn't come this far to fight under any flag of Mexico. Sterne mildly protested, but the men noticed that he joined the rest when the wine appeared and they roared a toast, "To the Republic of Texas!"

It was the same with all who came. Men who had never given a thought to Texas three months earlier suddenly found themselves the most violent patriots. "I am over the Rubicon and my fate is now inseparably united with that of Texas," wrote young John Sowers Brooks only three days after he arrived from Virginia. "I have resolved to stand by her to the last, and in a word, to sink or swim with her."

And trying on their new patriotism, men felt an exhilaration, a tingling satisfaction that many had never known before. Micajah Autry—aesthete, poet, violinist, business failure—wrote his wife Martha from Nacogdoches, "I have become one of the most thorough-going men you ever heard of." He closed his letter with a piece of exciting news: "P.S. Colonel Crockett has just joined our company."

If the postscript was meant to impress her, it must have succeeded. There could be no stronger reference for a reformed poet than Colonel David Crockett, lately Congressman from Tennessee. His syntax jolted people even in an era that cared little about spelling and grammar. His coonskin cap, buckskin shirt and Indian moccasins made a virtue of backwoods ignorance. His rifle was his substitute for learning—it had brought him political success, national fame. He was the man who shot forty-seven bears in one month . . . who killed six bucks in one day . . . who rode alligators for exercise . . .

who grinned a bear into retreat . . . who once aimed up a tree, only to have the coon come down and surrender.

Typical Crockett humor. Unfortunately, most of his jokes were just a façade. A brave front for a simple man who had swum far out over his head. For warm, kindly David Crockett was as naïve as they came. Born with all the right instincts, he had little depth and was too lazy or restless to acquire it. He loved politics, but it was so much easier to get by with a joke, or the backwoods role he so carefully cultivated.

"When a man can grin and fight, flag a steamboat, or whip his weight in wildcats, what is the use of reading and writing?" he liked to say. Actually, he could do both perfectly well; but here too there was an easier way, and he gradually relied more and more on ghost writers.

The formula worked all right at first. Uneducated, gregarious, articulate, a marvelous hunter, Crockett was a political natural on the frontier. Appointed a magistrate in western Tennessee in 1817, he was fair, honest, and it took no great depth to referee bounty payments for wolf scalps. He was soon elected colonel of the local militia.

Advancing to the Tennessee Legislature in 1820, he found that warmth and color were still enough. He had the frontiersman's love of rough-and-tumble antics, the heavy practical joke. He once delighted his constituents by using his opponent's speech word for word during a joint stumping tour in the 1823 campaign.

He moved on to Congress in 1827 and for a while the old magic worked even in Washington. The capital quickly took to this friendly man with the tall stories and coonskin trappings. For his part, Crockett showed little interest in affairs—only a distaste for authority (particularly West Point) and a single-tracked desire to see that the people of the frontier could keep the open land they were squatting on.

The state and federal governments had other ideas. They

hoped to raise revenue by selling the land. Bitterly fighting this policy, Crockett narrowly lost a bid for re-election in 1831, squeaked in again two years later. Through it all, he never could adjust or compromise. In the Colonel's uncomplicated mind, every issue took the form of selfish interests against the honest poor. Andrew Jackson and the Democrats who opposed free land were clearly grasping villains. Anybody who supported his own position was automatically public-spirited. There was no need to look for deeper motives.

The Whigs found this very convenient. They were getting much too big a reputation as the party of affluence, of Nicholas Biddle and his powerful United States Bank. They badly needed a little backwoods respectability. Who better than David Crockett? And who easier to reach—with his love of the limelight, his gullibility, his weakness for the easy way?

They wined him and dined him . . . laughed at his jokes . . . sponsored his meetings. The great Daniel Webster shook his hand. The United States Bank lent him money. The Young Whigs of Philadelphia gave him a rifle, and Mr. du Pont came through with some powder. Whig clubs packed his rallies; Whig papers pushed his books; Whig ghosts wrote his speeches. By 1834, David Crockett—who liked to boast that he would never wear a collar marked "My Dog, Andrew Jackson"—was actually the best-trained dog in Washington. In one canned speech full of references that must have mystified him, he labeled Jackson "a greater tyrant than Cromwell, Caesar or Bonaparte."

At this point Old Hickory had enough. In the 1835 Congressional campaign, he tore into "Crockett and Co.," as he contemptuously called the Colonel. David fought back, told his constituents that he had done his best for them; if they didn't re-elect him, they could go to hell—he would go to Texas.

It was no use. Crockett lost the election by 230 votes. He

was already unwelcome in the Democratic camp; now the Whigs, having no use for a loser, quickly abandoned him too.

"I am on the eve of Starting to the Texas," he wrote his brother-in-law on October 31. "On tomorrow morning myself, Abner Burgin and Lindsy K. Tinkle & our nephew William Patton from the Lower Country—this will make our Company. We will go through Arkinsaw and I want to explore the Texas well before I return." Nothing about fighting for liberty; the Texas revolution was going full blast, but it was not for him. Crockett wanted only the tonic of exploring new places once again . . . the thrill of staking out a new claim on a new frontier . . . the fun of hunting, riding, joking and laughing with good companions . . . a chance to rinse out the bitter taste of Washington.

It was nothing new. He had always shoved on when things went against him. He did it as a 12-year-old, when he ran away after four days of school. Again, after the flash flood wrecked his little mill in 1817. Other times too. Nor was family a problem to this most casual of men. As he later explained to a shocked lady in Big Prairie, "I have set them free—set them free—they must shift for themselves."

It was all the more important, for time was running out. Crockett was nearly fifty now. His face was flushed; his 190 pounds were no longer distributed the way they used to be. This might be his last chance—his last great opportunity— nothing must interfere.

Starting down the Mississippi on November 1, Crockett felt truly content for probably the first time in years. By his side, significantly, was "Betsey"—the rifle he used in the old days—not "pretty Betsey," the fancy gun he got from the Whigs. Around him were long-time friends—none of those scheming Washington lackeys.

They caroused all night in Memphis—Crockett delivering his "go-to-hell" speech at the Union Hotel bar, again on a flatboat just below the Gayoso Hotel. More drinking and parties at every place the steamboat touched along the Mississippi. Then west on the Arkansas River, arriving finally at Little Rock on November 12. By now the group had increased to eight or ten; Crockett always seemed to pick up new companions on a trip like this.

When a committee of Little Rock citizens waited upon Crockett, they found him skinning a deer in the back yard of the City Hotel. They suggested a shooting match and Crockett was delighted—legend says he gaily put an extra bullet in the hole made by his first shot, to insure himself a second bull's-eye. Then to the banquet table, and past disappointments must have seemed far away indeed as the fife and drum burst into "Hail, the Conquering Hero Comes."

On through the thickets to the Red River country. At Fulton he accumulated still more followers. At Clarksville, Mrs. Isabelle Clark, a magnificent pioneer woman, galloped after the party, shouting a timely warning of hostile Indians. At Lost Prairie, Crockett found himself running out of money, worked out a swap with Isaac Jones. In exchange for Jones' silver watch and thirty dollars, Crockett handed over the magnificent gold watch given him by the Whigs in Philadelphia—to hell with that too.

Now south, across the Sabine, and Texas at last. The good news had gone ahead, and when Crockett reached Nacogdoches on January 5, the town's cannon banged out a salute. More cheers, more limelight. Another banquet, another chance to describe how he told them back home to go to hell. Another standing ovation.

Crockett was walking on air. Only a few months ago he felt crushed by political defeat; now "I had rather be in my present situation than to be elected to a seat in Congress for life." Last autumn he never expected to run again for anything; now "I have but little doubt of being elected a member to form a constitution for this province." In November, he wasn't remotely interested in Texas revolutions; now he was about to enroll as a volunteer and plunge into the fighting.

Liberty? He outdid them all. When Judge John Forbes administered the oath of allegiance, Crockett dramatically stopped the proceedings. He noticed that he was required to uphold "any future government" that might be established. That could mean a dictatorship. He refused to sign until the wording was changed to "any future *republican* government." The judge obligingly inserted the change and the ceremony continued.

The volunteers drifting around Nacogdoches were enchanted. The idealist Daniel Cloud and his lawyer friends yearned to join this magnetic man. John Purdy Reynolds, the crusading Pennsylvania doctor, and his old friend William McDowell couldn't wait either. Crockett told them to come along—there was always room for a good companion. The "Tennessee Company of Mounted Volunteers" was born and immediately prepared to head for San Antonio.

But first, a brief diversion. A quick trip to St. Augustine for another big welcome. More saluting cannon . . . a gala ball . . . then back to Nacogdoches for the long ride to the army. Just before leaving St. Augustine, Crockett found time for one of his rare letters to his children. It was a happy letter, bursting with enthusiasm and closed with the assuring words: "Do not be uneasy about me. I am among friends."

By now these "friends" also included James M. Rose and Micajah Autry, still relishing his new virile life. But there were times when even the most exuberant felt a twinge of sadness, a faint longing for things left behind. Standing guard under the January moon one crystal night, Autry's mind drifted to home and Martha. "With what pleasure did I contemplate that lovely orb," he wistfully wrote her, "chiefly because I recollected how often you and I had taken pleasure in standing in the door and contemplating her together. Indeed I imagined that you might be looking at her at the same time. . . ."

Every man knew these moments of loneliness—and other hardships as well. The banquets and toasts were always remembered longest, but in between were days of toil and drudgery . . . slogging hundreds of miles through rain, mud and racing streams.

There was sickness too—especially smallpox. It was all very well for Micajah Autry to say he feared the tavern bill more, but he was traveling with Crockett. Hundreds of others weren't so lucky: lower tavern bills, but miserable days of chill and fever. Falling by the wayside, they had little care except that provided by rough, kindly "doctors," whose chief medical qualification seemed to be an inventive mind. "A good receipt for a cough alcoholic," Dr. J. H. Barnard noted in his ledger: "Tincture Cannabis India three ounces; Extract of Calabria Liquorice half pound; salts of tartar one-eighth pound; warm water one gallon." Under such ministrations, it took a deep love of liberty indeed to march to the rescue of Texas.

Many preferred to come by sea. They had their hardships too—rolling in the coastal swells, thirsty under the hot Gulf sun, bumping over the off-shore sand bars—but at least no fever or mud or aching feet. The New Orleans shipping notices ticked them off—the second company of Greys on the schooner *Columbus* . . . 62 men on the steamboat *Quachita* . . . 15 more on the schooner *Santiago*.

The little group that boarded the *Santiago* on December 7 was typical. Impressed by Captain Lentner's glowing notice of his "splendid accommodations," they took passage—strangers from ten different states. Richard W. Ballentine was a 21-year-old country boy, fresh from a big family of brothers and sisters in Marengo County, Alabama; Cleland K. Simmons was a tidewater aristocrat from Charleston, South Carolina.

A couple of days out, they all jammed into the *Santiago's* cramped little cabin (they never found the "splendid accommodations") and put their feelings on record: "We hereby declare that we have left every endearment at our respective places of abode in the United States of America to maintain and defend our brethren, at the peril of our lives, liberties and fortunes."

Noble words but hard to prove. For as the new arrivals converged on San Antonio, they found little going on. By November 1, Cós was bottled up in town and the nearby Alamo, while the Texans surrounded him in a loose, sprawling circle. No one knew what to do next.

Leadership had all but disappeared. Stephen Austin left to rally support in the United States. General Edward Burleson, who replaced him, seemed to have no heart for fighting. Jim Bowie, although devoted to the cause, showed only flashes of his old fire. In October he led a force that routed the Mexicans at Concepción; on the other hand, he twice tried to resign.

Travis dashed about . . . scouting, burning grass, capturing Mexican horses. But these weren't the deeds of a Famous Man, and on November 6, he too tried to resign. He explained vaguely that he could no longer be useful "without complaints being made"—odd excuse for a Byronic hero. He was briefly mollified, but later in the month he did pull out. Riding to San Felipe, he joined the General Consultation that was setting up the Provisional Government of Texas.

The siege dragged on, with little to do. The inactive troops grew restless and quarrelsome. One damp November day a man named Conway killed Sherod Dover of Captain Coleman's Company. The men hung Conway from a pecan tree, and the incident would have been forgotten—except that

Dover's name was later enshrined in another, mistaken connection.

Then the camp snapped to life on December 2. Two of San Antonio's American residents, Sam Maverick and John W. Smith, escaped from town; reported that the Mexicans were starving, dispirited, low in ammunition. The newcomers urged immediate attack and offered a plan, backed by maps that Maverick had smuggled out.

For two days Burleson hesitated, still unwilling to fight. Then a leathery plainsman named Ben Milam finally lost patience, emerged from the General's tent shouting, "Boys, who will come with old Ben Milam into San Antonio?" A roar of approval, and 240 men joined up.

Shortly before dawn on December 5, they advanced on the town. For four days they fought house to house, hand to hand. It was slow, dangerous work—Ben Milam himself was shot by a sniper, fell dead in Sam Maverick's arms. But the Texans moved steadily forward, and one by one the strong points fell—the Navarro house, the Zambrano row, the priest's house.

At 6:30 A.M. on December 9 General Cós had enough. Surrender negotiations began, and by 2 o'clock the following morning the terms were set. Cós agreed to retire beyond the Rio Grande under parole; he and his officers would "not in any way oppose the re-establishment of the Federal Constitution of 1824."

"All has been lost save honor," bemoaned Captain José Juan Sánchez Navarro, appointed by Cós to sign the surrender document.

"A child's bargain," snorted volunteer William R. Carey of Baltimore, mulling over the same agreement. "However, it's done now and it's too late to alter until we have another fight, which we expect shortly."

Most of the Texans preferred Captain Sánchez' view—
Mexico had suffered a crushing defeat. The danger was over.
General Burleson went home to his family. Creed Taylor of
York's Company returned to his cabin on the Guadalupe with
enough trophies to pass for a Mexican—a sleek new horse,
silver-mounted saddle, costly bridle, splendid silk sash, silver
spurs. The scene was repeated everywhere as the colonists left
the army to rejoin their families, celebrate Christmas and
begin farming again.

Many of the American volunteers were equally anxious to
leave San Antonio now that the fighting was over. Dr. James
Grant, a shrewd Scot, sensed this and proposed an exciting
project. Why not carry the war to Mexico itself? The country
below the Rio Grande was full of liberals who would rally
around. If the volunteers took the port of Matamoros, they
would find plenty of friends—and magnificent booty too. Dr.
Grant happened to be a large landowner in that area; he stood
to gain immensely if his confiscated estates were liberated, but
nobody bothered to look for a hidden motive. The idea
sounded perfect. The men seethed with excitement; most
could hardly wait to get going. Colonel Frank Johnson, now
in command, was all for it too. He turned the post over to
Colonel James C. Neill and dashed off to get the provisional
government's blessing.

Grant didn't bother to wait. On December 30 he set out,
taking 200 of the men with him. They marched off in a blaze
of enthusiasm—their eyes on the loot of Matamoros, their
hands on the loot of San Antonio. For they appropriated practically everything in sight—money, clothing, saddles, arms,
food, blankets, medical supplies. Behind them they left only
picked-over Mexican junk that nobody wanted—30 useless
muskets . . . 2 trumpets, 1 large clarion . . . 15 carabines,
out of order.

"It will be appalling to you to learn and see herewith our

alarming weakness," Colonel Neill wrote the authorities in San Felipe on January 6, 1836. He had only 104 men. There was no food or clothing. Many of the volunteers were down to one shirt and one blanket. "If there has ever been a dollar here, I have no knowledge of it."

A week later, conditions were even worse. On January 14 the men were to get their October pay, but nothing turned up. Next morning Neill was down to 80 effectives: a few hungry colonists and volunteers, a handful of shivering New Orleans Greys. Clearly he couldn't hold both the town and the Alamo with a force like this. He ordered the men in Bexar back across the winding little San Antonio River and concentrated his whole strength in the rambling old mission just east of town.

"You can plainly see that the Alamo never was built by a military people for a fortress," Green B. Jameson wrote Sam Houston on January 18. Jameson, the mechanically minded lawyer, had cast aside his San Felipe practice to become the Alamo "engineer." He had no technical background, but it didn't require professional training to see the fort's many weak points.

The old mission, mostly built by 1750, was a large, sprawling compound of buildings taking up over three acres. Heart of this compound was a rough rectangle of bare ground, flatteringly called "the plaza." It was about the size of a city block and was bordered by various walls and buildings.

On the south side of the plaza was a long, one-story building called the "low barracks"; it was pierced by the Alamo's main entrance. Along the west side—which faced the town about 400 yards away—ran a haphazard line of adobe huts, linked and protected by a strong stone wall about twelve feet high. Across the north end ran a similar wall. The east side was banked by the so-called "long barracks." This two-story building was extremely strong and got extra protection from walls bordering a corral that lay in the rear. But the "long barracks" stopped considerably short of the southern side of the plaza, leaving the rectangle incomplete. The gap, however, was partly filled by the most eye-catching building of all—the Alamo church.

Through years of neglect, the church was now a ruin, but it still was the sturdiest building in the compound. Its walls were four feet thick, and although most of the roof was gone, the sacristy and several small rooms along one side were arched and well covered. The center was filled with debris— due mainly to Cós, who had ineffectually tried to fortify the place before surrendering in December. He built a platform at the eastern end, reached by a ramp of earth and timber that ran almost the whole length of the nave.

Although strong and durable, the church was set back so far that it still didn't meet the south side of the compound. There remained a diagonal gap of about fifty yards in the southeast corner. This gap was the Alamo's most glaring weakness, but there were other problems almost as big. Although the walls were wonderfully thick—usually two to three feet— they had no embrasures or barbettes. They were mostly twelve feet high, yet there were no parapets. An *acequia* or ditch provided water, but it could be blocked.

Worst of all, the place was so big. How could 80 men hope to do any good? Or even double that number? Colonel Neill had every right to feel depressed when the garrison assembled to discuss its situation the day after the Matamoros group left. And he had every right to feel surprised when the men passed the solemn resolution: "We consider it highly essential that the existing army remain at Bexar."

With what? They had no food, no clothes, no money. To make any kind of stand, it would take a miracle—not just supplies, but new men, new leaders, even new spirit. And yet, these things do happen, and within a few weeks the Alamo

would undergo changes that Neill, a conscientious but un-
imaginative man, couldn't hope to see. At the moment, however, there was nothing but a piece of paper expressing the
belief of a few hungry, ill-clad men that San Antonio was a
very important place to hold.

CHAPTER FOUR

"The Supreme Government Is Supremely Indignant"

Eight hundred miles south of the Alamo, a well-knit, middle-aged Mexican buckled on his $7,000 sword, mounted a saddle heavy with gold-plated trim, and turned his horse north toward the Rio Grande. General Antonio López de Santa Anna also felt that San Antonio was an important place to hold; and he planned to do something about it.

To Santa Anna, the Texans' seizure of the town was more than a strategic problem. It was a national outrage, a humiliating blow to his personal pride. It not only called for a remedy; it demanded revenge. "Don Santa Anna," reported the Tamaulipas *Gazette*, "feeling as every true Mexican ought, the disgrace thus sustained by the Republic, is making every preparation to wipe out the stain in the blood of those perfidious foreigners."

That was what hurt the most—"those perfidious foreigners." It was bad enough being beaten, but to Santa Anna, being beaten by Americans was the greatest indignity of all. He recalled so well his first brush with them in 1813. Then he had come to Texas as a young lieutenant in the Royal Spanish Army to help throttle an early uprising against the Hapsburg regime. At the Battle of Medina he saw the rebels crushed by a clever ambush—and some American hangers-on sent flying. Clearly, the undisciplined "Anglo" frontiersmen could never stand up to an army drilled in the European tradition.

Santa Anna had come a long way since Medina—mostly on the theory that if a man was nimble enough, he could end up on top. True, it didn't always work; there was that time in 1813 when he was caught forging his commander's name on a draft to cover some gambling debts. But he wriggled out of that, and since then it had certainly paid to be opportunistic. One March morning in 1821 the Spanish promoted him from captain to lieutenant colonel for beating some rebels; that afternoon he changed sides and got his full colonelcy. In 1822, now fighting for the Mexicans under Augustin Iturbi, he proved a dashing 28-year-old suitor for the hand of Iturbi's 60-year-old sister . . . and soon became brigadier general. Later in the year, when Iturbi became Emperor Augustin I, Santa Anna solemnly swore, "I am and will be throughout life and till death your loyal Defender and Subject." That December he launched a successful rebellion for a republic.

Sometimes on the winning side—sometimes not—Santa Anna was mixed up in one revolution after another over the next few years. Finally, he himself emerged on top in 1832: an apparently unwilling Cincinnatus whose liberal policies would end the chaos. "My whole ambition is restricted to beating my sword into a plowshare," he wistfully announced from his country estate, where he liked to retire at dramatic moments. "I swear to you that I oppose all efforts aimed at destruction of the Constitution and that I would die before accepting any other power than that designated by it," he scolded the clergy and the military men, who were against the liberal reforms he promised.

But all the time he was secretly dickering with these same conservative groups. And when finally convinced that he would remain in the saddle, he dramatically shifted his ground in 1834. Sure at last of all the power in his own hands, Santa Anna scrapped his liberal program, jettisoned the Constitution of 1824 with its emphasis on states rights, and revamped the government along "centralist" lines . . . meaning a government run by himself direct from Mexico City.

It was at this point that Stephen Austin—languishing in the capital under arrest—despaired of ever getting freedom for Texas under Mexican rule. And he was right too; for Santa Anna quickly forgot that he only wanted to beat his sword into a plowshare. Soon he was dashing about the country, ruthlessly suppressing every attempt by the individual states to preserve their constitutional rights.

Prancing ahead of the troops with his escort of thirty dragoons, Santa Anna cut quite a figure. He was a master showman with a great sense of timing. He knew just when to brood at his hacienda until the people begged him to come forward; or plunge into danger till they begged him to hold back.

He was also a mountain of vanity. He affected a gold snuff-box. His epaulets and frogging dripped so heavily with silver that later they were easily made into a set of spoons. He collected Napoleonic bric-a-brac and felt there was an obvious comparison between the Emperor and himself. "He would listen to nothing which was not in accord with his ideas," noted his top subordinate, General Vicente Filisola, who got to know him well.

Yet it would be so dangerous to underrate him. His boldness and energy revived a drooping army. His strength, his marvelous voice gave new hope to a nation weary of chaos. Even his appearance—he was much taller than the average Mexican—suggested an infinitely more promising leader than the shoddy collection of petty figures who had been wasting away the country's resources. His shrewd sense of timing made him not only a great politician, but often a skillful, imaginative general. And above all he was great at organization, and this more than anything was needed when Santa Anna once more emerged from "retirement" to develop the Texas campaign in the fall of 1835. At first he planned to invade next spring, but the capture of San Antonio changed everything. Now he would go at once.

The first problem was money. The Mexican Army was an appalling sieve. It had already consumed a back-breaking amount of money for a poor country worn out by civil war. And now more was needed. Undiscouraged, Santa Anna plunged into the task. He gave his personal security for a quick loan of 10,000 pesos. He hit the church for contributions—1,000 pesos from the Monterey Cathedral. He got rations on credit . . . but at double the usual price. He went to the loan sharks: Messrs. Rubio & Errazu supplied 400,000 pesos at an interest rate amounting to 48 per cent a year. Nor was that all. To make sure they got their money back, these gentlemen required the government to sign away the entire proceeds of a forced loan on four Mexican departments, plus various customs house duties, plus the right to bring in certain military supplies duty-free. Outrageous terms, Santa Anna agreed, but the money had to be raised.

Generals were much easier to find. Santa Anna's growing assortment included Vicente Filisola, second-in-command and perhaps the stuffiest Italian in history . . . Adrian Woll, a tough French soldier of fortune . . . Juan José Andrade of the cavalry, with his delicate golden cigar tongs. They were every kind, sharing only their jealousy and suspicion of each other.

Graft and intrigue swirled around headquarters. Through the always obliging firm of Rubio & Errazu, General Castrillón secretly managed to lend the army some of his own money at 4 per cent a month. General Gaona cornered supplies along the route and sold them back at 100 per cent profit. Colonel Ricardo Dromundo, master purveyor and another brother-in-law of Santa Anna, never even tried to account for the money given him for provisions.

Jockeying around headquarters, a good man to know was Ramón Caro, Santa Anna's ferret-like secretary. If he seemed unfriendly, it might be wise to work through Colonel Juan Almonte, a bland chameleon who could be counted on to undermine Caro.

Beneath this glitter and intrigue were, as in every army, the unsung professionals. Fine officers like Lieutenant Colonel José de la Peña of the *Zapadores* battalion. Or General Urrea's dull but conscientious paymaster Captain Alavez. (Everyone wondered how he rated such a beautiful wife.) But there were so few of these good men . . . and so many fops, dandies, favor-buyers, blackmailers. It all added up to one officer or non-com for every two privates in the Mexican Army.

No wonder the privates were so hard to catch. Bad leadership, poor pay and no glory were all that awaited them. Enlistments fell off, and local officials scraped the barrel to fill their quotas. The Yucatán battalion was loaded with helpless Mayan Indians—frightened, shivering men who couldn't even understand the language. If a man deserted, there was no better punishment than to send him back. After Juan Basquez, an unfortunate shoemaker from Durango, ran away twice, he was sentenced to ten more years in the army without pay.

Willing and unwilling, the troops began assembling toward the end of December, 1835. First at San Luis Potosí, where Santa Anna laid much of the groundwork; then at Saltillo, where he planned to whip them all into shape. This was the real starting point for the great expedition—about 365 miles from San Antonio.

Santa Anna arrived at Saltillo on January 7, 1836 and immediately collapsed with some sort of stomach-ache. For two weeks everything stopped while the Commander writhed in his bed. But if the experience did nothing else, it should have taught him that plans alone are not enough. The medical corps —so neat and impressive on paper—proved nonexistent. In his agony, the Commander-in-Chief finally hired a second-rate village practitioner named N. Reyes, who from that point went along as his personal physician.

Back at last on his feet, Santa Anna worked all the harder to get the men ready. An endless stream of orders poured on the hapless Ramón Caro, who sat at a portable *escritoire* frantically taking dictation: Tell Filisola to order 100,000 pounds of hardtack ("very, very necessary") . . . have him buy 500 horses as replacement mounts ("fat, saddle-broken"). Minister of War Tornel was told to issue a proclamation that might give the men more spirit . . . to establish a Legion of Honor with a cross as insigne—"silver for the cavalrymen, but of gold for all officers." General Cós, just back in disgrace from San Antonio, got special treatment. What did he mean by giving his word not to fight again? Forget it and join the march.

"His Excellency himself attends to all matters whether important or most trivial," noted Captain Sánchez, Cós' old adjutant, who dropped by headquarters hoping for a job. "I am astonished to see that he has personally assumed the authority of major general . . . of quartermaster, of commissary, of brigadier generals, of colonels, of captains, and even of corporals, purveyors, *arrieros* and *carreteros*."

Santa Anna thought of everything, in fact, except to teach the men how to shoot. Hating the recoil of their heavy, old-fashioned blunderbusses, the troops rarely fired from the shoulder. When they did, they never bothered to use the sights.

Otherwise nothing was omitted. Day after day the men drilled and deployed, marched and countermarched, until at last Santa Anna was satisfied. On January 25 came the final Grand Review. As the glittering generalissimo watched from his horse, the men wheeled by in more or less good order—the senior officers in their dark blue uniforms with scarlet fronts . . . the dragoons with their shiny breastplates . . . the endless rows of infantry, scuffing along in their white cotton fatigue suits, already grimy with dust. On their heads they wore tall black shakos, complete with pompon and tiny visor. The total effect was oddly antique—like something out of Napoleon's time.

But they were obviously soldiers; and if they looked a little Napoleonic, so much the better. Once again, how could the untrained American frontiersmen stand up to troops like these? As Minister of War Tornel put it, "The superiority of the Mexican soldier over the mountaineers of Kentucky and the hunters of Missouri is well known. Veterans seasoned by twenty years of wars can't be intimidated by the presence of an army ignorant of the art of war, incapable of discipline, and renowned for insubordination."

The comparison omitted an important element. The rifles of the Kentucky mountaineers were accurate at two hundred yards; while the Mexican *escopetas*—although authentic English surplus from the days of Waterloo—could barely reach seventy yards. Tornel would not have cared; tactics would win in the end; the Americans were pathetically "ignorant of manoeuvres on a large scale."

Hope soaring, the troops began moving out of Saltillo the day after the Grand Review. First, General Urrea's infantry . . . branching off to the east, heading for the Gulf Coast to serve as the army's right wing. This brigade would be pretty much of a side show for a while.

Next came the main force—the flower of the army—the brigades of Generals Gaona and Tolsa, the cavalry of General Andrade, and of course Santa Anna himself. Marching directly

Santa Anna marches to Texas. The General left Mexico City on
November 28, 1835, organized his army at San Luis during December,
reached Saltillo on January 7, 1836. Here he drilled his troops for
about three weeks, moved on to Monclova on February 1, reached
the Rio Grande on the 12th. He crossed into Texas on the 16th,
arriving at San Antonio on the afternoon of February 23.

north for the Rio Grande, they reached Monclova in the first
week of February. Here they picked up Filisola, who was organizing their supplies. A few days' pause; then on again. As
armies go, it was not large, but at this time and in this part
of the world it was impressive enough—some 4,000 men and
twelve business-like cannon.

Nor would that be all. Already waiting on the Rio Grande
was another brigade of 1,541 men and eight guns under General Ramírez y Sesma. He had originally gone north in the
fall to reinforce Cós. Too late for this, he halted instead at
the river. Now the plan was for the main force to join Sesma,
and together they would recapture San Antonio. But all that
lay in the future; first Santa Anna's force had to reach the
Texas border.

Winding north into the bare, dry hills of Coahuila, they
presented a picture of curious contrasts. Santa Anna and his
personal entourage now pranced in front—a glittering display
of military ostentation. Far to the rear plodded the lines of
infantry. The snappy formations learned at Saltillo were soon
forgotten as the men shuffled along in the choking dust.

Behind them crawled the army's supply train . . . strung
out for miles along the narrow, rocky trail. It was quite a
sight—1,800 pack mules loaded with hardtack . . . 33 huge
four-wheel wagons, looking a little like stranded canal barges
. . . 200 two-wheel carts drawn by oxen . . . hundreds of
smaller carts and barrows, the property of enterprising sutlers
who trailed the army with liquor, tobacco, bread, anything
that might sell.

None of the carts had any metal; pegs and thongs of raw-
hide were all that held them together. Nor was there any
lubrication, and soon the great seven-foot wheels produced a
frightful creaking and screeching that could be heard for
miles.

Jumbled among them tramped another army of sorts—a

horde of chattering women and children. These were the
soldaderas of the men—a somewhat unusual military institu-
tion. Apart from the companionship they provided, these
women served the purpose of cooking and even foraging for
the soldiers—especially useful since Santa Anna hadn't bothered
to provide any formal commissary. Yet they consumed provisions too, and they certainly were a distraction.

General Filisola—perhaps brought up to believe in sterner
European standards—was appalled. He protested bitterly that
the women were cluttering up the army, wrecking any trace
of efficiency. His complaint was politely rejected. Headquarters agreed that the *soldaderas* were a disconcerting influence, but philosophically pointed out that if they were sent
home, half the army would desert.

Soldiers, sutlers, *soldaderas*—all pushed on, moving ever
deeper into the barren, mountainous country of northern
Mexico. Days of blinding glare, sore feet, parched throats.
"There have been sufferings," conceded the military correspondent of *El Mosquito Mexicano*, "but surprisingly small.
These sufferings only spur them to greater efforts." And later,
a bright thought: "The hardships of the day are forgotten in
the pleasure and the coolness of the evening."

This proved a masterpiece of understatement. On February
13 the "coolness of the evening" was a howling blizzard that
swept across the hills, wiped out the trail, blinded the troops
and animals. General Andrade's cavalry became hopelessly
lost in a mesquite thicket; men and horses thrashed about,
crashing against one another, tumbling into the drifting snow.
Gaona's brigade, caught squarely in the middle of the storm,
lost fifty yoke of oxen. There were no tents for the men, and
they could only huddle against one another, trying to stay
alive. The Mayan Indians in the Yucatán battalion, away from
the tropics for the first time, fell by the dozen—pathetic
bundles lying motionless in the drifts.

Struggling on, the army finally left the snow behind, only to face a new peril. It had been a dry winter, and now there was neither grass nor water for the horses. Some dropped with *mal de lengua*, a swelling of the tongue from thirst and dry fodder . . . others died of *telele*, a fever caused by stagnant water. The team of eight mules pulling a great howitzer—pride of the army—fell completely exhausted. What to do? asked Filisola. Leave the gun behind and sell the mules, he was told; the army could use the money.

By now the men too were falling. Short of hardtack from the start, Santa Anna cut the troops to half-rations . . . forced them to shift for themselves on 12½ cents a day. Desperately, they took to the fields, chewing bitter mesquite nuts and munching reddish berries that looked possibly nourishing. Hundreds collapsed with dysentery and diarrhea. Others succumbed to a spotted itch. Still others dropped from sheer exhaustion.

Nor was anyone likely to pick them up. The lack of doctors, drugs and ambulances—so embarrassing when Santa Anna had his stomach-ache—now proved fatal to scores of his men. Trailing the infantry, General Ampudia's artillerymen were kept busy collecting fallen soldiers, stuffing them into the munitions wagons and gun carriages.

One night Ampudia himself helped pick up a crumpled wretch, so weak and weighted down by his gun and pack that he could no longer even move. The man died before morning, and it seemed a shame that Santa Anna had also forgotten to bring any chaplains.

Many tried to desert. Some succeeded, more were caught and thrown back in the ranks. No longer did the correspondent from *El Mosquito Mexicano* write glibly of sufferings that only spurred the men to greater efforts. The paper now reported bitterly: "By recent letters we learn that desertions are increasing daily and becoming scandalous. That hunger and nudity have the troops in despair; the troops are not getting their pay nor officers their salaries."

Still, with the stoicism of all soldiers in all armies, most of the men somehow carried on. Across the Sabinas on rafts and logs . . . by the hacienda at San Juan . . . through San Miguel de Allende . . . always north toward the Rio Grande and Texas beyond.

Santa Anna himself galloped far in the lead. Around him were his dragoons, splendid in their shining helmets and breastplates. Just behind, his ornate carriage rattled and swayed along the rocky road. Behind it lumbered his baggage train, loaded with the things he felt he needed—the striped marquee . . . the tea caddy and cream pitcher . . . the monogrammed china . . . the decanters with their little gold stoppers . . . the silver chamber pot.

At last, on February 12, the Rio Grande. With a final burst of speed, Santa Anna's caravan raced down the hard, flat road leading toward the river . . . clattered into the old Spanish town of Presidio de Rio Grande . . . and drew up at the military headquarters of General Ramírez y Sesma.

It must have been a welcome sight for Sesma. During the past months he had been having his own troubles. He too never had enough money. On his way north in November, the government promised him 25,000 pesos from the accommodating Señor Rubio, but only 14,000 were ever delivered. Sesma papered the province of Nuevo León with worthless I.O.U.s to get grain. He requisitioned mules everywhere, and when the people of Abasolo failed to provide the number he demanded, he seized and threatened to shoot the *alcalde*, until the rest were produced.

He reached the Texas border at Laredo two days after Christmas and found Cós already there, retiring from San Antonio. New orders arrived, sending Cós back to Monclova and Sesma to Presidio, eighty miles farther up the river. Here

Santa Anna felt the detachment would be safer till he himself arrived. Waiting for him, Sesma continued to live off the land, stirring fear and hatred among the local people.

Meanwhile he did what military commanders always do while marking time. He polished and paraded his troops. On January 18 he had them all out, drilling in the fields by the Rio Grande.

High in the hills across the river, a lone figure peered down on the scene with interest. Señor José Cassiano was one of those citizens of Bexar who cherished his constitutional rights more than the glamour of Santa Anna. He had volunteered for scout duty along the Rio Grande, and his reports made interesting reading back at the Alamo.

Today was no exception. Cassiano took out his pencil and meticulously noted what he saw—about 1,600 infantry . . . 400 cavalry . . . 80 wagons . . . 400 mules . . . 3,000 mule-loads of flour . . . 300 *fanegas* of biscuit . . . 2 mortars . . . 6 pieces of artillery "supposed to be twelves."

Enough. Satisfied with his arithmetic, he mounted his horse and turned toward San Antonio.

CHAPTER FIVE

"We Will Rather Die in These Ditches Than Give It Up"

Mexican troop figures meant nothing to Jim Bowie, as he rode slowly toward San Antonio on January 18. He was coming to blow up the Alamo.

He had left Goliad the day before with the necessary orders from Sam Houston, the Texan commander. Feeling that the outpost was far too isolated, Houston had given Bowie a letter, urging Colonel Neill to abandon Bexar, demolish the Alamo, and pull the artillery back to Gonzales and Copano.

Bowie was of course no man's messenger boy. He had been picked to see that the orders were carried out. In Houston's words, "There is no man on whose forecast, prudence, and valor I place a higher estimate."

So now he was on his way. With him rode some thirty men —a mixture of recent recruits like James Bonham of South Carolina and old hands like Louis Rose, a Napoleonic veteran who had wandered across the Atlantic, finally winding up in Nacogdoches around 1827. A shiftless drifter, Rose couldn't have been less like Bowie; yet they were apparently good friends—another example of the Colonel's ability to win the loyalty of all kinds of men.

The little party reached San Antonio on the 19th. Riding

into the Alamo, Bowie handed Houston's letter to Neill, then began checking things himself. The General's wishes were perfectly clear—destroy the fort and pull back—but there was more to it than that. As Houston had specifically told him last time out, "Much is referred to your discretion."

Bowie soon discovered that conditions were bad indeed. The garrison had no horses for scouting. There were no medical supplies, no rifle powder, no cannon balls for the 18-pounder.

Morale was down too. The troops refused to drill, or even go out on patrol. Roll call was a farce. Several of the New Orleans Greys settled in the Alamo church, living as they pleased amid the rubble. Just before Bowie's arrival one man actually mutinied and was finally drummed out of camp.

Yet day after day Bowie hesitated. Somehow he couldn't bring himself to carry out Houston's wishes. Was it the place —this dramatic outpost, standing alone between the colonists and the Mexicans? Was it the Alamo's twenty fine guns, probably the strongest collection between Mexico City and New Orleans? Was it the "frontier" in him—the pioneer's refusal to be shoved around? Bowie had plenty of that.

Perhaps all these factors played a part, and undoubtedly the men did too. Angry and discouraged just now, they were still magnificent material, and their refusal to be lured away on the Matamoros treasure hunt showed at least a basic sense of responsibility. Green Jameson, who knew them well, certainly thought so. He felt that if properly supported, they would "do duty and fight better than fresh men, they have all been tried and have confidence in themselves."

His interest stirred, Bowie soon found himself doing things that had little to do with retreat—and a great deal to do with defense. Using his marvelous local contacts, he found horses for long-range scouting. He visited his Mexican friends and came back with fresh intelligence. On January 22 he heard

from the Navarro family that Santa Anna was marching on
Texas with 4,600 men. A useful talk with the local padre
developed further information: the Mexican cavalry was
heading straight for Bexar. It was enough to make Neill think
again about leaving, but Bowie's spirit was soaring. He thought
more and more about holding out.

The men caught the spark of this hard, determined leader.
Their spirits perked up and so did their work. Captain
Almeron Dickinson, the Gonzales blacksmith, discovered he
had a born knack for handling artillery. Hiram Williamson
of Philadelphia turned into a surprisingly good drillmaster.
John Baugh of Virginia took on the adjutant's chores with a
vengeance. Supplies started to trickle in too—42 beeves, 100
bushels of corn, ammunition for the 18-pounder. Green
Jameson began to boast that with the Alamo's artillery they
could whip the Mexicans ten to one.

Jameson himself proved an extremely imaginative engineer.
The Alamo actually began to look like a fort. He built a
palisade of stakes and dirt to close the gap in the southeast
angle. He threw up platforms of earth and timber along the
walls to serve as parapets and gun mounts. He put the heavy
18-pounder in the southwest angle, where it commanded the
town. And all the time his head swam with still more ambitious plans—moats, aqueducts and "a contemplated draw-
bridge across a contemplated ditch inside a contemplated half-
moon battery."

Bowie pitched in wherever he could—playing a major role
not only in defense but in the garrison's political life as well.
For the defenders of the Alamo always had time for politics.
Right now they were absorbed in a battle raging at San Felipe
between the Provisional Council and Governor Smith. The
Council had just fired Smith, and the Governor had retaliated
by dismissing the Council. None of this made it any easier to
get supplies for the Alamo, but the men's main interest seemed

to lie in their fear that the Council might come to terms with the Mexicans. The troops were virtually all "independence men" and strongly for Smith.

On January 26 Bowie attended a mass meeting in support of the Governor, which ended by going far beyond that. It turned into a rousing rally for holding the Alamo. The garrison demanded $500 for defense, then declared that even if the money didn't come, "We cannot be driven from the post of honor." First man to sign the resolution, just after the chairman James Bonham, was none other than Jim Bowie.

With soaring enthusiasm, the men returned to work, and Bowie contributed more of his special brand of talent. Since the troops' demand for money seemed a long shot at best, he negotiated a $500 loan locally—quite a feat, considering the garrison's nonexistent credit standing. Bowie also extended the scout service. By the end of January he was able to send out a detachment of "active young men" as far as the Rio Frio.

"Active young men"—Bowie would never have used the phrase a month earlier. But now he felt dreadfully sick and it was only his determination that kept him going. The fort's surgeon, Amos Pollard, was baffled and called in Dr. John Sutherland, a new arrival from Alabama. Sutherland, who had learned his medicine under what was vaguely described as "the old Thompsonian System," was puzzled too. He could only say that the sickness was "of a peculiar nature, not to be cured by an ordinary course of treatment."

Bowie grimly carried on, bolstered by the mounting tempo of events. On January 27 Señor Cassiano galloped in with his details on Sesma's force. There was something starkly real about his neat, meticulous figures, and a courier rushed off to San Felipe with another plea for "men, money, rifles, cannon powder." On February 2 one of Bowie's special contacts brought additional details: Besides Sesma's men on the Rio Grande, there were 5,000 more Mexicans a little way back.

"They intend to make a descent on this place in particular, and there is no doubt about it."

Time was growing short. Bowie decided formal resolutions were no longer enough to wake the government up, make it see the importance of holding San Antonio. On the 2nd he scribbled a strong personal letter to Governor Smith, urging all possible help. In it he carefully explained his views: "The salvation of Texas depends in great measure on keeping Bexar out of the hands of the enemy. It serves as the frontier picquet guard, and if it were in the possession of Santa Anna, there is no stronghold from which to repel him in his march toward the Sabine."

And lest anyone think there was still any chance of their pulling back, Bowie sternly concluded, "Colonel Neill and myself have come to the solemn resolution that we will rather die in these ditches than give it up to the enemy."

Houston never knew, to approve or disapprove. Fed up with the endless wrangling at San Felipe, he had gone off on furlough to deal with the Indians and wouldn't be back till March.

The course set, Bowie and Neill continued to strengthen their defenses. Thirty more men were due any day under William Barret Travis, and Neill already had plans for this dashing young figure. He would send Travis to harass the approaching Mexicans—cut off their supplies, make mischief in their rear, chop down the bridges over the Leona and Nueces rivers.

It was just as well that Travis didn't know. He had lost none of his ambition, but burning grass and chopping bridges was the work of a junior officer, and he now had his eye on higher things. In fact, that was what bothered him as he sulked his way toward San Antonio with only 30 men. He had really worked to wangle his lieutenant colonelcy in the cavalry—had even turned down a major's commission in the artillery.

Now here he was, stuck with a company officer's command.

Of course orders were orders, and when Governor Smith told him to reinforce the Alamo, Travis had to go. (He even put out his own money to buy tinware, twine and a five-dollar flag.) But that didn't mean he liked the assignment any better. Still fuming, he slipped off to pay a last visit to his small son Charles, then headed for Bexar on January 23, leading his unimpressive little squad.

Things grew rapidly worse. There was still no money, and Travis spent more of his own for blankets, coffee, sugar, more blankets. Morale sagged, and by January 28, nine of his original 39 men had deserted. As if supplies weren't short enough already, deserter Andrew Smith even took a horse, bridle, blanket, rifle and gunpowder.

"Volunteers can no longer be relied upon," Travis gloomily wrote Governor Smith from the Colorado River on the 28th. "The patriotism of a few has done much, but it is worn down." The more he thought about it, the more discouraged he grew. Here he was, making all these sacrifices, while nobody else lifted a finger. How little anybody appreciated him.

He fretted all night, and on the 29th again wrote the Governor:

> I beg that Your Excellency will recall the order for
> me to go to Bexar in command of so few men. I am
> willing, nay anxious, to go to the defense of Bexar,
> and I have done everything in my power to equip
> the enlisted men and get them off. But Sir, I am un-
> willing to risk my reputation (which is ever dear to
> a volunteer) by going off into the enemy's country
> with so little means, so few men, and these so badly
> equipped—the fact is there is no necessity for my
> services to command these few men. The company
> officers will be amply sufficient.

He added that if his request was turned down, "I feel it is due to myself to resign my commission." Dispatching this ultimatum by express, Travis then halted on the Colorado to await results.

The Governor never even answered. Perhaps he was too used to Travis' threats to resign—after all, this was the third time since November. Perhaps he knew his man well enough to feel that the storm would pass. In any case, he ignored the letter.

Travis waited, seethed, finally gave up. He gloomily led his men on toward San Antonio. Just now he looked like anything but a man of destiny. Yet even heroes get discouraged. All men know such moments, and perhaps in the end the hero is the one who does march on.

They arrived on February 3—William Garnett, a wandering Baptist preacher; John Forsyth, the restless medical student from Avon, New York; altogether some thirty tired, dusty men in buckskin shirts and blanket coats. Far from the snappy uniform prescribed in his cavalry regulations, Travis himself wore only a set of homemade jeans.

In his impulsive way, Travis soon forgot his problems and jumped into the affairs of the Alamo. The political pot was boiling again, and on February 7, he played an active role in electing Sam Maverick and Jesse Badgett to represent the garrison at the coming Convention, called to set up a permanent government for Texas.

Even politics were forgotten on the 8th. Into town from the east rode an unexpected group of gay, casual men. Colonel David Crockett had arrived with his amiable companions, "the Tennessee Mounted Volunteers." Soldiers, citizens, everyone dropped what they were doing, poured into the Main Plaza to greet the great man. Someone got a packing case, and Crockett climbed on it. The air erupted with cheers and yells.

He gave them the full treatment—all the best stories. And of course, he described once again how he told his constituents that if they didn't elect him, they could go to hell and he would go to Texas. "And, fellow citizens, I am among you," he concluded quietly, with a sudden change of pace that was quite unusual for him: "I have come to your country, though not, I hope, through any selfish motive whatever. I have come to aid you all that I can in your noble cause. I shall identify myself with your interests, and all the honor that I desire is that of defending as a high private, in common with my fellow citizens, the liberties of our common country."

It was a curiously touching finish that showed once again how the mere idea of liberty could capture a man's mind at this time. Six weeks ago Crockett had never seen Texas—now he was speaking of "our common country." In the past he had loved the favors and honors that were showered on him. Now all he wanted was to be a "high private."

This past week had brought in some remarkable men—and more were on the way. Three inseparable brothers named Taylor turned up from the town of Liberty. David Cummings delivered his father's guns to the government and headed down too. Cleland Simmons and R. W. Ballentine arrived to make good their pledge "to defend our brethren at the peril of our lives, liberties, and fortunes." Asa Walker, a young volunteer from Tennessee, hurried toward the Alamo with an almost haunting sense of urgency. Reaching Washington-on-the-Brazos, he took time only to scrawl a quick note to an involuntary benefactor:

> Mr. Gant—I take the responsibility of taking your overcoat and gun—your gun they would have had anyhow and I might as well have it as any one else. If I live to return, I will satisfy you for all. If I die I leave you my clothes to do the best you can with. You can sell them for something. If you overtake me,

you can take your rifle, and I will trust to chance—
the hurry of the moment and my want of means to
do better are all the excuse I have. . . .

As these came, a few others left. Most of the adventurers
and overnight patriots were already gone; now it was the turn
of the sick, the tired and the rascals. Lieutenant S. Y. Ream
came down with measles and was carted off to Gonzales.
Nathaniel Kerr died of an unnamed fever. A Tennessee man
returned home, saying there was absolutely no money in Texas
at all.

Watching them go, David Cummings wrote his father in
Pennsylvania, "Many it is true have left the country and returned home to their friends and pleasures, but of such Texas
has no use. . . . We want men of determined spirit that can
undergo hardships and deprivation."

And this was exactly how the garrison was shaping up. By
the 10th of February it numbered 142 hard, tested, dedicated
men. They came from everywhere—but two-thirds were
recent arrivals from the States and only a couple had been in
Texas as long as six years. They were everything in peace-
time: clerks, doctors, blacksmiths, lawyers, brickmasons—but
not one was a professional soldier.

On the night of the 10th, they jammed a fandango celebrating Crockett's arrival. Like most good fighting men, the
Alamo defenders liked to play hard too, and the party was
going strong around one o'clock, when a courier arrived with
fresh word of the Mexican advance. Bowie, Travis and
Crockett huddled over the message together. In the end they
correctly decided that it was nothing urgent, and the party
rolled on.

But the huddle itself was significant, for Colonel Neill was
not included. It was no particular mystery. He had simply
suffered the fate of many a good second-rater when abler,

84   *A Time to Stand*

more imaginative leaders appear on the scene of a crisis. He had been gently nudged aside.

Next morning Neill left on "twenty days' leave." The explanations were various—sickness in the family, a special mission to raise defense funds. Colonel Travis, at least, sensed he wouldn't be back.

Before pulling out, Neill appointed Travis to take command of the garrison. A logical choice, for he was the senior regular army officer present, but the free-wheeling volunteers weren't inclined to be logical. It was one thing to put up with the somewhat pedestrian Neill—he had at least been in charge from the start—but Travis had been around only a week. Moreover, Neill was 46; Travis only 26. Why take this emotional, melodramatic boy when they also had Jim Bowie, the best-known fighter in Texas?

Bowie did nothing to discourage the mood. He had always gotten along with Travis—but serving under the man was quite a different matter. He didn't need his big knife to prove no one was his master; those cold gray eyes and his quiet, firm manner took care of that. Sam Houston understood, usually let Bowie run his own show. How could a 26-year-old newcomer hope to command him?

Travis felt the pressure. He wavered, then ordered an election for command of the volunteers. If he hoped to win through, it was a poor gamble. The men happily voted for Jim Bowie.

The result was an impossible split. The proud, moody Travis, still commanding the regulars and the volunteer cavalry, had no intention of suffering further humiliation. For his part, Bowie always did what he wanted anyhow. And to make matters worse, he was ill again—feeling worse than ever.

On the 12th he burst into town, roaring drunk, his resistance shattered by sickness. He loudly claimed command of the whole garrison. He stopped private citizens going about their business. He ordered town officials to open the *calaboose* and let everyone go. When one of the freed prisoners, Antonio Fuentes, was thrown back in jail, Bowie exploded with rage. He called out his men from the Alamo, paraded them back and forth in the Main Plaza. They were all drunk now, shouting and cheering, waving their rifles.

"I am unwilling to be responsible for the drunken irregularities of any man," Travis primly wrote Governor Smith on the 13th, describing the whole sorry mess. He went on to say he would leave in an instant, were it not for the Alamo. But he too had fallen under the spell: "It is more important to occupy this post than I imagined when I last saw you. It is the key to Texas. . . ."

Sick and drunk as he was, Bowie knew it too. In the harrowing morning after of February 14 he was more than willing to let bygones be bygones. As quickly as the storm had broken, he and Travis came to an amazingly simple agreement. They would keep their separate commands, but take all major steps together. And high time; as they jointly wrote Governor Smith, "There is no doubt that the enemy will shortly advance upon this place, and that this will be the first point of attack. We must therefore urge the necessity of sending reinforcements as speedily as possible to our aid."

Under the new joint command, the Alamo hummed with increasing excitement. There was still no money, still not enough food, still a lot of grumbling; but there was greater determination than ever. Almeron Dickinson and his artillerymen wrestled their guns into place—by mid-February all but three were mounted. Dr. Pollard bustled about his hospital on the second floor of the long barracks—somehow he found instruments, all he needed except syringes and catheters. Sam Blair, the fort's 29-year-old ordnance chief, supplemented the meager supply of cannonballs by chopping up horseshoes.

The men now worked hard too, although they still had an exasperating way of wandering off at odd moments. On February 14 David Cummings went to the Cibolo Creek to do a little prospecting. William Garnett, the Baptist preacher, went back to Velasco, "to clean up business." Travis of course stayed at his post, but he too thought about business. All February he ran an ad in the *Telegraph and Texas Register* about his new law partnership with Franklin J. Starr: "One or both of them will be constantly found in the office at San Felipe."

And of course they all continued to play. The Alamo garrison was determined, but no band of angels. Men like the Arkansas jockey Henry Warnell and wild young William Malone of Georgia weren't about to ignore the pleasures of the town. Seaman William Jackson and John McGregor, the jaunty Scot from Nacogdoches, felt the same. Nor were the officers immune—Captain Carey talked not too seriously of marriage with a pretty *señorita*.

Over them all—whether at work or play—there was a new spirit in the air. The volunteers discovered that Travis wasn't so bad after all—a little self-centered perhaps, but no one worked harder. Travis' regulars, in turn, soon fell under Bowie's spell. The garrison had finally become a solidly knit group of men—resourceful and self-reliant, yet drawing strength from each other too.

On February 16 Green Jameson wrote one of his most optimistic letters to Governor Smith. He was full of his latest improvements, full of new ideas for an even stronger, "diamond-shaped" fort. Pleased with the garrison's accomplishments, he also had a few caustic words about an earlier Mexican attempt to fortify the Alamo: "They have shown imbecility and want of skill in the fortress as they have in all things else."

That same day a dusty horseman galloped into town from the south. Riding up Potrero Street, he reined in at the last house before the rickety bridge over the San Antonio River. This was Ambrosio Rodríguez' place, and the horseman was Mrs. Rodríguez' cousin Rivas. As a good member of the family, he had come all the way from Laredo to warn them that they must leave at once. Santa Anna was about to cross the Rio Grande and head for Bexar.

Señor Rodríguez, friendly to the Texans, sent for Travis at once. The Colonel came readily—he had grown to know the Rodríguez family well, liked to stop by and chat with them on his way to and from the Alamo just across the river. Now he listened carefully as Rivas repeated his warning. No, Travis finally decided, it just couldn't be. The Mexicans were coming —no one knew better than he—but not so soon.

On the 18th Rodríguez heard another alarming report, again passed the news on to Travis. But again the Colonel was politely skeptical. Rodríguez, a bit of a strategist himself, suggested pulling the garrison back. Travis had heard that advice all too often.

On the 20th still another horseman appeared. This was Blas Herrera, who had been recruited by his cousin, Captain Juan Seguin, to serve in a company of local Mexicans supporting the Texan cause. This group was an important addition to the defense, for Seguin came from an influential family in San Antonio, and his men knew the country intimately. As tension mounted, he had sent Herrera to the Rio Grande to watch for enemy movements; now Herrera was back with his own piece of alarming news—he himself had seen Santa Anna's army crossing the Rio Grande, plunging into Texas.

At nine o'clock that night a council of war convened in Travis' room. Herrera repeated his story, and the Texans argued for hours whether to believe him. Some were convinced, but more were doubtful—they had heard these stories before and nothing ever happened. In the end, Travis ignored the warning.

It was not a case of contempt. Travis had a healthy respect for Santa Anna's troops; he knew perfectly well that several thousand Mexicans could overwhelm 150 Texans. But he could not believe anything would happen very soon. Santa Anna would probably wait for the spring grass before bringing his cavalry north. John W. Smith, a shrewd observer, thought that the invasion would come in March. David Cummings wrote his father on February 14, "We have nothing to apprehend before a month or six weeks, as the enemy have not yet crossed the Rio Grande." Travis himself felt the Mexicans might be expected "by the 15th of March."

"Wretches! They will soon learn their folly," thundered General Antonio López de Santa Anna in a proclamation to his invading troops on February 17. He had left the Rio Grande the day before; now he was at the Nueces River, already forty-five miles inside Texas. Here he joined the vanguard of Sesma's brigade, which had started out on the 12th. Before them lay San Antonio—now only 119 miles away.

His Excellency felt rather elated. Everything at last was going smoothly. So well, in fact, that just before setting out from the border, he dictated a long, complaisant letter to Minister of War Tornel. "The campaign being over," he explained, "it is but natural that the causes that gave rise to it be analyzed." He went on to suggest various steps that might be taken in the wake of his triumph: The Texans must pay for the campaign . . . "industrious" Mexicans should resettle their lands . . . Anglo-Americans must be completely excluded . . . land bounties should go to the victorious troops.

Greeting Sesma's bedraggled soldiers at the Nueces, he was still bursting with confidence, and his proclamation of the 17th was designed to give them his own sense of mission.

"You," he assured them, "are the men chosen to chastise the assassins!"

Next day the "chastisers" struggled on. Since the Texans had burned the Nueces bridge, they were forced to build another of branches and dirt; but that was the least of their troubles. It rained torrents—soaking their white cotton jumpers, turning the hardtack to soggy pulp. Ironically, the drinking water was foul; and rations grew slimmer than ever, leaving the men to chew on mesquite nuts. Indians were an added hazard—pouncing on wagon trains, stealing the cattle, even killing Governor Musquiz' son.

On they trudged, gauging their progress by the shallow little rivers that laced the prairie. February 19, the Rio Frio—that meant only sixty-eight miles to go. February 20, the Hondo—less than fifty miles now. On the 21st, Santa Anna personally moved to the front, reaching the banks of the Medina at 1:45 P.M. Across this stream lay twenty-five more miles of waving grass—and then San Antonio.

At the Medina he found Sesma's dragoons already waiting—these fast, dependable horsemen had arrived the previous night. Now they waited together as the slower detachments straggled in throughout the afternoon. The exhausted men threw themselves down on the banks, soothed by the mere sight of the Medina's emerald waters rushing over a dazzling white limestone bottom.

Santa Anna himself had no time to rest. A delegation mysteriously turned up from San Antonio, and they brought important news. It seemed there would be a fandango this very evening at Domingo Bustillo's place on Soledad Street. It seemed the Alamo men would attend . . . they could easily be trapped. And incidentally, it seemed that the smiling civilians of San Antonio weren't all so friendly to the Texan cause as they appeared.

Quick, sharp orders to Sesma's cavalry. A detachment of dragoons were to take infantry officers' horses (better rested)

. . . attack the town that night . . . seize the dancing Texans by surprise. As the men saddled up around five o'clock, it began to rain. By the time they got going, a blinding storm lashed them from the north. The pretty green Medina, so easy to ford a few hours ago, was now a deep, foaming torrent. One glance convinced them—it just couldn't be crossed.

Too bad. It was the kind of operation Santa Anna loved— like the time his men dressed up as monks to seize an unsuspecting rival in Veracruz. But it couldn't be helped, so new orders went out: Sesma's whole force would attack on the 23rd.

Meanwhile, the men rested, and Santa Anna received some more interesting visitors from San Antonio—an old priest . . . a Señor Manuel Menchaca . . . one of the prominent Navarros. His Excellency didn't worry: an extra day or two would make no difference against men who spent their time at fandangos when the enemy was twenty-five miles away.

There were no fandangos at Goliad, the main Texas stronghold about ninety-five miles southeast of San Antonio. The Alamo might be disorganized and short of men, but not Goliad. Colonel James Walker Fannin had 420 troops—many of them from the Matamoros expedition, which had finally petered out. The fort was strong too—another of those old Spanish compounds, but it seemed more compact and in much better shape than the sprawling Alamo. And above all, there was organization. For Fannin was a genuine West Pointer, the only one with any significant command in Texas.

True; he hadn't exactly graduated. He ran away after two years under somewhat cloudy circumstances. And there was a good deal of speculation about his later activities. He came to Texas from Georgia around 1834, always flashed plenty of money, seemed to be mixed up in all sorts of shadowy deals— especially slave-running. Yet the fact remained that Fannin was a military man; he proved it in drilling the Brazos Guards, and even more persuasively in his fighting at Concepción.

His military training rang in everything he did. Professional recommendations flowed from his pen—establish a War Bureau, bring in West Pointers. His headquarters bustled with bright young aides like Captain John Sowers Brooks, who had been a U.S. Marine. His proclamations glowed with assurance: *"To the West, face. March!"* began his call for men during the Matamoros affair. He always had eloquent words for the fresh volunteers arriving from the United States, and they in turn recognized, to use the words of one committee, "that Georgia's honor and chivalry stood proudly vindicated in your person."

He seemed to think of everything, even though he did turn down James Butler Bonham when the South Carolinian appeared on February 18 with an urgent appeal for help from Travis. Yet the Alamo clearly fitted somewhere in Fannin's master plan, for on the 8th he assured San Felipe that he would "make such disposition of my forces as to sustain Bexar." And again on the 16th: "I have taken measures to forward provisions to Bexar, and forwarded orders there today to place that post in a state of defense, which if attended to will make it safe."

It took careful reading of his correspondence with Lieutenant Governor Robinson to find some unexpected words of self-doubt. These remarks were tucked away in bold, bristling paragraphs—but they were there. "I *feel*, I *know*, if you and the Council do not," he wrote Robinson on February 14, "that I am incompetent. . . . I do most earnestly ask of you, and any *real friend*, to relieve me, and make a selection of one possessing all the requisites of a commander."

And on February 21—the same evening that Santa Anna's surprise attack on the Alamo misfired—Fannin again beseeched Robinson, "I hope you will soon release me from the army, at least as an officer."

CHAPTER SIX   *"The Enemy Are in View"*

          Lights flickered before dawn at Ambrosio Rodríguez' house in San Antonio on the morning of February 23. Mrs. Rodríguez' cousin Rivas had reappeared during the night, saying he saw Santa Anna in disguise at the last fandango. Imagination, of course, but the citizens had come to expect almost anything from His Excellency. Besides, there was nothing imaginary about the muddy courier who rode into town urging the local Mexicans to get out—the place was about to be attacked.

Señor Rodríguez was off with some of Captain Seguin's company at Gonzales, but Mrs. Rodríguez was a capable woman. She quickly buried the family savings, about $800, in the clay floor . . . got a big two-wheeled oxcart . . . piled six-year-old José and his cousin Pablo in the back . . . and set out for the safety of the Ximenes family *rancho*.

By sunrise the same scene was unfolding all over town. People hurried to and fro, huddled in excited conversations, dashed in and out of their houses with clothes, bedding, pots and pans. Creaking, bumping, rattling along—a steady stream of carts crawled off into the open country. And those who couldn't ride seemed glad to walk, bending under their bundles, yanking their children behind them.

Travis watched, wild with frustration. The fainthearted had been pulling out for weeks, but nothing like this. Yet no one would explain anything. Worse, they told obvious lies: they were going to the country to do a little farming. Townspeople? In February?

Exasperated, he ordered no one else to leave. The commotion only increased. He arrested and questioned people at random. The mystery only deepened. Nine o'clock . . . ten . . . it was nearly eleven when finally he learned. A friendly Mexican took him aside, described the visit from Santa Anna's courier, told him that last night the Mexican cavalry were already at the Leon Creek, only eight miles away.

Travis and Dr. John Sutherland raced to the San Fernando church, a squat pile of stone that slumbered peacefully between the Main and Military Plazas. The church was anything but impressive, but its short, square tower easily dominated the area. Up the winding stairs they scrambled, taking a sentinel with them. In the belfry all three strained their eyes to the south and west. In the bright morning sunlight there was only the chaparral, the mesquite thickets, the rolling prairies. Nothing else.

Telling the lookout to ring the bell if he saw anything suspicious, Travis and Sutherland clambered down to the street again. Travis went off to his room in town; Sutherland to Nat Lewis' store on Main Plaza. Lewis, a bald, jolly man who had never allowed his friendliness to interfere with his pursuit of the dollar, was busy taking inventory.

Ruefully remarking that he might not see his stock much longer, Lewis asked Sutherland to help him. The minutes ticked away as the two men counted the spools, the bolts of cloth, the pots and plates, the candy sticks reserved for the children of valuable customers. Outside it was quieter now; most of the townspeople seemed to be gone, or indoors as a result of Travis' orders. Noon . . . one o'clock . . .

The bell in the tower clanged wildly. Sutherland dropped the trays of dry goods, ran across the plaza to the church. Travis was already there; others were pouring in from everywhere. High in the tower the lookout called down, "The enemy are in view!"

Up the stairs raced several men, and together they all peered out to the southwest where the sentinel pointed. But again there was nothing in sight—just the bare plains, glaring bright in the noonday sun. Cries of "false alarm!" Then a shower of scorn for the sentry, who stood his ground cursing and shouting, "I seen them . . . they've hid behind the brushwood!"

It did no good; the crowd soon drifted off. But Sutherland had no more heart for counting spools of thread for Nat Lewis. He told Travis he would like to ride out and check the lookout's story, if someone would come along who knew the country. John W. Smith—that tower of strength during the December fighting—was soon at hand. They devised a simple signal: if Travis saw them coming back at anything else than a walk, he'd know the sentry was right.

Out the road they trotted. Now up the slope about a mile and a half from town. At last they were at the top, where they could see down the other side.

At first glance, it must have looked like a million Mexicans there in the thickets just over the crest. Sutherland later estimated 1,500; actually there could not have been more than 369. But there were enough. The sentry was right; the enemy had come. These were his cavalry, waiting for orders in a long restless line.

Gulping in the sight of the polished armor, Smith and Sutherland wheeled around and took off for town. Suddenly a terrific jolt, and Sutherland found himself flying through the air. His horse slipped in the mud, pitched him forward, and landed on top of his legs. Smith raced back, untangled the mess, and they were off again. Slithering, sliding, they frantically galloped down the road. Up in the church tower the vindicated sentry saw them coming, again began clanging his bell.

"Give me the baby! Jump on behind and ask me no questions," Captain Almeron Dickinson told his wife Susannah, as he rushed to his quarters in the Musquiz home. She handed him little Angelina, climbed up behind his saddle, and the three of them headed off. The bridge already looked dangerous—some commotion down Potrero Street—so Dickinson guided his horse across the ford, then turned up through the outlying huts and shacks to the gate of the Alamo.

Jim Bowie had the same idea. His adored Ursula was gone, but her adopted sisters Juana and Gertrudis were still at the Veramendi house—he must get them to safety. Juana especially must have been glad to see him. A young widow with a baby, she had remarried Dr. Horace Alsbury of Kentucky just a month ago, but now he was away when she needed him most. It was a situation made for Bowie—so loyal to his family and courtly to ladies. He rushed both girls to the Alamo.

Other Mexican women also streamed along with the sweating, shouting garrison—Trinidad Saucedo, a pretty teen-age girl . . . Petra Gonzales, an ancient crone. Half hidden in the crowd hurried Nat Lewis, carrying the cream of his stock. Antonio Fuentes was there too; it seemed a lifetime since his release from jail only ten days ago climaxed the feud between Travis and Bowie.

As the garrison swarmed up Potrero Street, across the footbridge, and on to the Alamo, the Mexican townspeople shook their heads. Some of them deeply wanted Santa Anna to win . . . most of them only prayed they could stay out of it . . . but all of them seemed somehow moved at the moment. Watching this ragged band—and knowing that the armed might of His Excellency would soon sweep the town—it was hard not to feel a pang of sympathy. "Poor fellows," a woman cried, "you will all be killed."

Surging into the Alamo, the defenders found a most unusual sight: Sergeant William B. Ward was sober. Normally an inveterate drunkard, Ward was now cool and collected, looking after the guns that covered the main entrance. Curiously, he seemed to be the only person who knew what he was doing in the place.

Otherwise bedlam. On their way up Potrero Street the men had seized some thirty cattle, and now the air echoed with curses and moos as they herded the animals into the corral on the east side of the fort. Bowie and another squad were ransacking nearby huts . . . lugging in sacks of grain which they dropped in the rooms of the long barracks. The artillerymen, quartered here, were swearing as only artillerymen could. Men who had lost or misplaced their equipment were clamoring for Mexican surplus, loading themselves down with hardware they could never hope to use. The women and children, trembling and crying, were crowding into the rooms along the sides of the church. Here they would be safe—or as safe as could be expected, considering the Alamo's entire supply of gunpowder was stored in the same rooms.

Looking on the scene, Nat Lewis had enough. Once again shouldering the best of his stock, he slipped out of the Alamo and headed east into the open country. So did two of the soldiers: Captain Dimitt and Lieutenant Nobles.

Undismayed, Travis worked in the headquarters room in the west wall. Time had run out, and still no reinforcements. Yet now that the enemy were really here, maybe somebody would do something. He scribbled another appeal to Colonel Fannin at Goliad, sent the message off with a young courier named Johnson.

A commotion outside, and Travis looked up to find David

Crockett and Dr. Sutherland clomping in. Crockett was supporting the doctor—his knee, wrenched when the horse fell on it, had stiffened and was now almost useless. Still, Sutherland could be used somehow. In fact, he was just the man to ride to Gonzales and rally the people there.

At this point, Crockett, fidgeting for some assignment himself, blurted out, "Colonel, here am I. Assign me to a position, and I and my twelve boys will try and defend it."

Travis had just the place—the diagonal palisade of stakes and earth that ran from the church to the low barracks on the south side. It was the soft spot in the defense, but it wouldn't be nearly as weak with the world's greatest hunters behind it.

Now back to Sutherland. Again the pen raced over the paper—short, crisp, almost breathless sentences:

> The enemy in large force is in sight. We want men
> and provisions. Send them to us. We have 150 men
> and are determined to defend the Alamo to the last.
> Give us assistance.

Folding the paper, Travis addressed it to "Andrew Ponton, Judge, Gonzales." Then, his dramatic instinct suddenly taking over, he impulsively crossed it out and wrote instead, "To any of the inhabitants of Texas."

Sutherland left shortly after 3 P.M., soon fell in with John W. Smith, who had been off closing his house in town. Smith was also going to Gonzales—to recruit some reinforcements—so the two men rode along together. Reaching a small ford, they glanced back for a last look at San Antonio. The very sight froze them in their tracks: pouring into Military Plaza, their breastplates gleaming in the afternoon sun, were the advance units of Santa Anna's cavalry.

As Smith and Sutherland watched in fascination, storekeeper Nat Lewis unexpectedly panted up. He was on foot, loaded down with saddlebags, and paused only to greet them briefly. Next day he was still going when he met Antonio Menchaca, a friendly Mexican. Asked by Menchaca why he hadn't stayed at the Alamo, Lewis succinctly summed up his philosophy: "I am not a fighting man, I'm a businessman."

Smith and Sutherland hurried on too. Fearing Mexican scouts, they first followed the unused old Goliad road, then took to the open prairie. They did their best to keep out of sight, winding through the mesquite thickets, always bearing east toward Gonzales. Sutherland's leg hurt terribly, and by the time they reached Salado Creek, he could hardly bear the pain. In fact, he was on the point of turning back when from the direction of the Alamo there came the distant, heavy boom of a cannon.

A cannon shot can mean different things. To Sutherland it meant to forget about going back—the fort must now be surrounded. To another horseman not far away, the same shot meant only to reach the Alamo as fast as possible. James Butler Bonham was returning from his unsuccessful attempt to get help from Fannin at Goliad. He was in no particular hurry, and that afternoon was prospecting a little land along the way. But that distant boom started him moving again. Meeting courier Johnson carrying Travis' latest message to Goliad, Bonham learned that the Mexicans had finally arrived and were probably opening fire. Bonham spurred his horse and rode all the harder for the Alamo.

Johnson continued toward Goliad. There was no time to lose, for the appeal he carried was urgent indeed. Signed by both Travis and Bowie, it declared:

> We have removed all our men into the Alamo, where
> we will make such resistance as is due to our honour,
> and that of the country, until we can get assistance

from you, which we expect you to forward immediately. In this extremity, we hope you will send us all the men you can spare promptly. We have one hundred and forty-six men, who are determined never to retreat. We have but little provisions, but enough to serve us till you and your men arrive. We deem it unnecessary to repeat to a brave officer, who knows his duty, that we call on him for assistance.

Perhaps because Fannin was the kind of officer "who knows his duty," Goliad seemed in better shape than ever. The men knew their jobs; their spirits were high. In a burst of enthusiasm they even held a lottery to pick a good name for their fort. "Milam" and "Independence" both had some backing, but "Defiance" was the name finally drawn from the wheel.

So now Fannin waited in Fort Defiance for whatever the future might bring. At last his men were ready for anything. The night before—February 22—he had written Lieutenant Governor Robinson, "I am now happy to say that I have got them quite well satisfied, and being well-disciplined, and doing good work."

It was much farther down in the letter that he also confided to his friend, "I am not desirous of retaining the present, or receiving any other appointment in the army. . . . I am a better judge of my military abilities than others, and if I am qualified to command an Army, I have not found it out."

CHAPTER SEVEN   *"I Answered Them
with a Cannon Shot"*

For General Santa Anna, the
day was looking better after a somewhat shaky start. The previous night he had sent Sesma and the dragoons forward in another attempt to take the enemy by surprise. But the fool halted at 7 A.M. on the Alazan—only a mile and a half from town—fearing, of all things, an attack by the Texans.

He was still there at 12:30 P.M., when the rest of the army came up. Then another two hours lost, while plans were remade and troops realigned for a general advance.

They finally got under way at 2:30 P.M., moving down both the Presidio and Laredo roads. By now the Texans of course knew they were coming, and as Santa Anna's skirmishers approached, a group of defenders appeared at the edge of town. They hoisted a Mexican tricolor with two stars in the middle—standing for Texas and Coahuila as separate states. It was a gesture of loyalty to the old Constitution of 1824, and probably meant that the men belonged to Seguin's militia— about the only people left on either side who still thought the revolution could be settled this way.

Santa Anna's advance guard ignored them. Sweeping steadily forward, the Mexicans were soon in the Campo Santo burial ground; His Excellency himself rode in the lead. The little knot of defenders lowered their flag and retired to the Alamo.

So the "perfidious foreigners" were routed. It was 1813 all over again. The skirmishers, the polished dragoons, the dusty ranks of white-clad infantry drove on. They splashed across San Pedro Creek . . . fanned out over the town . . . and were pouring into Military Plaza by 3 P.M.

Little Juan Indalencio could hear the band coming. Like all small boys, he rushed toward the music and came face to face with a tuba so big it looked like the mouth of an alligator. Terrified, he turned and ran home. Juan Díaz, son of the San Fernando caretaker, heard the music too . . . watched the band march into Main Plaza, followed by standard-bearers carrying the massed battle flags of Mexico. No legalistic pair of stars here; rather the angry, vengeful eagle of the proud Central Government.

But the flag that caught all eyes was no national emblem at all. High in the church tower a group of soldiers flung out a great red banner that flapped and snapped in the afternoon breeze—easily visible to the men in the Alamo some 800 yards away. That was important, for this blood-red flag was the traditional Mexican symbol of no quarter—no surrender—no mercy.

A moment's silence. Then the Alamo's 18-pounder thundered with a roar that shook the town . . . echoed through the nearby hills . . . reverberated over the distant prairies—reaching Bonham, Johnson, Sutherland and Smith, the fleeing townspeople, anyone else within miles. A cannon ball skimmed harmlessly into town, hitting no one—yet everyone—for it was a clear message of defiance addressed to them all.

But unexpectedly there followed hours of inaction and indecision—proving once again that real battles are never set pieces, neatly staged, unfolding with proper dramatic pace. In the Alamo word spread that the Mexicans had sounded a parley just before the cannon shot, and Bowie began wondering about the wisdom of defiance if there really was a chance for negotiation. Seizing the first paper in sight—page eight of an ordinary child's copybook—he dashed off a note to the Mexicans. He explained, almost apologetically, that the garrison had fired before hearing that the Mexicans wanted a truce . . . now he was sending his aide "Benito" Jameson to find out if this was really so.

If Bowie was conciliatory, he still was determined. After ending his note with the salutation "God and the Mexican Federation," he suddenly crossed it out and wrote instead, "God and Texas." On this most basic of issues, Jim Bowie too was committed to independence.

Perhaps that was what made Santa Anna so angry. He refused to receive Jameson; he refused even to answer the note himself. (Who did these rebels think they were, offering to negotiate as equals?) Scornfully tossing the message to his aide, Colonel José Batres, Santa Anna told him to give it the reply it deserved. "The Mexican army," Batres wrote, "cannot come to terms under any conditions with rebellious foreigners to whom there is no other recourse left, if they wish to save their lives, than to place themselves immediately at the disposal of the Supreme Government. . . ."

In other words, unconditional surrender. Jameson took the answer, headed back to the fort—but this was not the end of it. He was no sooner gone than another emissary emerged from the Alamo: this time Albert Martin, speaking for William Barret Travis.

No one ever knew why separate representatives came from each of the fort's co-commanders. Juan Seguin, in the Alamo at the time, later said that Travis wanted no truck with the Mexicans . . . that he was furious when Bowie sent Jameson without consulting him. But this can only be half-right, for Travis too got in touch with the enemy. It seems more likely

The siege tightens, February 23-March 5. (1) The Alamo; (2) the footbridge, scene of abortive parley on the 23rd; (3) San Fernando Church, where Santa Anna raised his red flag; (4) the Yturri house on Main Plaza, where he established his headquarters; (5) Military Plaza; (6) to (10) batteries described by Travis on March 3; (11) battery planted within 250 yards of Alamo on March 4, and later pushed still closer.

that Travis was indeed angry with Bowie, but not so much for making his overture as for breaking their agreement to do everything together. Hence—in a gesture typical of this touchy, sensitive man—Travis' own emissary appeared under his own flag of truce.

Martin walked to the river . . . met the smooth-as-syrup Colonel Almonte on the small footbridge just above Potrero Street. He explained that he was speaking for Travis, that if Almonte wanted to talk matters over, Travis would receive him "with much pleasure."

Officially, Almonte explained that "it did not become the Mexican government to make any propositions through me" . . . that he was there only to listen. Unofficially, he apparently stressed that the Texans' only hope was to surrender; but if they did lay down their arms—promising never to take them up again—their lives and property would be spared. After an hour's talk, Martin said he would return with Travis if the Texans agreed to the Mexican terms; otherwise they would resume fire.

Martin trudged back to the Alamo, and the reply came in the form of another shattering blast from the big 18-pounder. As Travis tersely reported in a message to Houston, "I answered them with a cannon shot."

As evening approached, strange noises replaced the usual sounds of San Antonio. Men stacking rifles . . . unhitching horses . . . fumbling with mess gear. In the Veramendi yard soldiers sweated with picks and shovels at an earthwork for the 5-inch howitzer. At the Nixon house Colonel Almonte pored over the inventory of captured matériel. What a disappointment—items like that barrel of pecans; all of it together worth no more than 3,000 pesos. Far more intriguing were the papers taken from John W. Smith's quarters: piles of maps and plans and lists of names, odd work for a simple carpenter.

In Main Plaza Santa Anna himself wearily dismounted, handed the reins to an orderly, went into the Yturri house on the northwest corner. A flat-roofed, one-story building like most others in San Antonio, it didn't make much of a headquarters. But at least it was strong; the Texans themselves had used it as an outpost.

The Mexican leader turned immediately to the task of organizing a siege. Yes, there must be a military government. Yes, Francisco Ruiz could stay on as *alcalde;* he seemed co-operative whoever held the town.

Outside, the darkened streets seemed almost gloomy. Gone were the tinkling guitars, the laughter and firelit yards. Here and there, people slipped along in the shadows, quietly bent on some mysterious errand. At Gregorio Esparza's house, all was suppressed excitement. Swiftly the family gathered a few things, collected their three children and made off into the dusk. Across the river by the ford, they turned left and headed for the Alamo.

The crumbling old mission was battened down now, silent in the dying light of day. Below the walls the Esparzas waited, while unseen sentries studied them closely. Nothing to worry about here—Gregorio Esparza was one of Seguin's best men, one of the few local Mexicans who could handle artillery. For some unknown reason the family had been delayed until now, but they were no less welcome.

A window in the church opened and one by one the Esparzas were lifted up and through. Twelve-year-old Enrique, tiny but alert and knowledgeable, stumbled over a cannon just inside the window. Finally they were all inside —the last of the defenders to retire to the Alamo.

In the headquarters room Travis and Bowie faced a difficult night. Here they were with the Mexicans just arriving, and already their command arrangement had broken down. Whether Travis was furious at Bowie or not, this much is certain: something had gone very wrong with their agreement to act jointly.

Now that the siege had begun, how to patch things up again? How to work out a mutually tolerable arrangement between the touchy, sensitive Travis and the stubborn, independent Bowie? Certainly friction, indecision, and divided responsibility could only lead to disaster.

At this point, events took a turn beyond the power of either man. Bowie, ill for weeks, collapsed completely. Literally overnight he was unable to carry on. In the medical ignorance of the day, some said it was "hasty consumption"; others pneumonia; others typhoid fever; others compromised on something called "typhoid pneumonia." Almost certainly it was not—as many claimed later—a fall or an accidental blow from a cannonball.

In any case, it immediately solved the command problem. Early in the morning of the 24th Bowie turned his responsibilities over to Travis. Then he had his men take him to a small room in the low barracks. As he was carried off, lying pale and weak on a litter, he called Juana Alsbury to his side: "Sister, do not be afraid. I leave you with Colonel Travis, Colonel Crockett and other friends. They are gentlemen and will treat you kindly."

With the command at last in the hands of one man, the defenders faced their first day of siege. It was clear from the start that the Mexicans meant business—the warm, cloudy morning found them busy digging a new earthwork on the river bank about 400 yards away. Still out of rifle range . . . but they were closer than the night before.

Early that afternoon they opened up. First a 5-inch howitzer . . . then a long 9-pounder . . . then still another 9-pounder. Shells rained on the Alamo. The garrison occasionally answered, but most of the time saved its fire. Everywhere the men huddled at their posts, dodging the flying dirt and stones. Almeron Dickinson on the church roof . . . William Carey at the artillery headquarters in the southwest corner . . . Crockett and his Tennessee "boys" behind the palisade. Others crouched in the irrigation ditches just outside the walls—an advanced line used for extra protection. In the dark little rooms of the church the women and children waited in uncertainty.

A crash in the corral—the cry of a wounded horse. Another crash on the southwest parapet—the 18-pounder sent spinning. Yet another along the wall—this time a 12-pounder dismounted.

At last, silence. It was dark when the Texans took stock. Incredibly—miraculously—no one killed or even hurt. In the gathering dusk, Travis used the lull to send off Albert Martin with the message "To the People of Texas & all Americans in the world."

The Mexicans made no attempt to stop him. Only 600 of Sesma's troops had yet arrived—just enough to cover the south and west. Taken by surprise, they were too far away to counter the move. Besides, they were busy getting organized and in no mood to worry about occasional enemy messengers. There would be plenty of time for that.

As the troops settled down, Santa Anna was everywhere, preoccupied as usual with even the most minor details. At nine o'clock that morning he personally supervised the distribution of shoes. At eleven he was off scouting with a small cavalry unit. By afternoon he was back in town, watching his guns bombard the fort. Local informants—always happy to accommodate either side—offered the good news that four defenders were killed.

That evening His Excellency made a gesture quite in keeping with the sardonic streak that ran deep within him; he ordered his band to serenade the besieged. To the blare of horns and trumpets, he added the blast of an occasional grenade.

There were other bizarre touches. Men out of gunshot were often within earshot, and insults were freely exchanged. Townspeople wandered between the lines without serious interference. Margarito García, a friendly local Mexican, slipped over to the Alamo after dark and chatted with his friends in the garrison. Estaban Pacheco even brought Captain Seguin his meals.

Later in the evening the festive touch suddenly evaporated. A sharp-eyed Texan spied something moving on the footbridge leading across the river. Shouts of alarm, and a blast of rifle fire caught Colonel Juan Bringas crossing the bridge with five or six men on a scouting mission. One Mexican toppled over dead; the others wildly stampeded back across the bridge. In the commotion Colonel Bringas himself fell into the river, barely managed to reach safety as the bullets cut the water around him.

Not all the Mexican efforts were as futile. In the gray drizzling dawn of February 25 the Alamo men found another enemy earthwork going up by the McMullen house just across the river.

More was to come. At 10 A.M. a blare of Mexican bugles . . . a hail of solid shot, grape and canister. Through the smoke the garrison could see little figures swarming across the river; scattering among the adobe huts and wooden shacks south of the main entrance. The defenders held their fire, as the enemy soldiers darted from building to building, always moving closer. Now 200 yards . . . 100 . . . 90.

A roar of cannon from the Alamo. Point-blank range, and Artillery Captains Carey and Dickinson made the most of it. Guns blasted from the church roof, the earthwork stockade, the sandbagged main entrance. The Tennessee "boys" joined in with their squirrel rifles, and David Crockett was everywhere cheering them on. Cavalryman Cleland Simmons, other volunteers, rushed over to lend support. Who wouldn't want to fight beside Crockett today?

The Mexicans wavered, stopped, dodged behind the ramshackle buildings that covered their advance. A serious problem for the Texans. This area, known locally as La Villita, was a jumble of shacks and huts, offering good shelter and dangerously close to the Alamo. Never a part of San Antonio proper, La Villita grew up in the days of the Spanish—a place where soldiers lived with their common-law wives. It had always remained a disreputable section, happily patronized by whatever garrison was holding the town at the moment.

Little matter its past; today La Villita was a valuable military asset. Protected by its buildings, the Mexicans could plant new batteries in the very shadow of the Alamo. Something had to be done.

The Alamo gate briefly opened. Through the smoke Robert Brown, Charles Despallier, James Rose, several others raced with torches toward the nearest buildings. Smoke poured from the thatched roofs; dry wooden walls crackled in flames. Hard dangerous work, for the enemy might be anywhere. James Rose barely escaped the grasping hands of a Mexican officer.

But the job was done. The nearest huts were burned; the Texans had a new field of fire; the Mexicans lost their best cover.

By noon they had had enough. Sesma's men pulled back to the river in confusion, dragging their casualties with them. The Texans relaxed, pleased with the morning's work. Taking stock, Travis discovered that—again miraculously—he had no serious casualties. Only two or three men clipped by flying rocks.

At Mexican headquarters Santa Anna was taking stock too. A definite repulse, but there were compensations. His own losses were also light—only eight casualties. Maybe the men were too cautious, but at least they knew how to take cover. Moreover, he was at last on the Alamo side of the river. Even if the Texans destroyed the buildings nearest the fort, he still held a few good houses close to the water.

To add to the bright side, only 300 Mexicans had made the attack—the Matamoros battalion reinforced by the Jiménez. Things would be different when the rest of the troops reached San Antonio. Where were they anyhow? Santa Anna sent for Colonel Bringas, by now dried out from his midnight swim. Bringas was soon on his way to General Gaona, marching leisurely from the Rio Grande. Gaona was ordered to hurry along his three best companies by forced march.

A hot, muggy afternoon replaced the morning drizzle. The Mexican guns died, the townspeople crawled out from their houses again. Once more noncombatants slipped back and forth across the lines, providing the gossip either side wanted most to hear.

But that evening there was no serenade by Santa Anna's band. At 9 P.M. the wind shifted and a norther soon lashed at attacker and defender alike. Still, it was not an idle night for the Mexican Army. Sesma's rear units had been arriving all day, and finally there were enough troops to start maneuvering in true European fashion.

Colonel Morales led a detachment to dig trenches protecting the hard-won ground in La Villita. Two new batteries were also planted across the river—one about 300 yards south of the Alamo, the other near the powderhouse 1,000 yards to the southeast. The Matamoros battalion moved up to support both. The cavalry occupied the hills to the east and the Gonzales road by the old slaughterhouse—it was now

time to stop that absurd stream of enemy messengers gal-
livanting over the country.

Travis didn't let all of this go unchallenged. A hail of
grape and rifle fire greeted a Mexican unit testing the Alamo
defenses on the north. Later a group of Texans sortied out
on the east for a skirmish with some of Sesma's men. Another squad of defenders raided La Villita to the south.
They yanked down a few of the shacks for firewood—always
a problem at the Alamo—and burned others to clear the area
in front of the new Mexican earthworks.

But it was clear things couldn't go on this way. The
Mexicans were moving closer, drawing the ring tighter all
the time. Feeling the pressure, several of the local Mexican
defenders slipped out during the night, crossed the lines and
gave themselves up. They asked to be taken to Santa Anna, but
were coldly told that His Excellency had gone to bed and
couldn't be disturbed until morning.

In the Alamo Travis dashed off a new appeal for help—
this time addressed to Sam Houston himself. If anyone could
get action, it ought to be the Commander-in-Chief. But how
to send the message? Those ominous mounds of earth—the
mysterious noises in the dark—showed all too clearly that
the garrison now was completely surrounded. No one seemed
especially anxious for the assignment of carrying the message
out.

A council of war debated the problem. As the men talked,
the argument centered more and more on Captain Juan Seguin
as the logical courier. He knew the country; he spoke the
language; he even was a Mexican. But, Travis argued, that
was just why he needed Seguin in the Alamo. There might
be more dealings with Santa Anna; if so, who could be
more useful? Travis finally lost out. When it came to a
vote, Seguin was elected to carry the message.

Darting across the yard to the hospital, Seguin asked Jim Bowie if he could borrow his horse. Bowie, tossing with fever, was now so weak he could barely recognize anybody. Finally he understood. Yes, of course, it was all right.

Into the rain-swept night rode Seguin and his orderly Antonio Cruz. As they passed out of the fort, the two were briefly insulted by the sentry on the northern wall. In the time-honored tradition of all enlisted men everywhere, the man could only see that another officer was heading for a safe place.

Turning onto the Gonzales road, Seguin and Cruz soon came upon the Mexican outpost—a guard of dragoons, dismounted and resting by the wayside. Ever so casually, the two horsemen approached. A challenge in the dark. The answer—two friends, good Mexicans. Almost at the outpost, they suddenly spurred their horses, raced by the startled sentries. Excited yells . . . a fusillade of shots whizzed harmlessly overhead. The two men rode on, building a lead that even the superb Mexican horsemen could never overcome.

And just as well, for the message Seguin carried was the fullest, the most detailed yet. Describing Santa Anna's gradual encirclement, Travis concluded:

> Do hasten on aid to me as rapidly as possible, as from the superior number of the enemy, it will be impossible for us to keep them out much longer. If they overpower us, we fall a sacrifice at the shrine of our country, and we hope posterity and our country will do our memory justice. Give me help, oh my Country!

But a "relief expedition" was already 'n train. At Goliad, Colonel Fannin was now on the move, spurred to action by Travis' first message which had arrived that morning. Orders went out immediately to collect rations, get ready to march.

Niles' South America and Mexico, with a Complete View of Texas

This violent scene, copyrighted in 1837, is almost certainly the first picture ever published of the Battle of the Alamo. Having no idea what the Alamo looked like, the artist solved his problem with smoke and a fleeting glimpse of a castle right out of Sir Walter Scott.

Lieutenant Colonel William Barret Travis, commander of the Alamo, as drawn by his friend Wiley Martin two months before the siege. This sketch was found on the fly-leaf of an old Tennessee gazetteer and is the only contemporary picture of Travis said to exist. Even so, the likeness is questionable; Martin may well have been a better friend than an artist.

Culver Service

Jim Bowie, most famous fighter in the West, shared command with Travis until stricken with illness the first full day of the siege. From this point on, Bowie lay immobilized in bed and Travis took charge of the defense.

Antonio López de Santa Anna, President of Mexico and General-in-Chief of the Army of Operations, who personally directed the siege. The General's *équipage* included monogrammed china, crystal decanters, striped marquee and a silver chamber pot.

San Fernando Church—heart of San Antonio—looking east toward the Alamo, about 800 yards away. From the church's squat tower, Santa Anna hung a blood-red flag, the traditional Mexican symbol of no quarter.

The San Fernando tower, as seen from atop the roofless Alamo church. The artillerymen handling the three 12-pounders here had a good view of Santa Anna's red flag, if they needed any reminder to strengthen their will to resist. This sketch was made ten years later in the course of a U.S. Army survey during the Mexican War.

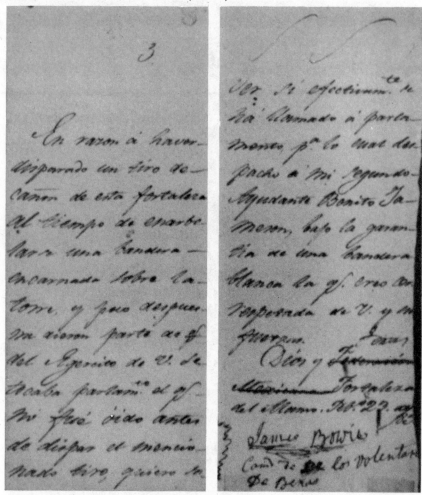

Message sent by James Bowie to the Mexicans as the siege began on February 23. He was trying to find out if a parley had been called—and soon found that this wasn't so. Bowie's fast-failing health shows up in his shaky signature, but his determination is clear from the salutation. After writing *"Dios y Federación Mexicano"* to indicate his loyalty to the old Constitution of 1824, he then crossed it out and wrote instead *"Dios y Texas"* ("God and Texas").

David Crockett, a late arrival in the Alamo, manned the weak southeast palisade
with his Tennessee "boys." As the siege dragged on day after day, Crockett
told his friend Mrs. Dickinson, "I think we had better march out and die in
the open; I don't like to be hemmed up." The remark seems in keeping with
his favorite motto, scrawled under this old engraving.

Sam Houston, Commander-in-Chief of the Texas Army, was strangely inactive during most of the siege. Bitter at being constantly circumvented, he was off dealing with the Indians when the battle began. Later he turned up at Washington-on-the-Brazos for the Convention called to set up a new government. Only after the Declaration of Independence did he move into action with his usual vigor and begin organizing his troops at Gonzales.

ARMY ORDERS.

----------※----------

CONVENTION HALL, WASHINGTON, MARCH 2, 1836.

War is raging on the frontiers. Bejar is besieged by two thousand of the enemy, under the command of general Siezma Reinforcements are on their march, to unite with the besieging army. By the last report, our force in Bejar was only one hundred and fifty men strong. The citizens of Texas must rally to the aid of our army, or it will perish. Let the citizens of the East march to the combat. The enemy must be driven from our soil, or desolation will accompany their march upon us. *Independence is declared*, it must be maintained. Immediate action, united with valor, alone can achieve the great work. The services of all are forthwith required in the field.

SAM. HOUSTON,

Commander-in-Chief of the Army.

P. S. It is rumored that the enemy are on their march to Gonzales, and that they have entered the colonies. The fate of Bejar is unknown. The country must and shall be defended. The patriots of Texas are *appealed to, in behalf of their bleeding country.*   S. H.

Houston issued this broadside the day independence was declared. Calling the citizens to arms, he then left for Gonzales to organize his army. Despite this appeal, the turn-out was at first disappointing.

Taken from *El Soldado Mexicano*

Dawn, March 6, 1836, the massed bands of Santa Anna played these stirring notes. Called the *Degüello*, the music was a hymn of hate and merciless death, played to spur the Mexican troops forward in their final assault on the Alamo.

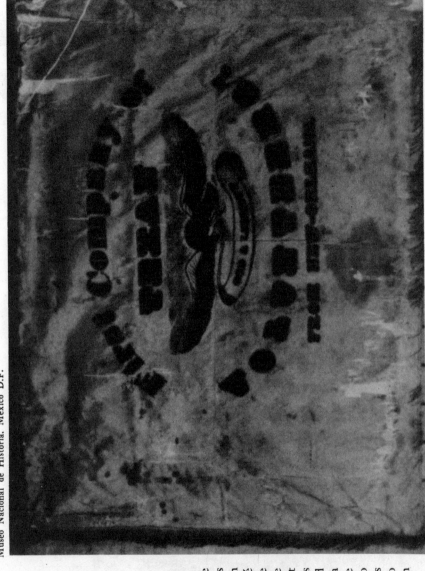

This flag of the New Orleans Greys was ripped down by Lieutenant José María Torres. The Mexican colors were raised instead, but Lieutenant Torres was shot and killed in the process. Santa Anna later sent the flag back to Mexico City, where it lies today—crumbling to pieces in brown wrapping paper.

Antonio Perez left the ranch of Don Jose M. Arocha on Sunday morning last and returned in the evening with the notice that the soldiers of Santa Anna had that morning entered the Alamo and kill'd all the men that was inside and that he saw about 500 of the Mexican soldiers that had been kill'd and as many wounded

Thrall's *A Pictorial History of Texas*

First word of the Alamo's fall was brought to Gonzales on March 11 by Andres Barcena and Anselmo Borgara, two Mexican refugees. Above is an extract from the interview with Barcena conducted by Houston's aide Major Hockley. Below, Hockley confers with the General during the retreat that followed.

VERY LATE FROM TEXAS.

"A sigh is heard on every gale,
A voice breathes from each *bloody grave;*
My country! hear they children's wail—
Rise and avenge thy MARTYRED BRAVE"

SAN ANTONIO HAS FALLEN!! AND THE GALLANT BAND OF PATRIOTS,

who defended its walls with undaunted heroism, born down and overpowered, have BEEN INHUMANLY BUTCHERED!!! COL. DAVID CROCKETT IS AMONG THE SLAIN—THE BLOOD OF FREEDOM'S MARTYRS CALLS ALOUD FOR REVENGE!!

By the documents below, the reader will find a melancholy confirmation of the rumors brought from Texas by Mr. William Butler of this place. To that gentleman we are indebted for a copy of the Declaration of Independence, and the documents which accompany it on our first page. The more recent intelligence below was brought express from Washington by Captain Benjamin W. Pedford of Sommerville, to whose polite attention, and that of Maj. Chalmers of this place, we are indebted for copies.

Copy of a letter from Calvin Henderson Esq.

My Dear [....]—I snatch a few [moments] from the press of preparation, to give you a small sketch of things here. The Convention is still in session and its members are acting like men: You will have seen before this reaches you, their gallant Declaration—'twas nobly done. At the moment that Santa Anna entered Texas, at the head of 8,000 men, breathing desolation in all directions, they took their manly stand.

Now comes the struggle. [....]

News of the massacre was a sensation throughout the United States. At a time when any headline was a novelty, this choice item—taken from the Columbia, Tennessee, *Observer* of April 14, 1836—was bound to stir immense excitement, propelling a flood of aid and volunteers to Texas.

TEXAS!!

Emigrants who are desirious of assisting Texas at this important crisis of her affairs may have a free passage and equipments, by applying at the

NEW-YORK and PHILADELPHIA HOTEL,

On the Old Levee, near the Blue Stores.

Now is the time to ensure a fortune in Land: To all who remain in Texas during the War will be allowed 1280 Acres.

To all who remain Six Months, 640 Acres.

To all who remain Three Months, 320 Acres.

And as Colonists, 4600 Acres for a family and 1470 Acres for a Single Man.

New Orleans, April 23d, 1836.

Exactly a week after news of the Alamo's fall reached New Orleans, this recruiting poster appeared on the city's streets. Appeals to idealism were all very well, but the broadside wisely included specific details on the free land that awaited the volunteers.

Six weeks after the massacre, Houston's little army pounced on the Mexicans at San Jacinto. The Texans' battle cry was "Remember the Alamo!" and the enemy thoroughly under- stood what was meant. As indicated in this taunting cartoon published in New York, many of Santa Anna's men sur- rendered, desperately pleading, "Me no Alamo."

Author's Collection

In 1846 a U.S. Army survey included this print of the ruined Alamo church (above). It was soon picked up by *Gleason's Pictorial*, embellished with romantic trappings, and passed on to an eager public (below). The epoch of the Alamo had already caught America's imagination, and the end is not yet in sight.

They would go to the Alamo, whatever the cost. As Fannin's young aide, Captain Brooks, wrote his sister that day: "We have resolved to do our duty and to perish under the walls of the Alamo, if stern necessity requires it."

Fannin too was firm now. Writing his friend Lieutenant Governor Robinson that day, there were no more self-doubts, no secret dread of command. He felt that his march to the Alamo was militarily unsound but it simply had to be done: "The appeal of Colonels Travis and Bowie cannot be resisted, and particularly with the description of troops now in the field—sanguine, chivalrous volunteers. Much must be risked to relieve the besieged."

CHAPTER EIGHT

"I Don't Like to Be Penned Up"

James Rose, who stammered when excited, must have been hopelessly lost for words. There to the east, in the first light of February 26, swept a detachment of Sesma's cavalry, circling toward the rear of the Alamo. A group of Texans raced out the northern postern to meet them head-on. Rifles blazed, the Mexicans veered off, and another threat was over.

There was little rest for anyone this cold, bleak day. The dramatic Travis was the last man to want a static defense, and he worked hard to hold the initiative, to keep the enemy off-guard until help could come. He sent a squad to the south to pull down more of the nearby shacks for firewood; another to the west to scoop up buckets of water from an irrigation ditch. After dark, still another group sallied out to La Villita, burning more of the huts that gave the enemy cover.

In the Alamo, Green Jameson's men dug more trenches, threw up more earthworks to bolster the walls and serve as parapets. Ticklish work, for they had to dodge a steady hail of Mexican shot—Sesma's eight guns were now to the west, south and southeast. The Alamo replied only occasionally; ammunition was running low and orders were out to hold fire. The gunners whiled away the time as best they could—Almeron Dickinson with his wife, John McGregor with his bagpipes, Henry Warnell with his endless opinions on horses.

No rest for the riflemen. They kept a keen, sharp-eyed watch on La Villita, happily blazed away at any Mexican rash or careless enough to show his head. By now the Texans had it down to a science. For cover, they used the nearby irrigation ditches as well as Jameson's earthen parapets. For faster fire power, each man kept four or five loaded rifles by his side. And of course they were all deadly shots.

Take the case of that Mexican engineer, reconnoitering across the river some two hundred yards from the Alamo. He worked in the open, apparently sure he was safe. A man in buckskin climbed up on the southwest corner of the fort —a living monument against the bleak, gray sky—and coolly shot the Mexican dead.

Of course everyone always said the Texan was Crockett. No one will ever know for sure, but Captain Rafael Soldana of the Tampico battalion later pictured a Texan that gives food for thought:

> A tall man, with flowing hair, was seen firing from the same place on the parapet during the entire siege. He wore a buckskin suit and a cap all of a pattern entirely different from those worn by his comrades. This man would kneel or lie down behind the low parapet, rest his long gun and fire, and we all learned to keep at a good distance when he was seen to make ready to shoot. He rarely missed his mark, and when he fired he always rose to his feet and calmly reloaded his gun seemingly indifferent to the shots fired at him by our men. He had a strong, resonant voice and often railed at us, but as we did not under-

stand English we could not comprehend the import
of his words further than that they were defiant.
This man I later learned was known as "Kwockey."

The Mexicans soon learned to keep down. Even if only
wounded, they faced the fresh peril of their medical service.
In contrast, the Texans sometimes stood in full view, openly
challenging the enemy to do his worst. It was hardly fair.
Sesma's troops were indeed poor shots, but even the brilliant
Tennesseans could have done little with ancient smoothbores
that reached only seventy yards.

All day on the 26th the Texan sharpshooters braved the
bitter north wind, nor was there much relief that evening.
The night was filled with alarms, bugle calls, distant shouts,
the nerve-racking feeling that the enemy was always inching
closer. Why didn't help come?

Saturday, February 27, found the norther still blowing.
Travis continued his strategy of active defense, but strain
and weariness were beginning to tell. No sorties, little firing
from the Alamo this day. And the defenders suddenly found
themselves facing a new peril—Mexican troops by the mill
to the north were blocking the irrigation ditch, hoping
to cut off the fort's water. Jameson put a squad to work on
a half-finished well at the south end of the plaza.

The men hit water all right, but they also undermined an
earth and timber parapet by the low barracks. The mound
collapsed, leaving no way to fire safely over the wall.

Midafternoon. The Alamo lookouts suddenly yelled and
pointed. A handsomely mounted Mexican general was passing along the enemy lines, surrounded by a glittering corps
of aides and dragoons. The Texans fired away at this inviting
target, but it must have been out of range, for no hits were
scored. The men's disappointment would have been even

greater had they realized the flashy horseman was Santa Anna himself.

In the cold, windy night Travis penned one more of his fervent calls for help. This time to Fannin again. And this time he handed the message to the man he trusted most. James Butler Bonham, the South Carolinian, had shown his devotion by getting back to the Alamo after the siege began. Now he would have another chance to prove his loyalty. The northern postern opened briefly and Bonham galloped off into the night.

February 28, and another gray day. The norther was dying down but a dreary drizzle seemed almost worse. The men huddled under soggy blankets, or vainly tried to keep warm by damp, smoky fires. Little rest, little food, little reason to be cheerful. They could see a Mexican squad making another attempt to cut off their water. A second enemy detachment was busily planting a new battery by the old mill, perhaps eight hundred yards to the north. The other Mexican guns were stepping up their fire; and finally there was always that red flag on the church tower. It had no snap today—just a wet rag hanging limp in the rain—but it still meant no quarter.

Bowie, though desperately ill, did his best to encourage the men. He had his cot brought out . . . urged them to keep fighting, whatever happened. Crockett turned on the tested charm that had never failed him yet. His favorite device during these dark days was to stage a musical duel between himself and John McGregor. The Colonel had found an old fiddle somewhere, and he would challenge McGregor to get out his bagpipes to see who could make the most noise. The two of them took turns, while the men laughed and whooped and forgot for a while the feeling of being alone.

Still, stunts and encouraging talk could only accomplish

so much. Nothing could hide the fact that the trap was closing, that the Mexicans were drawing the ring ever tighter.
Artilleryman Henry Warnell jammed his huge quid of tobacco against the side of his mouth and blurted the words
that so many felt: "I'd much rather be out in that open
prairie. . . . I don't like to be penned up like this."

Santa Anna would have been pleased. Along with Napoleonic tactics, psychological warfare was his forte. It was his
idea to fill every night with bugle calls, cheers, volleys of
musketry, bursts of artillery—all designed to harass the Texans,
break them down, wear them out.

But as the days passed, the Mexicans were wearing down
too. Colonel Almonte found practically no supplies in San
Antonio, and the troops' skimpy rations were fast running
out. Everything depended on the wagon trains somewhere
to the rear. If Travis wondered where Fannin was, Santa
Anna was growing no less concerned about Filisola, Gaona
and the rest. Miserable sluggards, were they never on time?

On the 27th, he sent more couriers to prod them along.
A barrage of orders pricked and needled the methodical
Filisola: "Speed up the march" . . . "Send ahead all supplies you can gather" . . . "Hurry the money held by the
Commissary General" . . . "Be sure to send us two to three
hundredweight of salt, none here—not a grain—and we need
it badly."

Actually, Filisola was still dawdling by the Rio Grande.
But he soon pushed ahead into Texas, trying his best to please
his impulsive, impatient chief. He was sadly aware that His
Excellency would never understand the problems—finding
water, spurring the men, giving them even an ounce of desire, when all along the way they saw nothing but the broken
debris of Santa Anna's own march—dead mules, abandoned
oxen, smashed cases, wrecked carts left even with their har-
nesses dangling.

In San Antonio, Santa Anna finally improvised. That local Mexican Manuel Menchaca had always been helpful. Now the General sent him to find some food. Menchaca knew just where to go. He led a raiding party straight to the Seguin and Flórez *ranchos*—both owners sympathized with the Texan cause. He soon cleaned them out of corn, beef and hogs.

Feeling better, Santa Anna despatched another courier on the night of February 27—this time to Mexico City, reporting his success to date. His Excellency glowingly described the capture of San Antonio, but totally ignored the fact that across the river over 150 defiant Texans still held out in the Alamo.

By now it was time for a brief dalliance. Always an admirer of beautiful women, Santa Anna had surveyed the local scene well, and a couple of accommodating ladies were soon incorporated into his entourage. Their presence was later wrapped in intrigue and romance by Sergeant Francisco Becerra, perhaps the most unreliable of all the Mexican participants who spun yarns for the Texans in years to come. Becerra loved to tell how a mock marriage ceremony was performed by a rascal disguised as a priest, linking Santa Anna to the purest of San Antonio's pure.

Be that as it may, there was certainly a girl. And delectable too, for His Excellency ultimately rewarded her well. He had his own carriage take her back to San Luis Potosí, where she might be saved from the confining life of the provinces. As a parting gift, he gave the girl and a companion 2,000 pesos.

Such pleasant interludes were rudely shattered on February 28. On that day word suddenly reached Santa Anna that Fannin was coming to the Alamo's rescue—marching from Goliad with 200 men.

Good espionage, but actually Fannin's force was even stronger. After frantic preparations, he had started from

Goliad on the afternoon of February 26 with 320 men and four cannon. Down the hill toward the San Antonio River his troops doggedly made their way. Heads bent low against the biting wind, for the norther was blowing hard. The men moved slowly, unevenly; most were on foot, and the oxen that drew their guns were never more stubborn.

Two hundred yards from town, while still in clear sight of the Goliad mission, a wagon broke down. Everything stopped for repairs; then the whole caravan crept on down to the river edge. Now two more wagons came apart; and worse yet, the single yokes of oxen weren't strong enough to drag the guns across.

Aimless hours of waiting around, while the oxen were double-teamed for each gun. It was late afternoon by the time all the artillery was over, and the men were weary and discouraged. Fannin decided to let them rest. They couldn't have gone on anyhow, for the ammunition wagon was still on the wrong side of the river.

As evening approached, Fannin made another carefully considered decision. They certainly couldn't march in the dark, so they might as well camp for the night and start fresh in the morning. He ordered the men to stack their arms and turn the oxen loose to graze. Spirits drooped lower, as the wind continued to blow.

Dawn on the 27th brought an unpleasant discovery. During the night the oxen had wandered off. Fannin sent out working parties to herd them back . . . and more hours passed.

It must have been midmorning when he got the request to hold a council of war. Normally Fannin dreaded the democratic process in military affairs ("Spare us, in God's name, from elections in camp"), but this time he seemed almost relieved. A meeting of all his officers convened in the bushes, and hesitantly someone raised the question that troubled more than one mind: was this expedition really a wise idea?

The firebrands seemed shocked, but Fannin had not been to West Point for nothing. He knew something about logistics, and he patiently pointed out their supply situation: they had only a little dried beef, half a barrel of rice, and no cattle except those needed to draw the guns. The nearest supplies lay at Seguin's ranch, seventy miles away, altogether a dismal prospect.

But ignore the Alamo's call for help? Fannin sympathized; however, he was a trained soldier, taught to weigh military odds realistically. Here they were—320 volunteers, four cannon, little ammunition. Against them—thousands of well-equipped, superbly drilled Mexican troops.

But *abandon* the men in the Alamo? Well, a professional military mind must consider the over-all strategic picture. If they went to San Antonio, Goliad would be left practically undefended. An enemy attack would easily overrun the small rear-guard—endangering the supplies at Dimitt's Landing, exposing the Texans' whole left flank.

Sound tactics ruled the day. The guns and wagons were painfully withdrawn across the river, and the relief expedition trudged back up the hill to the old stone compound they called Fort Defiance.

By the 28th—when Santa Anna got first wind of the march —Fannin's feet were planted firmly back in Goliad. In fact, if Henry Warnell hated being penned up in the Alamo, Colonel Fannin seemed to relish the prospect in his own stronghold. "I have about 420 men here," he wrote Joseph Mims, "and if I can get provisions in tomorrow or next day, can maintain myself against any force."

All that day the Goliad men worked to strengthen their fort. They were still at it around 6 P.M. when a mud-spattered courier galloped up with appalling news. Mexican forces under General Urrea had just fallen on San Patricio, fifty miles to the south. There they surprised Colonel Frank Johnson and the remnants of the once carefree Matamoros expedition. Johnson and a few of his men escaped, but nearly everyone was slaughtered. It seemed the Mexicans weren't taking prisoners.

For Fannin, it was the final vindication of his strategy. He rushed off a letter to his friend, Lieutenant Governor Robinson, breaking the news and carefully pointing out that it justified his decision to pull his men back: "The propriety of their retrograde movement will now be apparent."

Then, waxing furious at Texans who wouldn't help other Texans, he eloquently asked: "What must be the feelings of the Volunteers now shut up in Bexar . . . will not *curses* be heaped on the heads of the sluggards who remained at home?"

CHAPTER NINE

"30 Men Has Thrown Themselves into Bears"

At least it was warm again. The bitter north wind no longer whipped through the low barracks where Jim Bowie tossed in his cot. It no longer lashed at the high platform in the back of the church, where Almeron Dickinson worked over the long 12-pounder by the east wall. Monday, February 29, was another gray day, but the norther had given way to a mild, westerly breeze.

The men in the Alamo needed it. Worn down by six nights of siege—jittery from the endless shouts and wild bugle calls in the dark—they were bitter and discouraged. Yet they hung on. Partly because, bound together by common peril, none dared to be the first to give in. But another reason lay even deeper. They simply could not shake the conviction that here, above all, was the place to stand. Sooner or later everyone would see it. Meanwhile they must hold out till the rest of Texas woke up.

But when? Today rounded out their first full week in the Alamo, and still no sign of help. Nor, oddly enough, any all-out Mexican assault. Only the earthworks that moved steadily closer . . . the elaborate, complicated maneuvering that went on just out of range.

There was a lot of it today. First a whole battalion of infantry crossed the ford to the south, circled left, passed the Gonzales road, and took up a position in the open brush to the east. Then it marched back again. Night fell before the Alamo men could see where the battalion finally ended up, but something must be brewing.

And indeed it was. Santa Anna had been laying plans, deploying men ever since he heard that Fannin was marching from Goliad. Troops must be sent to wipe him out. But this took manpower, something he didn't have—wouldn't have—until that snail Gaona arrived. So he must improvise —borrow troops from here and there for a special force to intercept Fannin. This meant weakening his ring around the Alamo, but the risk must be taken. He loved to gamble anyhow.

Orders went out to Sesma—take the Allende battalion from the east, the Dolores cavalry from the Gonzales road; head down the river toward Goliad. Ten cases of ammunition authorized. Then a final, laconic reminder: "In this war, you know, there ought to be no prisoners."

That evening the Allende men wearily shouldered their muskets and shuffled off into the dusk, convinced in the fashion of all infantrymen that the officers were crazy. Only that afternoon they had been sent to these bushes east of the Alamo; now they were being sent away again.

Behind them, General Manuel Fernández Castrillón did his best to seal the gap they left. A hard-luck general, Castrillón always seemed to get the worst assignments. Now he spread his men in a thin line, running from the powder house on the Gonzales road to a new earthwork near the irrigation ditch 800 yards northeast of the Alamo. A weak position at best, and weaker still when another norther suddenly struck at midnight. In the howling blackness, it was hard to see or hear anything. Just the sort of night when the "perfidious foreigners" might try to break out.

As it happened, nobody had any plans for breaking out, but there were men in that darkness with very definite plans for breaking in. They had been laying these plans ever since Dr. Sutherland and John W. Smith burst into the little town of Gonzales, seventy miles away, on the afternoon of February 24.

In Gonzales that afternoon, Prudence Kimball had been doing the family wash on the banks of the Guadalupe River. She was busily scrubbing away at 4 o'clock when her husband George rushed up to break the news. Couriers had just arrived . . . the Mexicans were attacking . . . Travis was besieged in the Alamo . . . he desperately needed help. And then the words that came hardest—he must answer the call; he might not be back.

George Kimball was typical of the men who had come to Texas for a fresh start. He was no big land speculator or gambler—just a hatter from New York. He had come to ply his trade in Gonzales, which seemed like a promising town. And he had prospered; his little hat factory on Water Street hummed with activity. He was single when he came but soon found Prudence Nash, a pretty young widow. They now had a baby son, another child on the way. He had everything to lose by going to the Alamo—yet everything to gain, for this fine, new life seemed very much worth fighting for.

That was the way with most of Gonzales. John Flanders, weary of feuding with his father over business, had at last discovered a free, open life far better than any factory near Boston. Dolphin Floyd, the Carolina farm boy, never found his "old rich widow," but in Gonzales he met Ester House, a widow who was neither very old nor very rich. She suited him fine, and perhaps to his surprise he too had now happily settled down. Men like these were already proud of Gonzales' record as the "Lexington of Texas." Now they poured out in answer to Smith's and Sutherland's appeal.

George Kimball was the obvious choice to lead them. Only the day before he had been elected the lieutenant of a home-guard unit ambitiously christened "The Gonzales Ranging Company of Mounted Volunteers." There were only 22 of them, and nobody expected to have anything to do so soon, but they made a perfect nucleus for the relief force. The available members quickly came forward—Marcus Sewell, the English shoemaker; Jesse McCoy, recently sheriff; John G. King, a great friendly bear of a man. Most of them were young, but Isaac Millsaps was forty-one; he also had a blind wife and seven children.

New volunteers steadily swelled the ranks. Young Jonathan Lindley put aside his surveying tools. Albert Martin arrived with Travis' message of the 24th, could hardly wait to get back. Jacob Darst turned up after delivering supplies to Goliad, his head still swimming with the fervor of Fannin's oratory.

Earthier reasons—like family pressure or the questioning glance of a neighbor—also played a part. Thomas R. Miller, the richest man in town, lived just a few doors from Darst and Kimball; it was hard to ignore their summons. Besides, Miller was unlucky in love. He had recently lost his pretty young bride, Sydney Gaston, to a dashing 19-year-old named Johnnie Kellogg—a crushing blow to middle-aged pride. Miller also joined up.

Young Kellogg himself felt the urge. So did Johnnie Gaston, his new 16-year-old brother-in-law who would follow him anywhere. And if Gaston was old enough, so was Galba Fuqua, another enthusiastic 16-year-old. They all joined up.

It was 2 P.M. Saturday, February 27, when the group set out from the public square. At the head rode George Kimball; beside him, Albert Martin. Guiding them was John W. Smith, the versatile San Antonio carpenter who knew the country better than anyone. The rest trailed along—25 lean men, loaded down with rifles, blankets, food and ammunition.

As they reached John G. King's place on their way out of town, a tall, thin boy ran out and caught Kimball's reins. It was young William P. King, and he begged to go in place of his father. The elder King was badly needed at home; after all, there were nine children to feed. William was sure he could do just as well—he was the oldest, all of fifteen.

Kimball nodded, the switch was made, and the band continued on. They slipped across the Guadalupe ford, by the Batemans' lonely farm and on west over the empty prairie. Next day, they stopped at the Cibolo, looking for more recruits. They picked up seven, including David Cummings of the Alamo garrison, who had been off prospecting land when the siege began. They rested most of the 29th, gauging their time so as to make the final dash at night. At last, just at sunset they crossed the river and continued west— 32 men riding into the fading twilight.

"Do you wish to go into the fort, gentlemen?" asked a polite voice in English, as they groped their way toward the Alamo shortly after midnight. There, just ahead, sat a stranger on horseback calmly awaiting their answer.

"Yes," someone called out, tired of the black night and the norther that howled in their ears.

"Then follow me," said the polite stranger, swinging his horse into the head of the column. The men fell in behind, relieved to escape the ticklish problem of finding their way through the Mexican lines.

John W. Smith was puzzled. There was something about this man he didn't like. His voice perhaps . . . his failure to identify himself . . . the distance he kept. On the other hand, he spoke good English, wasn't wearing an enemy uniform, could well be some friendly colonist. It was clearly one of those situations where a scout must fall back on his intuition. "Boys," Smith suddenly blurted, "it's time to be after shooting that fellow!"

The stranger moved even faster than the Texans. With a great kick, he spurred his horse, bolted into the bushes, and was gone before a gun could be raised.

Cautiously, very cautiously, the Gonzales men pushed on through the brush. First to the left, then to the right, they heard the clanking of equipment. That meant stick to the middle . . . stay low . . . keep quiet. They edged on forward, squinting hard into the night. At last they saw it—looming out of the darkness directly ahead were the silent old walls of the Alamo.

Suddenly a rifle cracked from the fort. Hit in the foot, a Gonzales man exploded with an oath that could only come from an American. The firing stopped, and a dim light glimmered in the dark, as the postern swung open. Then with a final dash, the 32 men from Gonzales surged into the Alamo at 3 A.M., Tuesday, the first of March.

The morning dawned bitterly cold again—but who cared? For the Texans, the arrival of the Gonzales contingent was the greatest thing that had happened since the siege began. The reaction was what might be expected from men who had vainly waited a week. Crockett and McGregor, who conducted their musical duels at high as well as low moments, must have split the air with fiddle and bagpipes.

Later the garrison indulged in a more practical form of celebration. To save ammunition, Travis now had standing orders against using the guns except to repel an attack. But apparently in a burst of whimsy—extremely rare for this intense young man—he relaxed the rule that afternoon. Dickinson's men rushed to one of the 12-pounders that pointed out over the west wall; let fly a double blast at a house on Main Plaza where the enemy seemed especially active. One shot missed, but the other crashed into the building, sending stone, timber and Mexicans flying. Unfortunately for their celebration, the Texans never knew that they had just hit the headquarters of Santa Anna himself.

As luck would have it, His Excellency was out. He had gone off reconnoitering that afternoon and was now at the old mill, some 800 yards to the north, inspecting his camp there. A volley of orders told General Ampudia to build more trenches.

If Santa Anna seemed disturbed, he had reason to be. That fool General Gaona still hadn't come. With Sesma off chasing Fannin, the east was far too weak. And to cap it all, Sesma had found nothing. He ranged as far down the river as Tinaja, with no sign of Fannin at all. Now he was returning, and they were all right back where they started.

Santa Anna would have been even more agitated had he known the immense stir caused by Travis' letter of February 24. Signs multiplied that Texas was at last shaking off its lethargy. At Victoria, word spread that Colonel Wharton had crossed the Guadalupe with a relief party bound for Bexar. In San Felipe, Captain Moseley Baker ordered the local militia to get ready; as they prepared to march on the 29th, two blushing ladies gave them a homespun flag proclaiming independence—by now the goal of everyone.

In Washington-on-the-Brazos, where the delegates were assembling to vote for independence, the air was electric with excitement. On March 1 Sam Houston reappeared, setting off a roar of acclaim. On the 2nd, the Convention rammed through its declaration of independence—another wild demonstration. Later the delegates were again in a tumult when word arrived that the Gonzales men had marched to the Alamo's relief. Lieutenant Governor Robinson excitedly wrote Colonel Fannin the news: "This moment information has been given that about 30 men has thrown themselves into Bears. . . ."

Gonzales itself was again in an uproar. Late on the 27th a letter had arrived from Colonel Fannin. He had written it early that morning while sitting in the bushes wondering what to do, but he said nothing about his various misgivings. Instead, he was full of the boldest plans. He explained that he was on his way to the Alamo with 300 men, and laid out an intricate plan for a rendezvous on the Cibolo. As he described it, all the various relief forces would link up there and then march together on San Antonio.

It was too late to tell Kimball—he was already on his way— but Dr. Sutherland and Horace Alsbury quickly recruited twelve more men and prepared to join this ambitious project. Across the Guadalupe, Juan Seguin rallied 25 of his local Mexicans. The two groups set out together on the 28th, hoping to overtake Kimball's company and incorporate them too, but they reached the Cibolo too late for that. Little matter. The 300 men from Goliad were the main thing anyhow. Seguin and Sutherland settled down to wait for Fannin's arrival.

In Goliad, Fannin too was settling down—to await the delayed arrival of the Mexicans. He had completely forgotten the master plan for joining all parties together for a grand-scale march. He thought only of the siege he faced. "I am pretty well prepared to make battle," he wrote Lieutenant Governor Robinson. "I have nearly completed my fortifications, and have beef enough for 20 days, and will have more. . . . I am resolved to await your orders let the consequence be what it may."

But as the days passed and still no Mexicans, Fannin began to take heart again. Hearing that Colonel Wharton had crossed the Guadalupe en route to the Alamo, he revived his old rendezvous plan. On March 1, he wrote Captains De Sauque and Chenoworth foraging on the Cibolo. Reporting Wharton's advance, he stressed: "If you can find him or communicate with Gonzales and know how many volunteers will form a junction, if informed speedily, I will push out 200 and co-operate. . . ."

The more he thought about the idea, the better he liked it. By March 2, the men of Goliad were once again getting ready to start out for the Alamo. "If the division of the Mexican Army advancing toward this place has met any obstacles," Captain John Brooks wrote his mother, "200 men will be detached for relief of Bexar. We will probably march tomorrow or next day, if we can procure fresh oxen enough to transport our baggage and two 6-pounders."

CHAPTER TEN

"I Will Report the Result of My Mission"

Colonel Fannin was coming—the rumor raced through the Alamo. To William Ward at the main gate . . . to Micajah Autry at the stockade . . . to Gregorio Esparza in the church . . . to Eliel Melton, slaughtering beef in the corral to the east. No one knew how it started—perhaps with some Gonzales man; perhaps out of thin air, the way rumors so often begin among soldiers.

In any case, it made sense. After all, Fannin was the leader who had always called for action: "March to meet the Tyrant" . . . "Kick at the moon, whether we hit the mark or not." He was the man who asked less than a month ago, "Will the freemen of Texas calmly fold their arms, and wait until the approach of their deadly enemy compels them to protect their own firesides?"

And now, the arrival of the Gonzales contingent showed it could be done. If these 32 lightly armed men had made it, certainly Fannin's 400 could get through. They even had artillery.

Best of all, James Butler Bonham had been sent to fetch them. There was no more forceful man in the garrison than this young South Carolinian. He went after what he wanted —within two weeks of coming to Texas, he was taking things up direct with Sam Houston. And people listened to him. "His influence in the army is great," Houston observed, "more so than some who would be generals."

So from the moment Bonham left for Goliad on February 27, the men in the Alamo began counting the days. He should get there early on the 29th . . . Fannin's force would start that morning . . . they were bound to arrive before dawn on March 2 . . . at the very latest, March 3.

Yet March 2 came with no sign of Fannin. Only another Mexican battalion to the east. Then March 3, and still no Fannin. Just a new Mexican battery going up on the north. Had even Bonham let them down?

In a way he had. Reaching Goliad on February 29, Bonham found Fannin in one of his low periods. Just back from his abortive relief march, the Colonel was in no mood to try again. Nor did it help when Colonel Frank Johnson arrived that day, fresh from the disaster at San Patricio. He poured out harrowing stories of Mexican butchery. It all made Fannin less anxious than ever to leave his fort. He urged Bonham to stay with him in Goliad.

No, Bonham explained, he had promised to get help; he must try somewhere else.

He next headed for Gonzales, probably arriving late March 1. Here he found only a town of women and children. Kimball's little band had already marched. Sutherland's and Alsbury's men were on the way too. Seguin's company was supposed to be with them. Most of the older men were at Washington-on-the-Brazos, thrashing out the declaration of independence.

But Bonham did find a 19-year-old named Ben Highsmith. He had left the Alamo with an appeal for Fannin shortly before Santa Anna arrived. Turned down, he headed back for San Antonio alone, only to discover the enemy had come. Reaching Powder House Hill, he found his way hopelessly blocked by the Mexicans. Worse, they spied him and the Dolores cavalry chased him a good six miles. Turning up in Gonzales at last, Highsmith now poured out the story of his close escape. He was sure no one could get through the Mexican lines. Better stay here, he urged Bonham; reinforcements would soon be coming from San Felipe and the other towns to the east. Then they would have some chance.

"I will report the result of my mission to Travis or die in the attempt," Bonham stubbornly answered. And next morning, March 2, he crossed the Guadalupe ford and headed off toward the Alamo.

It took more than a brave man to make this decision. It called for the chivalry of Scott, the fire of Byron, a love of the *beau geste*, and a romantic attachment to desperate chances for a noble cause. Qualities of the age, and James Butler Bonham had them all.

Born in 1807 near Red Bank, South Carolina, he came from the best family in the area. On a distinctly lower plane, the Travises lived a few miles away, but they moved to Alabama when Barret Travis was nine and Jim Bonham eleven. It's doubtful whether the two boys ever knew each other really well.

Bonham grew into a tall, dark boy with black wavy hair and flashing brown eyes. He looked rebellious and was. Entering South Carolina College in 1824, he was always in trouble. Senior year, he battled the authorities over going to class in bad weather, the meals served in commons. But where other college boys might only complain about the food, Bonham dressed in deep mourning, rallied his classmates to the cause, staged a giant demonstration. Not surprisingly he was expelled.

Odd training for a lawyer, but by 1830 Bonham was practicing in Pendleton, South Carolina. Then the Nullification crisis and another stormy interlude. Bonham was, of course, in the thick of it—boy colonel, aide to Governor Hamilton, dashing artilleryman with a flaming red sash and silver epaulets.

The crisis over, he went back to his practice in Pendleton. Then, less than a year later, another storm—this time in the courtroom. His client was a lady in distress . . . the opposing lawyer insulted her . . . Bonham caned him. When the judge ordered an apology, Bonham threatened to tweak His Honor's nose. Ninety days for contempt of court.

Inevitably the ladies of Pendleton filled his cell with flowers, deluged him with delicacies. Finally released, he was the town hero, the dark Galahad who made every fair heart beat faster—except the one he wanted. The last person to take defeat in love lightly, Bonham was crushed. Filled with despair he left Pendleton early in 1834, joined the restless tide to the West. By April he was starting practice all over again in Montgomery, Alabama.

He cut loose the past completely. Out with the sash, the epaulets, all the other trappings of the old days. ("Sell them as well as you can, but sell them, for they are of no use to me.") Yet the patient, upward struggle had never been for him, and when the Texas storm broke in 1835, Bonham was immediately in the thick of it. His descendants later said he joined at Travis' urging. Maybe, but the evidence is lacking. The fact is, Bonham being Bonham couldn't possibly have stayed out.

He went to Mobile, the center of excitement, and led the rally that jammed the Shakespeare Theater on October 17. At a second rally three nights later, the citizens appointed him to take their resolutions direct to Sam Houston. Two more weeks, and he was organizing the Mobile Greys.

The Greys reached San Antonio December 12—just too late to share in the glory of beating Cós. But this didn't stop Bonham. His life in Texas became a whirlwind of activity.

On the 20th he was commissioned lieutenant in the Texas Cavalry . . . the 26th he was starting a law office in Brazoria . . . the 30th he was back in the Alamo writing Houston about a good officer. In the middle of January he turned up in Goliad; on the 19th he was back in the Alamo with Bowie; on the 26th he led a political rally for Governor Smith. With a man like Bonham, it didn't matter that he was only a lieutenant or that he had never heard of Smith six weeks earlier.

All this left little time for renewing any boyhood memories with Travis, but when the Colonel arrived in the Alamo on February 3, the two men took to each other right away. Bonham was a man after Travis' own heart. He liked Houston and Smith, didn't like Robinson, Fannin, the Matamoros crowd.

Maybe this made him less than an ideal choice to send to Fannin for help. The commander at Goliad was not only in the other camp, but it was a matter of record that he didn't like cavalrymen. Still, Travis knew no one more forceful, more trustworthy than Bonham. So off he went to Goliad twice in two weeks—on February 16 and again on the 27th.

And now he was coming back alone. Over the dark, silent prairie . . . across the Cibolo in the first light of dawn . . . through the thickets and mesquite trees to the top of Powder House Hill. Here he could look down on the Alamo less than a mile away.

Clearly the fort was still holding out. Around it, on all four sides, were the Mexican camps—the earthworks for Sesma's guns, the dozens of smoky fires, the troops in their white fatigue suits. The lines were closer than when he left; yet with luck, it was still possible to get through. Bonham was the last man to feel he couldn't make it.

He pulled off the road to his right, quietly worked his way east through the brush and thickets. At last he reached a point well between the Mexican-held powder house on the Gonzales road and Sesma's batteries northeast of the Alamo. As near as he could judge, he was safely between the two enemy positions.

Now to run for it. Digging in his spurs, Bonham swiftly gathered speed, flashed into the open, pounded straight for the Alamo gate by the corral. He hunched low on his horse, making himself small against an expected hail of bullets. But the startled Mexicans never fired a shot, and at 11 A.M. on Thursday, March 3, Jim Bonham hurtled safely into the Alamo. He was reporting back—as he had promised—to his commanding officer.

Travis wasn't discouraged. He had written off Fannin anyhow. He still felt help might come from San Felipe, Brazoria, a dozen other towns. Sooner or later they would see the importance of the Alamo. Meanwhile, he had food for twenty days; he had made the fort much stronger; he had no casualties.

But even if no one came, he was determined to stick it out. He would make the Mexican victory so expensive, it would be worse than a defeat. He could count on his men for that.

Indeed he could. Their spirits were remarkable, considering the danger, the weariness, the frustration of waiting for help that didn't come. True, there were some glum faces and several more of the local Mexicans had vanished. But Henry Warnell still chattered about horses; Jacob Walker still bragged about his children; David Crockett still could get a laugh. There was little fighting to be done, but Green Jameson kept them busy digging trenches in the big open square, piling up more dirt against the walls to make them stronger.

They were hard at this work after welcoming Bonham, when they suddenly heard the sound of distant cheering.

Rushing to the church roof, the gun platforms, the makeshift parapets, they peered into the noonday glare. Could this at last be some reinforcements?

No, the sound came from town. A great celebration was going on. People swarmed in the streets, waving and shouting, "Santa Anna! Santa Anna!" In the bright sunlight the Texans made out a long column of troops—over a thousand soldiers streaming in from the west.

Gaona's men had at last arrived. Not the whole brigade, to be sure—it was strung out all the way to the Rio Grande —but at least the picked companies. And these were the troops Santa Anna had been demanding.

For picked companies, most of them looked a little seedy. The Toluca men were all *activos*—a term that belied their status as inexperienced reservists. The Aldama battalion seemed anything but smart in its dusty white rags. But there was nothing wrong with the *Zapadores*, a crack unit of 185 sappers, who served the brigade as a whole.

Santa Anna now had 2,400 men and ten guns to deploy about the Alamo, and he spent the afternoon galloping around the perimeter planning new batteries, trenches and earthworks. His brother-in-law, General Cós, trailed along behind, while Cós' adjutant, Captain Sánchez, hovered in the background. They both had arrived the day before—ahead of the reinforcements—and were now being introduced again to the scene of their disgrace last December. Santa Anna rushed about, pointedly showing them the right way to handle troops.

Sánchez was suitably impressed. "It amazes me," he confided to his diary, "how Santa Anna seeks and dashes to places of danger, while General Sesma avoids even those that are safe."

There was always time for carping in the Mexican Army, but even the most dedicated practitioner forgot his complaints that afternoon. A messenger burst into town with the glorious news of Urrea's victory at San Patricio. Actually, the Texan losses were unimportant—16 killed and 21 prisoners later shot—but victories are not judged by numbers alone. Ever since the revolution began, the Mexicans had lost one battle after another. Now at last the tide was turning.

Joy erupted once again on Potrero Street. The bells of San Fernando pealed out the tidings. The blood-red flag in the church tower fluttered bright in the breeze. And to the east, someone raised another red banner on Powder House Hill. Here the setting sun would play on it, lighting it up for the hated Texans to see.

Victory was in the air. Colonel Juan Almonte was sure of it. Writing his sister that day, he told her to send his mail to Bexar; within three months the campaign would be over.

Certainly it looked that way on General Urrea's sector to the east. With Johnson under his belt Urrea next caught Dr. Grant at Agua Dulce Creek. The doctor was returning with fifteen men from a horse-hunting expedition along the Rio Grande, when he fell into a Mexican ambush on March 2. By the time the firing was over his force was annihilated.

Urrea now sent scouts toward Goliad. He moved very cautiously, for this next step should not be easy. Fannin had 400 troops, good guns, and sounded like a man spoiling for a fight. Surprisingly, when the scouts returned to the Mexican lines on March 3, they reported no sign of unusual activity at Goliad.

They were right. By the third, Fannin had shelved all plans for another march to the Alamo's rescue. Once again, he seemed mesmerized by the thought of the Mexican Army advancing toward him. His bright young aide, Captain Brooks, no longer talked of "marching tomorrow or the next day." He too spoke only in terms of hanging on. "We are in hourly expectation of an attack," he wrote his sister, "but we are resolved to die, to a man, under the walls we have thrown up. . . ."

Not all of the men were satisfied with their leader's decision. The Goliad group of New Orleans Greys desperately wanted to help their friends in the Alamo. The camp surgeon, Dr. Joseph Henry Barnard, felt the men had lost their confidence in Fannin. A young private, Joseph G. Ferguson, put it bluntly in a letter to his brother: "I am sorry to say that the majority of soldiers don't like him, for what reason I don't know, unless it is because they think that he has not the interest of the country at heart, or that he wishes to become great without taking the proper steps to achieve greatness."

CHAPTER ELEVEN   *"Take Care*
                      of My Little Boy"

                        In the dim moonlight that
bathed the Alamo plaza, John W. Smith saddled up once
again. It was nearly midnight, Thursday, March 3, and Smith
was about to leave on another attempt to rally help for the
garrison.

Word soon spread that he was going. Private Willis A.
Moore of Raymond, Mississippi, scribbled a few private lines
to his family, folded and handed the note to Smith. Others
did the same.

In the headquarters room by the west wall, William Barret
Travis was also writing messages. First, he put the finishing
touches on his latest official report—this time a ringing appeal
to the President of the Convention at Washington-on-the-
Brazos. He stressed the garrison's resilience, praised its spirit,
spelled out its needs: "at least 500 pounds of cannon powder,
200 rounds of six, nine, twelve, and eighteen-pound balls, ten
kegs of rifle powder . . ."

And once again he urged all possible help, for this could be
"the great and decisive ground." He closed with a few bitter
words about the local Mexicans—he charged nearly all had
deserted the fort—but on the whole he was game and optimistic.

Now he turned to his own personal messages. First came a little note so secret no outsider ever saw it. Just the cryptic request in the covering letter: "Do me the favor to send the enclosed to its proper destination instantly." It was hard for anyone then, or more than a hundred years later, not to think of Rebecca Cummings.

Next, a warm, intimate letter to his friend Jesse Grimes. In it he again stressed his good spirits, his determination to die rather than give up the Alamo. But this time—much more eloquently than in his official correspondence—Travis explained why he was making this stand. His reason went far beyond any views on strategy . . . beyond the bond that now welded the garrison together . . . even beyond his fierce desire to defend the new homes that dotted the land. More than all these (and they were a lot), he felt the spirit of the times—the conviction that liberty, freedom and independence were in themselves worth fighting for; the belief that a man should be willing to make any sacrifice to hold these prizes. With them, he had everything. Without them, nothing. Explaining his views, Travis minced no words:

> Let the Convention go on and make a declaration of independence, and we will then understand, and the world will understand, what we are fighting for. If independence is not declared, I shall lay down my arms, and so will the men under my command. But under the flag of independence, we are ready to peril our lives a hundred times a day. . . .

It was late in the evening now—Smith must be leaving soon —but Travis had one last message on his mind. It would be for David Ayers, who was boarding little Charles at the Ayers home near Washington-on-the-Brazos. No one in the world— even Rebecca—meant as much to Travis as Charles. A river of

memories must have flowed through his mind: persuading
Rosanna to leave the boy in Texas . . . saying good-by on his
way to the Alamo . . . the way Charles wangled fifty cents
from him to buy a bottle of molasses. Enough. Maybe he
would see him again someday, but there was always the other
possibility. He jotted a quick, simple note on a sheet of torn
yellow wrapping paper:

> Take care of my little boy. If the country should be
> saved, I may make him a splendid fortune; but if the
> country should be lost and I should perish, he will
> have nothing but the proud recollection that he is the
> son of a man who died for his country.

Walking out into the plaza, Travis handed his packet of
messages to Smith, then remembered something he forgot to
say in the official dispatch: tell the reinforcements to bring
ten days' rations with them. Next, another afterthought: he
would fire the 18-pounder three times a day—morning, noon
and night—as long as the Alamo stood. When they heard that,
they would know he was still fighting.

The northern postern once again swung open. A party of
Texans slipped outside, worked their way north toward the
sugar mill, and began firing at random. The Mexican guns
erupted in reply, and Santa Anna's patrols rushed to the scene
of the trouble. The way cleared, Smith whipped through the
Alamo gate, turned east, and vanished into the dark.

It was just about midnight—the end of a long, hard day.
But legend to the contrary, it was not a day of giving up
hope. There's a great deal of hope in any commander who
orders two hundred cannon balls. The best clue to Travis'
real feelings lay at the start of his letter to Jesse Grimes: "I
am still here in fine spirits and well to do."

Dawn, March 4. The new Mexican battery north of the

Alamo crashed into action, searing the early morning quiet. The guns were within rifle range—perhaps 250 yards away— and every shot smashed the fort's north wall, showering the plaza with earth and stones. Jameson frantically worked to shore up the defenses—piling up still more dirt against the wall, hammering extra bracing into place. The sound of the shovels and mallets drifted to the Mexican lines, and the rumor spread that the Texans were mining the walls, planning to blow everyone up together.

Certainly it was clear that the Alamo couldn't take this kind of punishment much longer. Yesterday Travis had been opti- mistic: "The walls are generally proof against cannon balls." Today his defenses seemed like a sieve.

The men never felt more trapped. Besides the new battery to the north, the Mexican ring seemed tighter than ever. The two long 9-pounders just across the river continued to pound the west wall, while Sesma's howitzers made life especially miserable by lobbing bombs into the innermost areas. Enemy entrenchments were now on all sides; to use Travis' own esti- mates, "in Bexar, four hundred yards west; in La Villita, three hundred yards south; at the powder house, one thousand yards east of south; on the ditch, eight hundred yards north- east, and at the old mill, eight hundred yards north."

Even Crockett now felt the strain. Echoing the sentiments of Henry Warnell in an earlier moment of discouragement, the Colonel announced, "I think we had better march out and die in the open air. I don't like to be hemmed up."

Jim Bowie, failing badly, was brought out more than once to rally the men. He weakly begged them to carry on, to stand by Travis whatever happened. Loyal Bowie men like Captain William Baker of the Volunteers took heart, but it was hard to be hopeful when they could clearly see new Mexican reinforcements streaming into town; when there in plain sight were Mexican work details fitting together scaling ladders.

The local Mexicans remaining in the Alamo were especially discouraged. All had good friends in the occupied town, some even relatives in Santa Anna's militia. Others merely wanted to be on the winning side, and it began to look as if they might have guessed wrong.

Still others had even deeper misgivings. They found themselves more and more uncomfortable in what had clearly turned into a collision between Mexicans and Anglo-Americans. After all, they *were* Mexicans. It was all very well when the struggle had been more of a family fight—which Mexican leaders; which Mexican constitution—but it was no longer that, and these Mexicans had a growing fear that they wouldn't do very well under any government dominated by "Anglos." Names like Flores, Rodríguez, Ramírez, Silvero, and Garza faded from sight.

On the evening of the 4th, still another Mexican disappeared—this time one of the women in the Alamo. Slipping through La Villita, then across the river, she made her way to His Excellency's headquarters. It turned out that she brought extremely interesting news: the defenses were crumbling . . . the men were weak . . . the ammunition low . . . the place could easily be taken.

A rumor swept the Mexican lines that the visitor had been sent by Travis himself, specifically to sound out the possibility of surrender. Conceivable—the Colonel had his moments of moody despair—but most unlikely. He was now committed, and he took a fierce pride in seeing things through. Take that day when he couldn't get through to Rebecca and angrily wrote, "the first time I ever turned back." Chances are no second occasion arose at the Alamo.

But the Mexican woman's report remained just as valid. The Texan defenses were weak, on the verge of collapse.

The clear, warm dawn of March 5 brought more bad news for the garrison. During the night the Mexican battery on the north had been pushed still closer—it was now only 200 yards from the fort. Brisk fire again pounded the crumbling walls, and the defenders again huddled behind whatever protection they found. By now they were pretty good at dodging enemy cannon balls—miraculously, not a man had yet been killed.

The Mexican fire tapered off sharply in the late afternoon, and at 5 P.M. the Texans puzzled over the sight of several columns of troops filing out of town. As the heavy firing stopped, the defenders emerged from shelter, began cooking supper on open fires in front of the church. Mrs. Dickinson persuaded a grimy Jim Bonham to have a cup of tea.

The lull meant more than tea to Colonel Travis. Shaking off what must have been an overwhelming desire to relax, he suddenly summoned the whole garrison to assemble in the open plaza. The men wearily ambled over, and Mrs. Dickinson hovered in the rear as the Colonel addressed his men.

He was brief and to the point. He declared that there was no longer any real hope of help. Their choice was to surrender, to try and escape, or to stay and fight to the end. Because it might delay the Mexican advance, he was determined to fight it out. He urged the garrison to join him, but he left every man to his own choice. If anyone desired to escape, now was the time to let it be known and step out of ranks.

It was later said that Travis gave his speech on March 3, but Mrs. Dickinson declared it was the 5th in the only account she ever gave without an enthusiastic assist from the press. It was also said that the Colonel drew a line with his sword to be crossed by all who chose to stand by him. Certainly in character, but in her unvarnished account Mrs. Dickinson never mentioned it. She did, however, remember well that one man stepped out of the ranks—the only member of the garrison who preferred to escape. "His name to the best of my recollection was Ross."

There was no man in the Alamo named Ross, but Louis Rose of Nacogdoches was very much there—and far from moved by Travis' eloquence. War was an old story to this Napoleonic veteran: when things went wrong, you lived and fought again another day. He wasn't about to die now.

His friend Bowie, lying pale on his cot, urged him to stick with the rest. Crockett pointed out that escape was impossible. Rose merely measured the defenses and thought to himself, "I have often done worse than to climb that wall."

He was gone by dark, edging his way downstream along the river till he came to the ford that led to town. He waded across, passed along a street, turned downstream again, and tramped out into the open country. No one saw him—perhaps because the town was surprisingly empty.

General Santa Anna could have explained. No troops lolled about the streets tonight, because he had methodically withdrawn them. They were off preparing for the grand undertaking that would finally redeem Mexican honor . . . that would teach these "perfidious foreigners" a lasting lesson. This ambitious project, now racing to its climax, had been brewing for nearly twenty-four hours.

It was early evening on the 4th when Colonel Almonte first knew that something was up. Ordered to report immediately to Santa Anna's headquarters, Almonte was joined by practically every general and colonel in the army. Strange, for His Excellency hated conferences and practically never asked anyone's opinion.

But this time was different, and Santa Anna stated his problem right away. Had the time come to take the Alamo by storm?

The officers exploded in a babble of advice that quickly

confirmed His Excellency's distrust of these sessions. Sesma and Almonte could hardly wait to attack, and Santa Anna himself was inclined to agree. But others were clearly opposed. Cós, who knew the Alamo well, felt that the light Mexican howitzers and 9-pounders weren't enough to really soften up the place. Castrillón, an old hand from Spanish days, backed him up—why not wait for Gaona's two 12-pounders, which should be up by March 7? Colonel Romero of the badly mauled Matamoros battalion eagerly agreed. Someone also pointed out that they were still short of doctors and medical supplies. The General-in-Chief drily replied, all the better; the men would know that it was "not as bad to die as to come out wounded."

Colonel Francisco Duque and Colonel Amat couldn't make up their minds at all, and a major representing the San Luis battalion maintained a discreet silence. After all, he had the lowest rank in the room.

Finally Santa Anna could stand the indecision no longer. He abruptly dismissed the council and returned to the old way—the best way—of handling these problems. He would do it all himself.

Mulling it over, he certainly saw Castrillón's point—those 12-pounders would come in handy. But there were other things to consider: the Alamo was bettering its defenses every day . . . the siege was draining his own men's strength . . . he needed these troops for later operations, really brilliant strokes into the heart of the country. Then there was the matter of those reinforcements from Gonzales. How easily they got in! If they could do it, so could others, and he might be pinned down here forever. Better strike before a strong force like Fannin's could come to the rescue, and he had "positive knowledge" that the Goliad troops were ready to march.

If Santa Anna had any lingering misgivings they were doubtless removed by that co-operative lady visitor, straight from the Alamo, who offered such interesting details on the garrison's weakness.

By two o'clock next afternoon, March 5, his plan was complete. Secretary Ramón Caro brought out the portable *escritoire*, dipped his quill in the little gold ink pot, and did his best to keep up as his commander poured out the details.

Four columns would hit the Alamo at the same time—Cós would strike the northwest corner . . . Duque the northeast . . . Romero the east . . . Morales the south. Sesma's cavalry would deploy to the east, prepared to cut down any Texans who tried to escape. Santa Anna himself would control the reserves from the new battery north of the fort, ready to throw them in wherever needed.

The main blow would fall on the north wall—Cós and Duque had 700 good men between them. Romero had to get along with 300, but they were all from the battle-hardened Matamoros and Jiménez battalions. Morales had only 100; but his target, the palisade, was the fort's weakest point. The reserves totaled no more than 400, but His Excellency surrounded himself with the cream—the grenadiers of the five infantry battalions and the hard, tough *Zapadores*.

Counting Sesma's 300 cavalry, the whole force added up to some 1,800 men—about three-fourths of the troops now on hand. Santa Anna felt that the rest, mainly convicts and raw recruits, would do more harm than good.

They would attack at 4 A.M. tomorrow, March 6. By that time everything must be in perfect order. And as usual, the Mexican leader immersed himself in even the smallest details: Cós' troops must carry ten ladders, two crowbars, two axes . . . all chin straps down . . . two spare flints for each man in the center companies . . . "the arms, especially the bayonets, to be in perfect order."

He had thought of everything; now it was up to the men. Early that afternoon couriers raced from post to post, distributing copies of his orders. The Mexican lines snapped to life. The battalion colonels studied the beleaguered old mission with new interest; even the jerry-built palisade began to look formidable. The company officers hurried here and there, collecting and sorting the ladders, the axes and crowbars, the flints and cartridge packs—His Excellency specified exactly ten packs for each grenadier. Everyone seemed to sense the quickening tempo and knew once again the empty feeling that always comes in the hours before a battle.

Lieutenant Colonel José de la Peña, in the service eleven years, self-consciously found himself praying for his soul. Captain Sánchez had different thoughts, almost blasphemous. Taking a moment off from his duties, he scribbled in his diary, "Why is it that Santa Anna always wants to mark his triumphs with blood and tears?"

Now it was 5 P.M. The grenadiers swung jauntily through town, headed up stream to join the *Zapadores* battalion at the reserves' assembly point. Seven o'clock, the Matamoros and Jiménez men near the powder house stacked their arms and turned in for sleep. The Aldama and Toluca battalions followed suit. Eight o'clock, the San Luis men pulled out of the line, munched some hardtack and bedded down too. As each group turned in, the firing fell off, until at ten o'clock a heavy, oppressive silence hung over the lines.

Midnight. Faint stirs in the darkness. Sergeants and company officers rustled among the men, quietly waking them up, mustering them into line. Officers moved silently up and down the formations, checking a dozen last-minute points: make sure the ladder carriers sling their guns on their shoulders . . . make sure the men leave their blankets behind . . . make sure they're wearing shoes or sandals . . . make sure their bayonets are sharp—His Excellency was very specific about that.

In the Yturri house on Main Plaza, Santa Anna nervously gulped a cup of coffee as he ran over the last details with Colonel Almonte. While they talked, the Colonel's orderly Ben waited nearby, keeping the coffee hot. Ben, a wandering American Negro, had once been a ship's steward, and tonight he needed all the patience he had ever accumulated in keeping passengers happy. Santa Anna was never more snappish. To Ben's relief, the two officers finally stalked off into the night.

One o'clock. The four columns began moving toward their positions. No sound but the dull tramp of marching feet, an occasional grunt as someone stumbled in the darkness.

Two o'clock. Santa Anna and Almonte unexpectedly reappeared at headquarters. His Excellency—now more nervous than ever—demanded coffee, threatened to run Ben through if he didn't bring it instantly. Ben bustled about the table setting the cups and serving the pot, as Santa Anna and Almonte discussed the situation. The Colonel said something about a costly fight, but Santa Anna cut him off: "It doesn't matter what the cost is; it must be done."

Three o'clock. Santa Anna and Almonte were off again, and Ben sank back to rest. Outside the troops shuffled steadily toward their posts. Cós' column reached its position 200 yards behind the Alamo, sank shivering in the cold, damp grass. A little to the rear, the reserves crossed the rickety bridge over the river, headed for the earthworks to the north. Now the cavalry saddled up and cautiously curled its way around the town to the grove in the east.

Four o'clock. Complete silence. No longer even the sound of troops marching, just the men breathing as they lay on the ground awaiting the signal to attack. Crouching there, Lieutenant Colonel Peña had a curious thought: if he died, he would never again be able to speak to anybody. Santa Anna now moved into the earthworks on the north. The reserves hunched nearby, and right beside him, oddly enough, were the massed bands of all the battalions.

The minutes dragged on—4:30 . . . 5:00. Bugler José María Gonzales glanced inquiringly at His Excellency. It was hard to see, for even the moon was co-operating—it lay behind a thick blanket of clouds.

Actually the moon knew no favorites. In the Alamo Colonel Travis also decided to take advantage of this cloudy night. He would try one last, desperate appeal to Fannin. By now the most experienced scouts were all gone, but 16-year-old Jim Allen was a marvelous rider and he had a first-rate mare. Once again the postern opened. Riding bareback—his arms around the horse's neck—young Allen raced out, darted through the Mexican lines, and was safe on the open prairie.

"We have heard again from Bexar," wrote Captain Brooks after Allen reached Goliad. Then, noting that the new Mexican batteries were pounding the Alamo to pieces, Brooks sadly concluded, "It is feared that Bexar will be taken, and that the devoted courage of the brave defenders will be of no avail."

There was no time for melancholy thoughts at the Alamo. With Allen on his way, Travis again gave his attention to the fort. Normally it might be time to turn in, but not tonight. They must take advantage of this lull in the Mexican bombardment. They needed every possible moment to repair and strengthen the walls, battered by two days of point-blank gunfire.

Hard work, but at some point Travis managed to fit in a quick visit to the church, where the women and children sat in growing fear and uncertainty. The moody, temperamental Travis always had a weakness for children—there was the comb he gave little Dilue Rose, the candy money for little Charles—and now at this hour of mounting peril his affection came to the surface once more. Going over to 15-month-old

Angelina Dickinson, he took from his finger a heavy hammered gold ring with black cat's-eye stone. Threading it with a bit of string, he looped it around Angelina's neck as a keepsake, and hurried back to the walls.

At last Travis was satisfied, and the garrison lay down for a few hours' rest. For some it must have been hard to sleep—at a time like this there was much to think about. Antonio Fuentes could wryly recall that only three weeks ago Bowie and Travis were arguing whether to let him out of jail. Well, Bowie had finally gotten him out, and here he was now.

Johnnie Kellogg and George Kimball had gentler things to ponder: both were about to become fathers. Andrew Kent had a different kind of family worry; he was the father of nine.

For Thomas Miller there was the irony of his will. Few Texans bothered with such formalities, but as the richest man in Gonzales, Miller had painstakingly covered everything. Even careful directions that "my body be decently interred."

Jim Bowie had made a will too, but in his case it didn't matter. Whether he died from fever or Mexican bayonets, he knew all too well he was leaving the world absolutely broke. What had happened to it all? Just paper profits.

Dolphin Floyd also had something to think about. As midnight passed and the Alamo entered its thirteenth day of siege, he realized that today, March 6, was his twenty-first birthday.

Four o'clock, even Travis was finally resting, wrapped in a blanket in the headquarters room, sword and double-barreled shotgun by his side. Lying nearby was his Negro slave Joe, a husky 23-year-old who by now had earned his spurs as a full-fledged member of the garrison. Five o'clock, all was quiet —only one man stirring. Adjutant John Baugh, officer of the day, was just starting his rounds on the north wall.

CHAPTER TWELVE   *"Great God, Sue,
the Mexicans Are
inside Our Walls!"*

Bugler José María Gonzales glanced again at Santa Anna. It was now just after 5 A.M., and the first streaks of dawn faintly tinged the eastern sky. Around the Alamo 1,800 Mexicans crouched in tense, mounting, irrepressible excitement.

"Viva Santa Anna!" a man suddenly yelled, unable to contain himself any longer. Others took up the cry, and a wild burst of cheering filled the air.

His Excellency knew that the moment had come. Already, these cheers must be warning the fort—any further delay would cost the last edge of surprise. He gave the signal, and Gonzales sounded the hard, strident call of attack. From company to company, battalion to battalion, other buglers picked it up and passed it on. There were seventy confusing, complicated bugle calls in the Mexican Army, but it's safe to say every man in the four attack columns knew exactly what this one meant.

"Arriba!" shouted General Cós to the men in the first column, lying in the grass 200 yards north of the Alamo. The men jumped up, grabbed their ladders and pikes and crowbars, and with a mighty shout surged forward toward the fort.

On the Alamo wall, Captain John Baugh came to startled

attention. Alarms in the night were an old story to him—but never anything like this. No word yet from the pickets outside, but this growing bedlam could mean only one thing—they were already overrun. He turned and raced for the barracks, crying for all to hear, "Colonel Travis! The Mexicans are coming!"

Travis sprang from his blanket . . . seized his sword, double-barreled shotgun and homespun jacket of Texas jeans. Telling his slave Joe to follow, he ran across the plaza, leaped to the wall by the north battery. No enemy in sight yet, but the yells, the bugles, and now the rockets exploding in the sky told enough. "Come on, boys!" he shouted. "The Mexicans are upon us and we'll give them Hell!"

Men were running everywhere—the infantry scrambling to their posts on Jameson's parapets, the artillerymen stumbling from their quarters in the long barracks. In the church, 12-year-old Enrique Esparza shrank from a flash of flame, as the Alamo's long 12-pounders swung into action.

Travis remained at the north battery, urging the men to hurry, shouting again and again, "Hurrah, my boys!" No time to put on his coat, he slung it over a peg by a cannon and turned back to the troops. Spying a couple of Seguin's company, he switched briefly to Spanish: "*No rendirse, muchachos!*"

They needed all the encouragement they could get. The first Mexicans had now reached the protective ditch—too close to bring cannon to bear. Soon planks and ladders were rising uncertainly against the wall, as the attackers struggled to find a firm footing.

Travis grasped the threat, aimed his shotgun down at the Mexicans, gave them a blast at point-blank range. At almost the same moment, a volley rang out from the darkness. Travis spun, hit in the head. His shotgun fell among the enemy; he himself within the fort, rolling down the bank of earth piled against the wall. He ended up sitting on the slope near a cannon, stunned and dying.

Joe took one look and fled to the barracks. Here he hid in a small room and saw no more. From this point on, he knew only the agonizing uncertainty shared by all the noncombatants. Very little seen; just the harrowing sounds of battle—cheers, explosions, cries, thuds, running feet.

In the dark sacristy of the Alamo church, Mrs. Dickinson listened too. Beside her, Angelina clutched at her apron as the tumult steadily grew. Suddenly 16-year-old Galba Fuqua of Gonzales burst into the room. He looked pale and haggard; both jaws were shattered by a bullet, and blood trickled from his mouth.

He painfully tried to tell Mrs. Dickinson something, but she just couldn't understand. Desperately, he held his jaws together and tried again. Still no luck. Shaking his head, he turned and rushed back to the fight.

The walls were now alive with rifle and cannon fire. As usual, every Texan had four or five guns stacked beside him, and Dickinson's ragged artillerymen proved fast, skillful workers in a pinch. To Santa Anna, standing behind the earthwork to the north, the whole fort seemed lit up by the blazing guns.

The four Mexican columns pushed into this hail of fire, heads bowed like men bucking a storm. To the east and the south, the troops slowed to a stop, pinned down by the guns on the Alamo church. On the northwest two blasts of grapeshot ripped the Aldama battalion—40 men lost. On the northeast, another blast swept the Tolucas—half a company down. The battalion commander Colonel Duque fell with a shattered leg, and his men—blindly plunging ahead—trampled over his crumpled body.

A few reached the walls—the men Travis fired at—but most of them wavered and finally fell back. Re-forming, they came

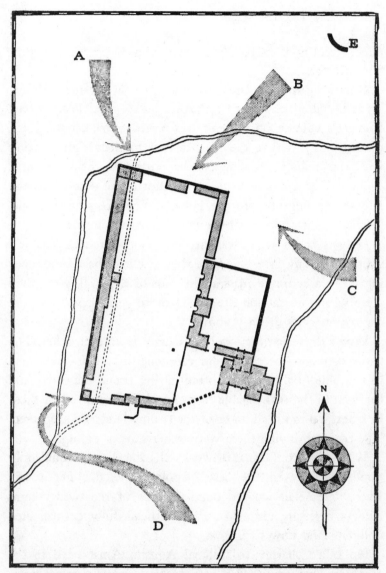

Storming the Alamo, dawn, March 6. (A) Cós' column, attacking
from the northwest; (B) Duque's column, striking from the northeast;
(C) Romero's force, coming from the east; (D) Morales' troops,
charging from the south; (E) Santa Anna, the reserves, and the band,
stationed by the northern battery. Heavy Texan fire forced the first
three columns to converge on the north, drove Morales' men to the
left, where they finally hit the fort at the southwest corner.

on a second time—and again the withering fire, again the stubborn retreat.

Now a third time. Once more the troops advanced, shouting and yelling, cheering Santa Anna and *la república*. Colonel Romero's column on the east was again stopped, but instead of retiring, this time the men drifted to their right, mixing with the Toluca battalion on the north. At the same time, Colonel Cós' column—held on the northwest—veered to the left, also ending up with the Tolucas. The effect was a single, jumbled mob of men—all surging toward the north wall.

Perhaps that's what was needed: more strength and less strategy. In any case, this time they reached the Alamo, ending up in a confused mass at the foot of the wall. Now they were safe from cannon fire but in more peril than ever from the Texan rifles directly above.

Worse than that, they were in danger from each other. The three columns—merging from different directions—continued to fire blindly ahead, more often hitting friend than foe. And the men in the rear, unable to see, took a fearful toll of those in front. To top it all, most of the scaling ladders disappeared. The troops bringing them were either shot or hiding.

Watching from the earthwork, His Excellency could only ponder how even the best Napoleonic tactics might fail. Every last detail worked out . . . each of the twenty-eight ladders carefully assigned . . . four beautifully co-ordinated columns—and now this.

He called sharply to Colonel Agustin Amat—send in the reserves. Then crisp orders to Secretary Caro, Captain Urizza, the smooth Almonte, all the rest of his fancy staff—go to the fort and encourage the men. The startled aides fluttered about and uncertainly took off for the fight.

Now the reserves—the grenadiers and the tough *Zapadores* —raced across the rough ground, firing and cheering, wildly

excited that their chance had finally come. And above the din
rose a new sound—the massed bands of all the battalions blaring out some special music. It was the thrilling, blood-curdling
strains of the *Degüello*, the traditional Spanish march of no
quarter . . . of throat-cutting and merciless death.

Fifteen incredible minutes. The Mexicans jammed together
at the foot of the north wall . . . the Texans firing down on
them from the top. Even the few ladders on hand were now
gone, trampled underfoot. Despite their overwhelming numbers, Santa Anna's troops were in serious trouble.

But at this point it turned out that the Texans had un-
wittingly played into Mexican hands. Trying to strengthen
the wall—especially by a breach near the east end—Jameson
had built a timber redoubt in front of the crumbling stone.
He was no finished carpenter, to say the least, and the barrier
had plenty of chinks and uneven beam-ends. Hard climbing,
but it could be done.

Up . . . up, the Mexicans scrambled. Clawing at the chinks
and notches, stamping on each other's hands, they would fall
back and then start all over again. The Texans blazed away
as never before, but even four or five guns to a man were no
longer enough.

A handful of Mexicans rolled onto the parapet, led by
General Juan V. Amador. For the General it was an especially
satisfying moment. Only two days ago he had been in disgrace—relieved of all duty by His Excellency for some minor
breach of decorum.

About the same time, General Cós hurled his Aldama battalion at a new spot some yards away. Tired of the jumble by
the north wall, Cós had halted his troops, executed a smart
right-oblique, and charged the west side of the Alamo. He hit
the north end, neatly flanking the Texan battery at the northwest angle.

There was no redoubt here—the climbing was far more dif-

ficult—but there were unexpected advantages. At several points
the Texan guns fired through freshly made embrasures,
rather than over the walls, and the assault troops squirmed
through the holes, pouring in faster than the Texans could
handle them. Soon the northern postern was opened, and
Cós' men surged through in an uncheckable stream.

"Great God, Sue, the Mexicans are inside our walls!" cried
Almeron Dickinson, bursting into the sacristy where his wife
sat trembling. There was just time for a last embrace and a
final plea, "If they spare you, save my child." Then he rushed
back to the guns on top of the church.

His men were already yanking around the cannon, taking
aim at the enemy pouring into the fort. On a high platform
in the plaza, another squad did the same. Their gun was light
but perfectly placed—a shower of grape ripped the Mexican
ranks.

The advantage was brief. Even as the gunners turned to the
north, the fourth Mexican column charged the south side of
the Alamo. It had been a bad half-hour for this detachment
under Colonel Morales. The "weak" palisade proved anything
but that, when guarded by Crockett's Tennesseans. But then
came the diversion at the other end of the fort, and Morales'
men had their chance.

Steering well clear of Crockett's barrier, they seized some
stone huts near the southwest corner. Here they regrouped
and quickly struck again. Racing across the few exposed yards
to the fort, they climbed the barbette and pounced on the
surprised Texas gunners. A few seconds of bayonet practice—
just as His Excellency wanted—and the prize 18-pounder was
in Mexican hands.

Pouring into the plaza, Morales' troops now charged the
main gate from the rear, as other Mexicans attacked from the
front. William Ward fired a last broadside and fell under an
avalanche of bayonet-slashing men.

As the Texans desperately turned this way and that, resistance on the north collapsed completely. The columns of Romero and Duque (now led by Castrillón) poured unchecked over the wall, flowed through the plaza, joined up with Morales' men fanning out from the south. It was too much for Quartermaster Eliel Melton. With the walls gone—the enemy surging behind him—he leapt the palisade where the barrier was lowest. A few others followed, and together they raced pell-mell into the graying dawn.

The Dolores cavalry had been waiting for just this moment. Sweeping down on the scene, they hacked away at the fleeing men. Here and there a cornered Texan fought back—one man killed a lance corporal with a double-barreled shotgun—but mostly it was child's play. The superb Mexican horsemen simply toyed with the fugitives, slashing them with sabers or running them through with brightly decked lances. Only two men escaped immediate slaughter. One Texan wriggled under a bush, where he was ultimately found and shot; another hid beneath a small bridge, where he was later reported by a local woman washing laundry. He too was executed.

Most of the Texans fought it out in the Alamo, giving ground foot by foot as the Mexicans continued pouring into the fort.

Crockett's Tennesseans, at bay near the palisade, battled with a wild fury that awed even the attackers. Individual names and deeds were lost forever in the seething mass of knives, pistols, fists, and broken gunstocks; but Sergeant Felix Nuñez remembered one man who could stand for any of them, including Crockett himself:

He was a tall American of rather dark complexion and had on a long buckskin coat and a round cap without any bill, made out of fox skin with the long tail hanging down his back. This man apparently had

a charmed life. Of the many soldiers who took de-
liberate aim at him and fired, not one ever hit him.
On the contrary, he never missed a shot. He killed at
least eight of our men, besides wounding several
others. This being observed by a lieutenant who had
come in over the wall, he sprang at him and dealt him
a deadly blow with his sword, just above the right
eye, which felled him to the ground, and in an instant he was pierced by not less than 20 bayonets.

In one sense, Crockett and his "boys" were a special case,
for they were too far away to head for the barracks, where
Colonel Travis always planned his last stand. Now with Travis
dead, it was Adjutant John Baugh who gave the signal to hole
up. The men quickly dropped from the walls—Lieutenant
Kimball and his band from Gonzales . . . Cleland Simmons
and the dismounted cavalry . . . William Carey and the artillerymen on the west side.

They didn't run blindly. Rather, they moved toward the
barracks with almost grim determination. Colonel Peña of the
advancing *Zapadores* was especially fascinated by a rangy
blond man, whom he mistook for Travis: "He would seem
to hesitate . . . take a few steps, stop, turn on us and fire,
shooting like a soldier. At last he died—a life sold dearly."

Once in the barracks, the Texans again faced the enemy.
The past thirteen days had been profitably spent, and now the
doorways were blocked by parapets. These were semicircular,
made of earth rammed between stretched hides, and just high
enough to rest a rifle. Some of the rooms also had holes bored
in the walls, and some even trenches dug in the dirt floors.
There was little communication between the rooms—and none
at all between the buildings—but that didn't matter. Everyone
knew what to do.

A searing, deadly fire crashed out from the loopholes and

doorways. The Mexicans wavered, scattered frantically for cover, but there was no cover in the bare, open plaza. The troops fell in heaps in the early morning light.

On the north wall, General Amador knew something had to be done right away. He snapped out an order; some men swung around the cannon by Travis' body; and a makeshift crew began blasting the barricaded doorways. On the south, Colonel Morales did the same with the big 18-pounder; he fired a devastating salvo at the long barracks.

As the battle raged in the plaza, Lieutenant José María Torres of the *Zapadores* battalion suddenly spied something that made his blood boil. There on the roof of the long barracks—easily seen in the growing light of day—flew a strange blue flag. He couldn't make out the design but it certainly wasn't Mexican—it was clearly a flag of rebellion and treason.

Torres, of course, couldn't know it, but this was the fine silk banner of the New Orleans Greys—brought all the way from the Sabine to proclaim the group's faith in "God and Liberty." There were at least two other flags in the Alamo this morning—one brought by Travis himself—but somehow only the Greys' colors were raised in the black predawn hours of chaos and tumult.

Lieutenant Torres raced for the roof . . . found others had been there before him. Three color sergeants of the Jiménez battalion lay dead near the flag—shot before they could reach it. That meant nothing to Torres. As Texan bullets whined around him, he ran over and ripped it down; then planted the Mexican colors instead. Lieutenant Damasco Martinez, who arrived to help, was killed beside him; and next instant Torres himself was shot to death. No one moved any longer on the barracks roof, but the flag that now flew in the morning breeze was red, white and green—with the angry eagle of Centralist Mexico.

Down in the plaza, Santa Anna's troops had little time to cheer the change in colors; they were much too busy storming the buildings. They moved methodically, from doorway to doorway, always using the same tactics: first a blast from the captured cannon to smash the doors and barricades . . . next a storm of musket fire to clear away the defenders . . . and then the final charge.

As the Mexicans crashed into the barrack rooms, new struggles broke out—more desperate, more fearful than any before. It was an intensely personal business now—pairs of men clutching and wrestling in the smoke-filled darkness. But there were always too many Mexicans, and one after another the defenders were beaten down.

Occasionally some Texan had enough. Colonel Peña remembered one man waving a rifle with a white sock tied to the end. But most of the defenders were doing their best to make Travis' prediction come true: "Victory will cost the enemy so dear, that it will be worse for him than defeat."

Yet they couldn't last forever, and one by one the buildings were taken—the long barracks to the east . . . the low barracks on the south . . . the collection of huts along the west wall. In one of these rooms on the west, Mrs. Horace Alsbury crouched with her baby and sister Gertrudis. For some reason they lived apart from the other women in the church—perhaps because their protector Jim Bowie felt they rated more privacy. In any case, they were no better off now: the sound of fighting drew steadily closer.

Gertrudis finally opened the door, hoping to show there were only women inside. A passing Mexican soldier snatched off her shawl, and she ran back in terror. As troops poured in after her, a young Texan (Mrs. Alsbury thought his name was Mitchell) appeared from nowhere and tried to protect them. He was quickly bayoneted at Mrs. Alsbury's side.

Then a Mexican officer arrived, chased out the troops, and turned on the two frightened women: "How did you come here? What are you doing here anyhow?"

He didn't even wait for an answer. He simply ordered them out, had them stand against a wall where they were comparatively safe.

To the south, Morales' men were mopping up resistance in the low barracks. Breaking into a room just to the right of the Alamo gate, they came upon a startling sight. Propped in his cot, brace of pistols by his side, pale as the death that faced him, was Jim Bowie. He undoubtedly did the best he could, but it must have been over very soon.

Now only the Alamo church was left. Dickinson's crew still fought the 12-pounders on the high platform in back. Bonham had joined them—eleven men altogether. Just below, Gregorio Esparza worked his small gun by the south window, and Robert Evans kept the ammunition coming from the powder magazine by the entrance.

A shower of nails and scrap iron flew from a gun on the roof, ripping the Jiménez men in the plaza. Colonel Morales knew the answer to that. He pulled around the 18-pounder and began raking the church—the timbered platform, the thick stone walls, the strong oak doors, everything.

Bonham fell . . . Dickinson too . . . gradually the rest of the men on the platform. Unable to stand the pounding any longer, one man took a small child in his arms, ran to the edge, and hurtled to the ground below. Colonel Peña, Felix Nuñez, other Mexicans gasped at the sight.

The heavy double doors splintered and sagged on their broken hinges. The Jiménez and Matamoros men raced through, and spread out in the smoke-filled church. Gregorio Esparza quickly fell under their bayonets. Robert Evans—now wounded—grabbed a torch and crawled for the powder room, hoping to blow up the magazine. A Mexican bullet got him first.

The women and children huddled in the rear, almost too frightened to move. One young boy stood up, uncertainly faced the advancing troops. He was unarmed and made no move, except to draw a blanket around his shivering shoulders. He found no mercy.

Twelve-year-old Enrique Esparza shrank against the wall, sure that his turn would come next. But fate was capricious, as always in war. Gunner Antony Wolfe's two boys—they looked less than twelve—were ruthlessly slaughtered, but Enrique somehow was missed in the crush. Stranger still, old Brigido Guerrero—one of the local Mexican defenders—managed to talk himself free. Desperately he pleaded he was just a prisoner, had really been for Santa Anna all the time. For some reason they believed him and let him go.

In the dark little sacristy, just off the transept, Mrs. Dickinson calmly awaited the end. There were other women in the room, but she didn't notice them. She was only aware of the shouts, the cries, the screams, always drawing nearer. She held Angelina close, deep in the folds of her apron.

Suddenly Jacob Walker, the little gunner from Nacogdoches, burst into the room. He ran to a corner and seemed trying to hide. But it was no use. Four Mexican soldiers rushed in, and as Mrs. Dickinson fell to her knees in prayer, they shot Walker and savagely hoisted him on their bayonets like a bundle of fodder.

The sounds died away. All grew still. By 6:30 A.M. the last firing was over—the Mexicans weren't even shooting at the bodies any more. A cheerful sun rose in the east, bathing the silent, smoking Alamo in the golden light of a bright new day.

CHAPTER THIRTEEN "*It Was But a Small Affair*"

"It was but a small affair," shrugged His Excellency, General Antonio López de Santa Anna, greeting Captain Fernando Urizza in the fallen Alamo.

In some ways, perhaps it was. A minor frontier outpost. Only 183 defenders. And these not even trained soldiers, but mere amateurs who saw fit to stand between the "ungrateful colonists" and the authority of the Central Government. Well, they learned.

His own losses? Easily swallowed. True, the toll was high—some 600 killed and wounded—one-third of the actual assault force. Yet this was still only 10 per cent of the army. Most of Gaona's men were fresh . . . Tolsa's battalion completely intact . . . Urrea's troops all-victorious. With San Antonio safely out of the way, they would now move on to far greater things. The Alamo was, in short, a slight distraction, a small pebble cast in the waters of a very large pond.

But if this was just a pebble in the pond, the ripples from the splash went far indeed. "The effect of the fall of Bexar throughout Texas was electrical," reported the New Orleans *Commercial Bulletin*, and that was just the beginning.

At a lazy plantation near Jackson, Tennessee, little Mary

Autry was gathering dog blossoms on a lovely April morning, when a strange horseman clattered up the drive. A few moments later, one of the slaves came running to her: "You must come to the house! Your father has been killed, and your mother is half-dead with the news."

In bustling Nashville, Edmund Goodrich tore open a letter from his brother Benjamin in Texas: "It becomes my painful duty to inform my relations in Tennessee of the massacre of my poor brother John." At a country home in Alabama, Sally Menefee read a distraught note from her sister Fanny Sutherland: "Yes sister, I must say it to you, I have lost my William. O, yes he is gone. My poor boy is gone, gone from me. The sixth day of March he was slain in the Alamo. . . ."

In South Carolina, James Bonham's family learned from the April 6 Charleston *Courier:*

BY THE RAILROAD:
IMPORTANT FROM TEXAS!
FALL OF SAN ANTONIO AND MASSACRE OF
THE TEXAN TROOPS

The dispatch had been picked up from the New Orleans papers of March 28, and was in turn relayed on to the North. New York, April 11 . . . Boston, April 12 . . . Portland, April 13. News spread slowly in these days before the telegraph, but it was no less fresh when it arrived. Everywhere the Alamo produced an immense sensation.

Santa Anna's "small affair" quickly shoved aside the other stories of the day—Robinson the Murderer . . . the plans for a steamship line across the Atlantic . . . the auction sale of "the remaining lots in the town of Chicago." And as people read the details, the private sorrow of a few families quickly turned to national grief and anger.

"The news is melancholy indeed," declared the New Orleans *Commercial Bulletin*, "and here is opened another field of action for the noble hearts now returning triumphant and covered with laurels won on the banks of the Withlacoochee." This last referred to General Scott's campaign against the Seminoles, and a young nation that found idealistic fulfillment in chasing several hundred Indians through the Florida swamps needed little stimulus to support this new, far more glorious crusade.

"Tyrant" . . . "butcher" . . . "bloody tiger" were only a few of the more printable invectives hurled at Santa Anna. "He will shortly see," the New York *Post* shrewdly observed, "that policy would have required that he govern himself by the rules of civilized warfare. Had he treated the vanquished with moderation and generosity, it would have been difficult if not impossible to awaken that general sympathy for the people of Texas which now impels so many adventurous and ardent spirits to throng to the aid of their brethren."

Indeed it was so. The "small affair" crystallized sentiment, welded the nation together as it hadn't been for years. Benjamin Lundy might warn of a slave-owners' "plot"—and the die-hard Whigs might grumble—but America as a whole went all-out for Texas. The previously neutral Frankfort *Argus* hesitated briefly, then kicked over the traces and urged that Santa Anna be taught "the virtue of American rifles and republicanism." Even the opposition papers were caught in the tide. "We have been opposed to the Texan war from first to last," admitted the Memphis *Enquirer*, "but our feelings we cannot suppress—some of our own bosom friends have fallen in the Alamo. We would avenge their death and spill the last drop of our blood upon the altar of Liberty."

Crockett's loss especially won many skeptics over. He had been the darling of the Whigs, the bitter foe of the expansionist Andrew Jackson—and now here he was, martyr for one of Jackson's pet causes. Thousands of Crockett's political followers suddenly saw new virtue in Old Hickory's Texas policy.

Even more moved was the ordinary citizen. He may have taken no sides in the Texas question, but he certainly adored Davey. It was impossible to dislike this warm, gentle, companionable man. How could anybody want to massacre him? The Natchez *Courier* perfectly expressed the feelings of most Americans everywhere:

> *Poor Davey Crockett!*—We lament the fate of the sick Bowie—we feel sad and angry, by turns, when we think of the butchery of the gallant Travis—but there is something in the untimely end of the poor Tennessean that almost wrings a tear from us. It is too bad—by all that is good, it is too bad. The quaint, the laughter-moving, but the fearless upright Crockett, to be butchered by such a wretch as Santa Anna—it is not to be borne!

In their mounting indignation, the papers outdid each other in calling for vengeance, in appeals for action, in summoning their readers to march to the rescue. "Let your patriotism finish a sentence too sublime for the quill—your rifles publish a theme too exalted for the press!" urged the Louisville *Journal*. The editor of the Memphis *Enquirer* quickly topped this—he offered to go himself: "If volunteers are few, our quill shall be placed in the hand of some one of 'the fair', and with trusty firelock and bristling bayonet, ourself shall be a host against tyranny—and for Liberty."

Few editors went that far. Most preferred to retain the "quill," but it has rarely been used with more fury. Perhaps the New Orleans *Commercial Bulletin* achieved the high point with this bit of poetry:

Vengeance on Santa Anna and his minions,
Vile scum, up boiled from the infernal regions,
Dragons of fire on black sulphuros pinions,
The offscouring baseness of hell's blackest legions,
Too filthy far with crawling worms to dwell
And far too horrid and too base for hell.

The nation responded with enthusiasm, and it was soon clear that the "small affair" had produced far more tangible results than indignation and angry poetry. The night the news reached Mobile, crowds packed the courthouse, raised nearly $5,000 on the spot. The ladies of little Bardstown, Kentucky, held a fair, collected $516 from their quilts and pies.

But the real money came from New York. Here a big throng jammed the Masonic Hall on April 26, whooped it up for a great fund-raising drive. Books for the "Texas Loan" opened on the 28th with $100,000 subscribed immediately, another $100,000 the following day.

Philadelphia, home of five Alamo defenders, seethed with excitement. Donations poured in from a rally at the Tontine, from another at the courthouse . . . from a flurry of theatrical benefits. The Arch Street Theater staged *The Fall of the Alamo or Texas and the Oppressors*, then followed it several nights later with a benefit performance of *Othello*. The curtain descended somewhat incongruously with the cast singing, "All for Texas, or Volunteers for Glory."

Representatives direct from Texas seemed to be everywhere —addressing the meetings, stirring up the crowds, enthralling them with new, thrilling stories of the Alamo. Texas Commissioner B. T. Archer harangued the largest citizens' meeting ever held in Richmond, Virginia. George Childress held the Natchez rally spellbound as he told how Santa Anna was boasting he might march all the way to Washington.

A roar of rage, and the Natchez citizens passed an immedi-

ate resolution, "That the proud dictator Santa Anna, like the
fort Alamo, must fall. And the purple current of valiant gore
that has moistened the plain in the cause of liberty must be
avenged."

Next week all Natchez came down to the river to see off
its first volunteers. Thirty of the town's finest men were leaving under Judge John A. Quitman on the steamer *Swiss Boy*.
Young John Ross of the newly christened "Quitman Fencibles" gave the farewell speech, and as the little white steamboat headed downstream, there was not a dry eye on the
wharf.

It was the same everywhere. A huge throng gathered at
Cincinnati's Exchange Hotel to honor 80 volunteers leaving
on the steamer *Ontario*. The lake-front workers of thriving
Buffalo cheered on another 80; the sleepy little town of
Greensborough, Alabama, came proudly to life one sweltering
April noon, as its own little company marched gallantly off.

Nor was the home front idle. At Lexington, Kentucky,
Mary Austin Holley organized a sewing group, and within
a month the girls turned out twenty-seven shirts, twelve shirt
bosoms, six collars, three roundabouts, and twenty-four pocket
handkerchiefs—just the thing, they felt, for the hot, dusty
plains.

What was it that stirred people so? What was there about
this "small affair" that made Americans not only angry but
wildly anxious to join the fight?

The massacre of the whole garrison was of course shocking.
The facts were bad enough, and an imaginative press was
happy to embellish them. The *Arkansas Gazette* described the
Mexican troops as "more brutal than the untutored savages of
the desert, bent only upon glutting themselves with the blood
of helpless victims."

But massacres were an old story on the frontier—Indian
raids were a constant terror—and it was not just the killing of

men that aroused the nation. It was the killing of *these* men. They were not remote frontiersmen—they were friends from Natchez, Charleston, Boston, home. With few exceptions, they were not rough adventurers—they were farmers, artisans, professional men, idealists. As the Memphis *Enquirer* put it, "Some of our own bosom friends have fallen in the Alamo. They were refused quarter and life—young men with whom we have associated—endeared to us by the power of goodness and greatness. We would avenge their death and spend the last drop of our blood upon the altar of liberty."

And when the citizens of little Russellville, Kentucky, heard the news, they didn't regard it as a massacre of Texan patriots; it was the murder of their own Daniel Cloud. The young men of the town solemnly assembled, and in the way of the times, recorded their sorrow in the form of some revealing resolutions:

> *Resolved,* That the many ties of friendship which he twined about our hearts—the high respect we cherished for his talents and enterprise, and our admiration of his amiable deportment, and his virtues, shall embalm his memory in our recollections.
>
> *Resolved,* That the early fate which closed his mortal career, has stricken from his profession a scion among the most cultivated and flourishing our country has reared.
>
> *Resolved,* That if any reflection can lighten the gloom that is spread in our hearts, it is the conviction that he has nobly bared his bosom as a patriot, and received the fatal shaft in the defense of liberty and humanity.

This last was important. For above all, these good friends had died for a cause that was sublimely in keeping with the spirit of the times. The Alamo fitted so perfectly with the young republic's somewhat mauve memories of '76 . . . with its heartfelt conviction that America was the true custodian of liberty. The lesson of the Alamo, in fact, seemed lifted right from Byron's stanzas:

> For freedom's battle, once begun,
> Bequeath'd by bleeding sire to son,
> Though baffled oft, is ever won.

So the "small affair" became also a symbol, inspiring men to great deeds by the example it set of courage, determination and sacrifice. And because the symbol matched the era so beautifully, the defenders of the Alamo enjoyed a happy windfall. Unlike many of history's heroes, they did not have to wait for immortality; they achieved it right away.

"We shall never cease to celebrate it," predicted the *Telegraph and Texas Register* less than three weeks after the siege. "Spirits of the mighty, though fallen! Honors and rest are with ye: the spark of immortality which animated your forms, shall brighten into a flame, and Texas, the whole world, shall hail ye like the demi-Gods of old, as founders of new actions, and as patterns of imitation!"

Perhaps it was impossible to see such things through the dust and smoke of the Alamo at 6:30 A.M. on the morning of March 6. In any case, Santa Anna devoted himself to poking around the rubble and idly inspecting a few of his victims. He was still at it when a commotion erupted toward the main gateway. The troops had just found six Texans still alive, hidden under some mattresses in one of the barracks rooms.

Several Mexican soldiers rushed at the group, but General Castrillón intervened. He ordered the soldiers away, and with an almost courtly gesture offered the Texans his protection.

He then led them across the littered plaza to Santa Anna and his staff. "Sir," Castrillón announced, "here are six prisoners I have taken alive; how shall I dispose of them?"

"Have I not told you before how to dispose of them?" the General exploded. "Why do you bring them to *me?*"

Turning on his heel, he impatiently told some passing troops to shoot the men. When the officer in charge hesitated, Santa Anna's own staff saw an opportunity to show their loyalty. They drew their swords and set upon the prisoners. In the carelessness of their enthusiasm, they almost killed Castrillón too.

Colonel Peña and Almonte, standing nearby, always remembered the scene—partly because it seemed so unnecessary; partly because they both were told that one of the victims was the famous David Crockett.

In the Alamo church Mrs. Dickinson sat listening to the occasional cries that still came from outside. As the last firing died away, she and Angelina had been ordered from the sacristy to a little room just right of the main entrance. Soon Mrs. Esparza, her children, and the other women in the church were also brought in. Apparently the Mexicans planned to keep them all here together, until somebody decided what to do with them. As the only "Anglo-American" in the place, Mrs. Dickinson's prospects seemed anything but bright.

Suddenly a Mexican officer appeared in the doorway and called in broken English, "Is Mrs. Dickinson here?"

No answer.

"Is Mrs. Dickinson here? Speak out! It's a matter of life and death."

"Yes," she finally answered.

"If you want to save your life, follow me."

He quickly led her outside—how long it seemed since she last saw the sun. Across the yard they went—the officer lead-

ing, Mrs. Dickinson carrying Angelina close behind. There
was little time to look around, but she couldn't help seeing
many familiar figures crumpled on the ground. Among them
was the mutilated form of David Crockett, lying between the
church and the long barracks.

The whole scene was so hideous it should have been etched
on her mind forever. Oddly enough—perhaps through some
blessing of Fate—she remembered almost nothing. The only
thing that stood out in this weirdest of settings was the one
thing that looked perfectly normal: Crockett's coonskin cap
lying neatly by his side.

The rest of the women soon followed. Mrs. Esparza and the
others in the church; Mrs. Alsbury, her baby and sister
Gertrudis from their shelter by the west wall. Of them all,
Mrs. Alsbury was the only one whose heart felt a lift on this
heaviest of mornings. She had been found by Manuel Pérez,
the brother of her first husband. He lived in town and had
come to inspect the ruins.

"Sister!" he cried, discovering Mrs. Alsbury standing in the
debris. "Don't you know your own brother-in-law?"

"I'm so upset and distressed that I scarcely know anything."

It was the same with them all. In a dazed, frightened group
they stepped through the litter to the gate. Numb with
fatigue, they were taken to town—Mrs. Alsbury and Gertrudis
to their family home, the Navarro place; the others to the big,
handsome house of Ramón Musquiz on Main Plaza. Behind
them, they left the Mexican Army now happily pillaging the
Alamo. It was quite a celebration—at one point the rejoicing
troops even killed a stray cat because it was "American."

But one American was still very much alive. From the room
where he hid after Travis' death, the Colonel's slave Joe
crouched and waited in trembling uncertainty. The battle was
over now—the noise of the firing gone—but there were new,
equally harrowing sounds: the shouts of rampaging Mexicans;

the last cry of some dying Texan. It was not very reassuring.

"Are there any Negroes here?" An officer appeared in the doorway.

"Yes, here is one," and Joe emerged slowly from his corner. For a moment it must have seemed like a mistake: one nearby Mexican fired at him, another nicked him with a bayonet. But the officer shoved them aside and took Joe safely away.

Minutes later, he stood face to face with Santa Anna himself. It turned out there was nothing to fear. His Excellency assured Joe that this was no war against Negro slaves—he would soon be freed. Meanwhile, would he kindly point out the bodies of Bowie and Travis? Joe grimly obliged.

Satisfied, Santa Anna then assembled all the troops in the plaza and rewarded them with a victory address. No one paid much attention to what he said, but the air was filled with *vivas*. The men were finally dismissed, and the celebration roared on.

Off to one side, Captain Sánchez felt in no mood to celebrate. He was depressed, dreadfully depressed by the casualties. Some 400 wounded—and no hospitals, doctors or medicines. Not even any mattresses or blankets. The town supply had been taken over by Santa Anna's enterprising brother-in-law, Colonel Dromundo. He would make bedding available, if a man could pay the price.

Santa Anna was much too busy for such details. He had to make his official report. Calling in Ramón Caro and the portable *escritoire*, he dictated a letter to Secretary Tornel in Mexico City.

"Victory belongs to the army," the message began, "which at this very moment, 8 o'clock A.M., achieved a complete and glorious triumph that will render its memory imperishable." This was, of course, poetic license, for the battle was actually over by 6:30. But Santa Anna loved dramatic effect and could be forgiven a mild exaggeration. Less pardonable were his casualty figures—over 600 Texans killed; "about" 70 Mexicans dead and 300 wounded.

Anyhow, it would read nicely in Mexico City, and as a final touch he sent along the captured flag of the New Orleans Greys. It was more than a battle trophy; it was dramatic proof that this time he hadn't beaten just another group of tattered peons—he had crushed the "perfidious foreigners" themselves. There it all was: the American eagle, the call for liberty, the very word "New-Orleans" arrogantly written on the banner. Lest anyone fail to appreciate the full meaning of this flag, he triumphantly concluded, "The inspection of it will show plainly the true intention of the treacherous colonists and of their abettors, who came from the ports of the United States of the North."

That over, Santa Anna turned back to the pressing matters at hand. First, a series of orders for Francisco Ruiz, the town's *alcalde:* have the fallen Mexicans buried . . . confirm the identification of Travis, Bowie and Crockett (nothing like being sure) . . . get some wood and burn what was left of the Texans. Yes, he'd allow an exception: the Esparza family could bury Gregorio; their other boy, at least, was a good Mexican.

Now a quick trip to town with Almonte. A stop for some coffee, while that clumsy Ben fumbled with the cups and the Colonel jabbered something about "another such victory will ruin us." Well, Almonte couldn't hope to understand, but there was more to a battle than casualty figures. Here the real fruits would come when the news got around Texas . . . when the people learned what happened to those who opposed authority.

One by one Santa Anna summoned the local leaders to make sure they got the point. He was glad to see most of them did. Even Louisiano Navarro, always so friendly with the "Anglos," now seemed ready to come back to the fold.

Navarro agreed to send a letter to his friends in Gonzales urging all Mexicans to "come forward and present themselves to the President to receive their pardon and enter on their own proper pursuits."

The Alamo survivors could help here too, and by the 7th Santa Anna was ready to receive them. One by one they came to headquarters and listened to the gospel: resistance was hopeless, Texas must lay down its arms. Through the generosity of the Central Government, the survivors were now free to travel through the colony, spreading the word. Joe was even invited to attend a military review, and it had just the right effect. He came away swearing he saw 8,000 troops—more than twice as many as could have been there.

His Excellency treated the women most courteously. Two dollars and a blanket for each. For Mrs. Dickinson, he had an extra treat. He would send her and Angelina to Mexico City, so the little girl could be properly raised. Mrs. Dickinson desperately pleaded against it, and even Almonte came to her aid.

Reluctantly, Santa Anna gave up the idea. She and Angelina would go to Gonzales instead, carrying one more message that resistance was hopeless. He arranged for Ben to serve as escort, and on the morning of the 11th the little party set out. They made a strangely touching picture—the worldly-wise Ben trotting along on his pony; the grief-stricken widow with her baby, silently guiding her horse by the now deserted Alamo and into the open country.

CHAPTER FOURTEEN *"Remember the Alamo!"*

Mrs. Dickinson jumped with fright at the rustle in the tall grass beside the road. She, Angelina and Ben were now across the Salado—well east of San Antonio—and it never occurred to her that anyone else might be near.

A head popped out of the brush, and a familiar voice hailed her—it was Joe, Travis' slave. Leery of Mexican promises, he had fled town on foot and was trying to get to Gonzales too. Hearing horses approach, he was sure the Mexicans were after him and plunged into the grass until he saw who it was.

Overjoyed, Joe emerged, attached himself to the little group, and happily trudged along beside Mrs. Dickinson's horse. He was dubious protection—he dived back into the grass at every unusual sound—but at least he was company, and she needed that too. Mile after mile, the little party continued on—all day March the 11th and 12th.

By noon on the 13th, they were about twenty miles from Gonzales, when once again Joe plunged into the underbrush. This time it was no deer, no stray cow, no fluttering prairie hen. There in the distance, cautiously coming toward them, were three horsemen.

Comanches, Joe whispered, and begged Mrs. Dickinson to join him. But she would have none of it; she was too tired and heart-broken to care any longer. "I'd as soon die one way as another."

The horsemen drew closer . . . close enough to see they were riding with martingales. No Indian ever did that. Joe leaped to his feet, wild with joy.

It was a Texan scouting party led by "Deaf" Smith, riding out from Gonzales to check on the Alamo. It didn't take long to hear enough, and soon they were all heading for Gonzales together. As Mrs. Dickinson wearily lagged behind, scout Henry Karnes left the rest and dashed ahead with the news.

It came as no surprise. All signs had pointed to the fall of the Alamo for days—almost since the moment Sam Houston reached Gonzales on March 11 to organize his army. That very evening Anselmo Borgara and Andres Barcena, two Mexicans from the *ranchos* near San Antonio, turned up with hair-raising details on the final assault. No, they hadn't been there themselves, but their friend Antonio Pérez had, and he was a truthful man.

The story caused wild dismay in town. To stop any panic, Houston jailed both Mexicans as spies, but in his heart he feared the worst. The silence of Travis' signal gun spoke louder than a dozen messengers. He canceled plans for a march on San Antonio. He ordered Fannin to pull back. He worried through March 12, waiting in vain for two of Seguin's spies to report. On the 13th he finally decided that the only way to get the truth was to send out "Deaf" Smith—the taciturn, almost legendary scout who could read footprints like handwriting and smell a Mexican ten miles away.

It was a typical Smith performance. Ordered to return "within three days," he was back by nightfall, complete with survivors. Now, as Mrs. Dickinson poured out the heart-breaking details, Houston could only hold her hand and weep like a child.

Clearly there must be no more of these sieges. They were simply wasting men. The only course was to hold the little army together and retreat, drawing Santa Anna along, always ready to turn and strike. "By falling back," Houston assured his highly nervous government, "Texas can rally and defeat any force that can come against her."

There was no time to lose. Mrs. Dickinson said the advancing Mexicans were already at the Cibolo. Houston ordered an immediate retreat, and by 9:30 P.M. men were collecting rations, loading the ammunition wagon, hitching the oxen. Others took the army's two brass 24-pounders and unceremoniously dumped them into the Guadalupe River. At a time like this, artillery seemed more a burden than a weapon.

As the commotion rose, one of the townspeople opened his door and called out in alarm: "In the name of God, gentlemen, I hope you are not going to leave the families behind!"

"Oh, yes," cracked a voice from the ranks, evidently no admirer of Sam Houston, "we are all looking out for Number One."

Hardly fair. Houston even turned over most of his wagons to the settlers, and they too were preparing to leave. Sydney Kellogg—wife of one Alamo defender, sister of another—had to move carefully: her new baby was due any day.

By 11 the families all seemed to be gone, and the troops were ready to follow. The men clumsily formed in ranks of four; the captains gave the command to march; and the little army tramped off to the east. There were some 374 men in all, and of every conceivable variety—Sampson Connell, an ancient veteran of Jackson's victory at New Orleans . . . John Jenkins, a lively 13-year-old . . . Colonel Sydney Sherman, who had the most dazzling uniform in Texas . . . Ben, late of the Mexican Army, who found no difficulty at all in making the transition from Almonte's chef to Houston's cook.

It was hard marching. The road was rough, the weather hot and muggy—blanket rolls weighed a ton. The night was black—pitch-black—and the men tripped and stumbled as they trudged along. They never knew it could get so dark.

Then unexpectedly it grew lighter. Not from the east, where dawn would break; but from the west, from the town they left behind. A lurid glare rose in the sky, lighting their way beyond complaint. A grim Sam Houston—determined to leave no shelter, no comfort for the advancing Mexicans— was burning Gonzales to the ground.

For a few of the men it was all too much. They had joined up to chase out the Mexicans—just like last fall. But this time everything was different. Butchered friends, burning homes, suffering families. They had families too, and it was time to protect them. Some twenty of Houston's men deserted, rushing home to save what they could, spreading stories of rout and disaster.

Head east, head east—that was the only hope. At Stafford's Point, the P. W. Rose family got the news in the afternoon . . . left at sunset, hauling clothes, bedding and food all jumbled together on an ox-drawn sledge. Dr. Rose was off saving the cattle, so Mrs. Rose had to make out alone. She piled the youngest children on the load and walked alongside, carrying the baby. Eleven-year-old Dilue trudged with her, weeping bitterly for Travis.

Head east, head east—the word spread everywhere. At San Felipe, Gail Borden ran an editorial in his *Telegraph and Texas Register*, urging everyone to stay put. Then he loaded his presses on a wagon and headed east himself. At Washington-on-the-Brazos, the country's fledging statesmen slapped together a constitution, elected an interim government, and joined the parade.

"It is with inexpressible regret that I observe the slightest indication of alarm among us," the new President David G. Burnet declared on March 18. Later that morning he was on his way east too—bound for the "temporary capital" hastily established at the little town of Harrisburg. Here the government resumed its functions, issuing frantic requests for stationery, blankets, cups and saucers, "liquors suitable for Genteel men to drink."

The "Runaway Scrape," the Texans called their flight, with a sort of embarrassed jollity in later years. At the time it was simply terrifying—a pell-mell rush of women, children, officials, speculators, everybody. But through it all, a small group of women stood out with unruffled grace and dignity. These were the Alamo widows. The blind Mrs. Isaac Millsaps —inadvertently left behind at Gonzales—waited patiently with her seven children, till Houston discovered the blunder and rescued her. Sydney Kellogg had her baby on March 19, then lay uncomplainingly in the back of an open wagon, bouncing along in the driving rain.

As the refugees streamed east, Houston's little army brought up the rear, guarding them from the enemy, prodding them along—like a scrappy shepherd dog herding the sheep. The troops reached the Colorado on March 17, waited there a week, hoping to blunt the Mexican advance. Much depended on Fannin, who had been ordered to pull back and be ready to co-operate.

But Fannin, of course, never moved. Rooted to Goliad, he waited too long to begin his march. Finally starting out on the 19th, he was quickly surrounded by Urrea's forces. A half-hearted fight, and early next morning he surrendered. Some 400 Texans were taken back to Goliad, where they spent a miserable week as prisoners. On the night of March 26 things began to look up—there were rumors of parole—and one of the men took out a flute and softly played "Home, Sweet

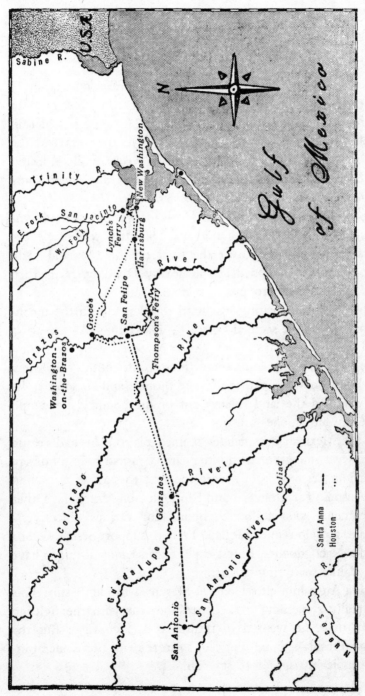

Rendezvous at San Jacinto. Houston's little army began retreating from Gonzales on March 13, leisurely followed by
Santa Anna. On March 31 the Texans halted on the Brazos
for two weeks to rest and regroup, while the Mexican leader
continued east, chasing the Texan government. An April 15

Houston resumed his march, now the pursuer instead of the
pursued. On April 21 he caught up with Santa Anna at the
mouth of the San Jacinto River, demolished the Mexican
force in eighteen minutes.

Home." The following dawn, Palm Sunday, they were led to the woods and shot.

News of Fannin's surrender reached Houston on March 25 and ended all hope of a stand on the Colorado. Next evening his troops were retreating again. On the 28th they passed Mill Creek, home of Travis' Rebecca; the 31st, they reached the Brazos. Here they rested and drilled two weeks, while Houston himself tapped reveille on a drum and spent the lonely hours of the night reading Caesar's *Commentaries*.

April 12, word came that the Mexicans were crossing downstream, and the retreat began again. The little steamer *Yellow Stone* ferried the men over the river on the 12th and 13th. Next night they camped at the nearby Donohoe farm, then the familiar orders to push on east.

This endless retreating was hard to take, and on the morning of the 15th it seemed especially frustrating. As the army left Donohoe's, a mysterious visitor appeared with a taunting message from Santa Anna somewhere to the south: "He knew Mr. Houston was up there in the bushes; and so soon as he had whipped the land thieves out of the country, he would come up and smoke him out."

If the Mexican commander seemed playful, he had reason to be. Ever since the Alamo, the campaign had been a holiday excursion. Sesma's troops were the first to start east, leaving San Antonio for Gonzales and San Felipe on March 11. Other detachments soon followed, bound for various objectives— Morales to help reduce Goliad, Tolsa to support Sesma, Gaona to take Nacogdoches. In less experienced hands, it might have seemed like scattering the army.

Santa Anna himself set out on March 31 to join Sesma. This was really something of a concession, for with the fighting nearly over, he wanted to return to Mexico City. But the stodgy Filisola seemed worried, so in the end the General-in-Chief amicably agreed to stay on.

It was really very easy. He reached Gonzales on April 2, crossed the Colorado on the 5th, took San Felipe on the 7th. Now he was on the Brazos and discovered that Houston had sunk or carried off every boat the Texans could find.

He knew a trick or two himself. First Almonte dashed to the edge of the river, and using his best American accent, yelled to the Texans guarding the other side, "Bring over that boat—the Mexicans are coming!" It didn't work, and after waiting around a few days, Santa Anna finally led the troops down the right bank toward Thompson's Ferry some thirty miles to the south.

On April 11 a clever ambush hauled in a frightened Negro —threats and bribes did the rest. He showed them a canoe hidden along the bank, and after much frantic paddling the Mexicans had a foothold on the east bank. Next morning they surprised the Texans guarding Thompson's Ferry, captured another canoe and, best of all, a fine flatboat.

As the last of the Mexicans were crossing on the 14th, they suffered their only shock so far in the campaign. The steamboat *Yellow Stone* suddenly churned into view. Houston had finished with her and now she was heading downstream. Her tall stack vomited clouds of smoke, her bright paddlewheels thrashed the water.

Many of the Mexicans raced in terror for the woods—they had never seen a steamboat before. Others dashed along the bank, firing their muskets at the paddles. A few intrepid souls laid a trap: at a narrow point along the river they tried to lasso the smokestack. All was in vain. The *Yellow Stone* rounded the bend and chugged from sight.

Small loss. Santa Anna now had far bigger game in mind. A friendly Mexican reported that President Burnet and his top officials were at Harrisburg. Only thirty miles away! Prompt action could capture them all and end the rebellion with one lightning stroke.

At 3 P.M., April 14, Santa Anna was on the way, leading 700 infantry, 50 cavalry and one 6-pounder. All afternoon and evening they rushed on, soaking the hardtack and drowning two mules in their hurry to get across one difficult creek. No one seemed to know where they were going—nor did Filisola, Sesma or any of the others left behind—but the men had rarely seen their commander more excited.

At 9 o'clock that night they flopped into camp, so tired they didn't even mind that His Excellency forgot to pick a site with water. Then on again next morning, driving hard all day—time out only to loot a small plantation. Even so, they weren't going fast enough. Finally, Santa Anna dashed ahead with some dragoons, swooping down on Harrisburg just before midnight.

They were too late. No President, no officials, almost no citizens. Only three printers, cranking out the latest issue of the *Telegraph and Texas Register*. Santa Anna indignantly pitched the press into nearby Buffalo Bayou and put the printers under arrest.

From them he learned that the government, warned in time, had fled to Galveston. They also confirmed that Houston was still up the Brazos with 800 men. A little at loose ends, Santa Anna now sent Almonte and the cavalry still farther eastward. He told them to check Lynch's Ferry and New Washington, both at the mouth of the San Jacinto River. See if anything was brewing in that direction.

There certainly was. On the 17th Almonte sent back some exciting news from New Washington: Houston was retreating again—heading for safety east of the Trinity—he would cross the San Jacinto at Lynch's Ferry.

Get there first and cut him off! Another golden chance to end the rebellion at a single stroke. Again Santa Anna's little force surged eastward, now driving harder than ever. First they would rejoin Almonte at New Washington, then move together up the San Jacinto estuary to Lynch's Ferry. They should easily get there before Houston.

Such an exciting prospect could make a man forget everything else. Where they were right now, for instance. Yet this was interesting country—especially for a student of military tactics. Hardly any room for maneuvering at all. On their left ran the sluggish waters of Buffalo Bayou . . . ahead was the estuary of the San Jacinto . . . to the right, the marshes and inlets of Galveston Bay. And as they swept across Vince's Bayou—spanned only by a narrow wooden bridge— there was now water behind them too.

On they raced. Soon Harrisburg lay far to the rear—and even farther, the rest of the Mexican Army. Sesma was still at Thompson's Ferry with 1,000 men . . . Filisola somewhere behind him with 1,800 more . . . Urrea at Matagorda with another 1,200 . . . Gaona lost near Bastrop with two whole battalions—he even admitted it. His Excellency had no patience with such men, and he certainly wasn't going to wait for them.

Noon, April 18, the little force reached New Washington. Almonte was waiting, as expected. No more word of Houston, and things seemed so quiet that Santa Anna decided to rest the troops a day before marching up the estuary toward Lynch's Ferry. On the 19th he sent Captain Barragan ahead to scout any sign of the Texans.

Eight o'clock next morning, Barragan came pounding back with stunning news. Houston was less than eight miles away —facing *them*, not Lynch's Ferry. Santa Anna leaped to his saddle, galloped to the head of his troops. They got under way immediately, marching "with joy and in the highest spirits." The Mexican leader never felt more confident; the battle was not shaping up quite the way he planned it, but the victory would be no less decisive.

A good many Americans would have agreed. To them, it

looked as though all the aid and money and enthusiasm had been too late. "The present campaign in Texas may be considered as closed," sighed the *Arkansas Gazette*, "and we would suggest to all persons who may intend taking up arms to assist the Texans to delay their departure for the present."

Then was the Alamo in vain, after all? Horace Greeley thought so. Lumping Bexar and Goliad together, he decided such disasters "must naturally, if not necessarily, involve the extinction of every rational hope for Texas."

Some things, certainly, the Alamo hadn't accomplished. Travis had vowed to make a Mexican victory worse than defeat; yet Santa Anna's losses were far from insuperable —he still outnumbered Houston six to one. Nor did the siege seriously interrupt the Mexican schedule. Writing his government on February 16—a week before he ever saw the Alamo—Santa Anna said he expected to have San Antonio by March 2. He was only four days late.

Nor did Travis' heroism inspire the Texans to rush to the colors. Volunteers were pouring out in the Mississippi lowlands, the woods of Tennessee, the streets of Philadelphia— but they were too far away. Men were needed on the spot. And in Texas, the Alamo had quite a different effect.

At first the turnout was heartening. The army increased from 374 on March 12 to perhaps 1,400 by March 25. But it didn't last. As details of the Mexican butchery spread and the "Runaway Scrape" began, hundreds of volunteers rushed off to protect their families. By mid-April the army was down again to 900 men.

To Houston, not even the government's flight was more damaging than the massacre at Bexar. "Your removal to Harrisburg," he scolded Secretary of War Rusk, "has done more to increase the panic in the country than anything else that has occurred in Texas, except the Fall of the Alamo."

Yet if the garrison's sacrifice achieved few tangible results, it accomplished something else far more important. Something less visible to Horace Greeley sitting in New York, but no less real in Texas.

It made the hard core of Houston's army—the staunch men who remained—blazing, fighting mad. Until the Alamo, it was difficult to take Santa Anna seriously. After the easy Texan victories in the fall, he seemed like something out of a comic-opera. But there was nothing comic-opera about this blood bath. "If such conduct is not sufficient to arouse the patriotic feelings of the sons of liberty," exploded Private G. A. Giddings, "I know not what will." And Benjamin Goodrich grimly promised, "We ask nor expect no quarter in the future."

Along with anger went another feeling, perhaps even more important. This was deep, gnawing shame—shame for failing to go to Travis' rescue. "Texas will take honor to herself for the defense of the Alamo and will call it a second Thermopylae," prophesied William Gray from Groce's Place, "but it will be an everlasting monument of national disgrace."

A little strong, but who didn't know in his heart that more could have been done? Who didn't feel secretly guilty about those interminable resolutions and indignation meetings, when they might have been marching? "My bones shall reproach my country for her neglect," Travis had written. The bones did their work well.

Men were ashamed they let Travis down, and now they were ashamed to be retreating. "Run, run, Santa Anna is behind you!" cackled an indignant old lady from her doorway, and the ears burned of every man who heard her. By mid-April the troops were raging to get at Santa Anna, and showed signs of revolting if they were held back much longer.

Few noticed that when Houston again moved eastward on April 15, he was no longer retreating; he was now following the enemy. That lunge at the fleeing politicians had drawn the Mexicans far past the little Texan army. Houston edged after them, but most of the men bitterly complained that it was just another march eastward. Nor did Houston enlighten them: "I consulted none—I held no councils of war—if I err the blame is mine."

April 18, they reached Buffalo Bayou, just across from Harrisburg. Here Houston paused uncertainly. There comes a time when any general needs more than a plan and his intuition . . . a time when he can also use a touch of luck.

It was just about dark when "Deaf" Smith burst into camp with astounding news. Santa Anna himself was leading the enemy force just ahead—the first time the Texans realized it. Better still, the Mexican leader was now far east of Vince's Bayou, groping his way down San Jacinto Bay. The Texans were between him and the main part of the Mexican Army. In short they had him cut off.

Could they be sure? Smith had prisoners to prove it—a Mexican courier and escort caught west of Harrisburg bearing important messages for Santa Anna. Not exactly proof, but no less meaningful for Houston's troops were the courier's saddlebags. They had been captured from the Texans; they were marked, "W. B. Travis."

The drum tapped reveille at daybreak on the 19th, and Houston addressed his men. He told them about the Mexican force just ahead; he told them about Santa Anna leading it; and as their eyes flickered in rising excitement, he told them a little about geography. To regain contact with the main army, Santa Anna must come back either by Lynch's Ferry or the bridge over Vince's Bayou. The Texans could get to either point first. "Victory is certain!" Houston cried. "Trust in God and fear not! And Remember the Alamo, Remember the Alamo!"

A wild yell erupted from the ranks. Then a mad rush

to get ready. The sick, the wounded, the wagons, the baggage would all stay behind. The rest shouldered their rifles and marched east. With them they took their new pride—two handsome 6-pounders christened the "Twin Sisters," a timely gift from the citizens of Cincinnati.

East three miles . . . then across Buffalo Bayou and east again . . . over Vince's bridge . . . by the dead Mexican campfires . . . through a beautiful moonlit night they marched. But the moon was dangerous too, for now they were in "Santa Anna country"—his scouts might be anywhere.

Whispered orders, and at 2 A.M. the Texans fell out for a few hours' sleep. Up at dawn and on again. Seven o'clock, a halt for breakfast, but they no sooner lit the fires than the inevitable happened. The Mexican scouts—specifically Captain Barragan's party—spied them and dashed off to warn Santa Anna.

No time to be eating. The Texans forgot breakfast and rushed on again. Just after 10 A.M. "Deaf" Smith's scouts swooped down on Lynch's Ferry, drove off an astonished enemy guard, and seized a Mexican flatboat loaded with flour. Maybe they'd have breakfast after all.

Houston laid out his camp along Buffalo Bayou, just where it joined the San Jacinto estuary, and the men fell out. But again, no time to eat. Scouts galloped in, reported the Mexicans coming hard. The Texans moved into line and waited. One o'clock . . . 1:30 . . . 2:00.

There they were. Across the prairie, through the tall grass they came swarming—those dusty white jumpers, the blaring bugles, the lancers prancing in their glistening armor.

The "Twin Sisters" crashed into action; the long line of Texan rifles cracked from the woods. The enemy wheeled up their own 6-pounder, traded a few shots. Then a halfhearted Mexican charge that quickly petered out. Firing died off. Toward sunset, Colonel Sydney Sherman led the cavalry to feel out the enemy's position, returned to camp badly mauled. Houston angrily replaced him with a bright young private bearing the highly military name Mirabeau Buonaparte Lamar.

Santa Anna too was less than completely satisfied with developments. The enemy wouldn't come out and fight. Instead of behaving like professional soldiers, they skulked in the woods, firing from trees and behind a low ridge. He did his best to lure them into the open, but nothing worked. Finally, he pulled back a thousand yards and camped for the evening.

He picked his camp site with infinite care and was extremely proud of his choice: "A hill that gave me an advantageous position with water on the rear, heavy woods to our right as far as the banks of the San Jacinto, open plains to the left, and a clear front."

Thursday, April 21, 1836. In the Mexican camp, it was a beautiful morning brimming with optimism right from the start. At 9 General Cós arrived with 400 reinforcements. Santa Anna had asked for them back in Harrisburg, and for once Filisola was prompt. Shouts, cheers and a special ruffle of drums celebrated the occasion.

No sign of enemy activity, so Santa Anna ordered the men to stack arms and rest in the nearby grove. For protection against any surprise, he improvised a barricade in front of the lines. It was made of branches. To the left—where the 6-pounder stood—he built a somewhat stronger breastwork. This was made of pack saddles, luggage and sacks of hardtack.

Around noon, General Cós suggested that the cavalry be allowed to eat and water their horses. Their job was to guard the camp, but all was quiet, and after all, the men had to eat. Santa Anna agreed.

He now retired for a nap. Not in his striped marquee, but under a spacious oak, where the shade seemed especially pleasant. He looked forward to big things once they all had their rest. With the camp back here, the Texans would have to come out of their woods, and then they would get their lesson. Meanwhile, he slept in peace.

Houston spent an even more unusual noon hour. He held the first council of war in his life. The question: "Shall we attack the enemy's position, or wait for him to attack us?" The staff aimlessly debated the matter, and Houston finally dismissed them. He had made his plans anyhow. Calling "Deaf" Smith, he told his dour scout to take a party and chop down Vince's bridge, the only way of retreat left open for Santa Anna.

Two o'clock, Houston quietly sent Colonel Joseph Bennett through the ranks, just to make sure the men were ready. They were ready, all right.

At 3:30 the order came: "Parade and prepare for action." The men fell in, deep in their thoughts. For one of them, at least, there was something quite special to think about. Alfonso Steele had deserted Travis en route to the Alamo. He hadn't felt like fighting then; but he felt very differently now.

Four o'clock, Houston raised his sword, turned his white stallion toward the Mexican camp. The 783 men surged forward—first in column, then in a long, thin line that swept like a scythe through the tall prairie grass. A fife and drum urged them on, serenading them with an old favorite about a long-awaited rendezvous: "Will You Come to the Bower I Have Shaded for You?"

It was all over in eighteen incredible minutes. Colonel Delgado's 6-pounder . . . the silver teapot . . . the sacks of crumbling hardtack . . . the brightly decked lances . . . the bugles . . . the portable *escritoire* . . . the whole Mexican force of 1,150 men—gone forever. More than that: gone were Santa Anna's plans for Texas and the Mexican dream of an empire running all the way to the Rockies and the Pacific. Other battles—another war—would follow, but for Mexico, San Jacinto was the real nightmare.

The luckless General Castrillón fell murmuring, "I've never showed my back; I'm too old to do it now." Others cared less. Colonel Delgado fled barefoot to a small grove by the bay, surrendered toward evening. The suave Almonte cheerfully turned himself in that night. Secretary Ramón Caro headed for Harrisburg, only to discover "Deaf" Smith had done his work well—Vince's bridge was down. Santa Anna simply disappeared.

The Texans celebrated and counted their own toll—ultimately 9 killed and 34 wounded. Next morning some of Houston's scouts found a nondescript little fellow hiding in the grass near the splintered remains of Vince's bridge. He wore a faded blue cotton jacket and red worsted slippers. When questioned, he finally acknowledged he was a simple private in the Mexican Army. They brought him back to camp, and no one suspected anything, until some of the Mexican prisoners spoiled the masquerade. Perhaps from force of habit, they just couldn't resist calling, "*El Presidente! El Presidente!*"

Brought before Houston, Santa Anna generously congratulated him on defeating the "Napoleon of the West." Houston took it calmly, and since a wounded foot kept him from rising, he politely invited His Excellency to have a seat. Months later, the Mexican leader was sent home unharmed on the understanding that he would support Texan independence.

Men were coolly reasonable once again, but it was just as well they didn't catch Santa Anna during the battle. There was nothing quite like the fury of those eighteen minutes. The flashing knives . . . the rifles used as clubs . . . the wrath of the infuriated Texan who even butchered one of the helpless *soldaderas*. As the slaughter continued, the terrified Mexicans could only fall to their knees, saying "Me no Alamo." For although they spoke a different tongue, they knew only too well what this was all about. Travis' stand—and Santa Anna's answer—had the same moral connotations in any language. Every man at San Jacinto understood the meaning, when in the late afternoon of April 21 Houston's line swept forward, shouting with an almost lofty rage, "Remember the Alamo!"

Riddles of the Alamo

"You know," the old Texan gently admonished, "legend is often truer than history and always more lasting." And yet the haunting questions remain—did Travis *really* draw the line, did Crockett *really* fall fighting, and so on.

The answers come hard, even when someone wants to know the facts. Traces of the frontier are few today in terms of towns, wild game, Indians, lawlessness, almost everything—except research. Here the frontier is still very much alive, for the pioneer's impatience with dates, spelling and record-keeping lingers on to plague anyone digging into the past.

Dates alone are a nightmare in the story of the Alamo. Ramón Caro had an exasperating way of saying things happened on February 30. Juan Seguin gave at least four different dates as the day he left the fort—February 26 (letter to W. W. Fontaine, 1890); the 28th (*Memoirs*, 1858); the 29th (talk with R. M. Potter, about 1878); March 2 (affidavit on behalf of Andreas Nava, about 1860). Actually, it appears he left on February 25. Seguin was almost certainly the man who carried Travis' message of the 25th to Houston, and was seen at Gonzales on the morning of the 28th by Dr. John Sutherland.

Under frontier conditions, dates could also get mixed up

in putting them down. Foote's 1841 history of Texas contains a letter from Colonel Fannin describing his abortive march to relieve the Alamo. Because the letter is dated February 29 and Fannin speaks of marching "yesterday," readers have understandably assumed he started out on the 28th.

Yet Fannin's letter is either misdated, miscopied or misprinted. At least seven other letters conclusively show that he actually marched February 26, and the letter in Foote should be dated the 27th. But because Foote is widely read, the error lingers on and Fannin becomes even slower than he was.

Names are another problem. Fannin ended his signature with such a fancy rubric that early historians often spelled his name "Fanning." In early documents Almeron Dickinson's name was sometimes spelled "Dickerson," and through the years a debate of medievalist proportions developed over which version was correct. At the time, of course, people didn't care as long as they knew who was meant. This book follows the spelling in his marriage certificate and application for headright land—but he would not have minded the other.

Place names are almost as complicated. People rarely saw a map and used the names they picked up from others, who perhaps used some personal description or association. Hence the same general spot on the Brazos is variously called Thompson's Ferry, Orozimbo, Old Fort and Fort Bend. In a later, better-organized day it became the town of Richmond.

Finally, so little was written down at all. Texas was acutely aware of the Alamo's importance, yet nobody had time to make a serious study until twenty-four years later, when Captain Reuben M. Potter issued his first little pamphlet in 1860. Potter, incidentally, was the first to add a fall to Bowie's various ailments. Later he changed his mind, wrote Henry Arthur McCardle in 1874 that Bowie had not been injured. But the story was now launched and still sails on, even though denied by the person who started it.

It is, then, a rash man indeed who claims he has the final answer to everything that happened in the Alamo. The best that can be done is to offer some careful conclusions—always subject to correction—that might throw new light on a few of the many intriguing riddles. . . .

Did Houston Order the Alamo Blown Up?

He later said he did, but his critics (of whom there were many) always maintained that this was just another example of Houston taking credit where no credit was due.

Actually, the evidence indicates that Houston did indeed try to avert the siege by ordering the Alamo destroyed and the garrison withdrawn. His orders to Bowie of January 16 have not been preserved, but a letter of the 17th to Governor Smith says, "I have ordered the fortifications in the town of Bexar to be destroyed, and if you think well of it, I will remove all the cannon, and other munitions of war to Gonzales and Copano, blow up the Alamo, and abandon the place. . . ."

While final action was apparently contingent on the Governor's approval, other evidence suggests that Houston—feeling sure of his grounds—had already given the necessary orders to Bowie. The Provisional Council certainly thought so and on January 30 angrily complained that Houston had ordered the destruction of all defenses at Bexar and the abandonment of the post.

Nor was this a case where Houston gained his foresight long after the event. Writing James Collinsworth on March 15—only two days after Mrs. Dickinson reached Gonzales—the General declared: "Our forces must not be shut up in forts, where they can neither be supplied with men nor provisions. Long aware of this fact, I directed, on the 16th of January last, that the artillery should be removed, and the Alamo blown up. . . ."

Did Travis Draw the Line?

Ever since William Zuber launched the story in 1873, historians have pondered over his tale of Colonel Travis' last appeal to his garrison. Did Travis really draw a line on the ground with his sword, ask all who were with him to cross, and give any others the chance to escape? Did Louis Rose really hang back—the only man in the Alamo who preferred to live? Did he really vault the wall and escape?

There were so many things wrong with the account, few scholars took it seriously for years. At best it was secondhand hearsay: Rose was illiterate and Zuber's parents, who heard him tell the story, never wrote it down. William Zuber himself was an incorrigible raconteur—another of his tales had a Mexican tearing Jim Bowie's tongue out.

Worst of all, the story just didn't fit the known facts: (1) Only one Rose was listed in the Alamo, and that was generally understood to be James M. Rose, ex-President Madison's nephew and an impeccable hero. (2) Travis had not lost all hope on March 3—his letters that day were full of high spirits and detailed instructions on what the relief force should bring. (3) John W. Smith, who left the Alamo later that night, never mentioned the speech or the line.

Nor, in fact, did any of the survivors, until long after the Zuber story was published. Then, versions by Enrique Esparza and Mrs. Dickinson began to appear . . . but obviously with heavy and not very skillful editorial assistance. In 1881, for instance, Mrs. Dickinson had the story backward—the line was to be crossed by anyone who wanted to leave. Far worse, she had it all happening on the first day of the siege.

Then in 1939 came a thunderbolt. R. B. Blake, a conscientious office worker long interested in the Zuber story, uncovered some amazing evidence in the Nacogdoches County Courthouse. It showed convincingly that there was indeed a Louis Rose, that he had been in the Alamo during the siege, and that his testimony was accepted by the local Board of Land Commissioners in deciding claims filed on behalf of six different Alamo victims. On Claim No. 254 by the heirs of John Blair, for instance, Rose testified, "Left him in the Alamo 3 March 1836."

So Rose was there. But did he leave under the dramatic circumstances described by Zuber? Freshly uncovered information suggests that he did. This consists of a formal statement, never published, given by Mrs. Dickinson to the State Adjutant General, who was trying to develop a more definitive list of Alamo defenders. Dated September 23, 1876, part of her statement declares:

> On the evening previous to the massacre, Colonel Travis asked the command that if any desired to escape, now was the time, to let it be known, and to step out of the ranks. But one stepped out. His name to the best of my recollection was Ross. The next morning he was missing.

Of course, she did say "Ross," not "Rose." But letters and spelling meant nothing to Mrs. Dickinson, who couldn't read or write. At this distance, her statement looks good enough —especially since there was no "Ross" in the Alamo. Nor does it seem damaging that her statement postdated the Zuber story by three years. It doesn't have the ring of a coached remark; and Mrs. Dickinson, who was exasperatingly uninterested in her historic role, didn't have it in her to take off all alone on a flight of fancy.

But the statement does throw great light on another point raised by Zuber's critics: How could Travis have drawn the line on March 3, when his letters were still so hopeful and John W. Smith never mentioned it at all? The answer: It didn't happen on March 3—it happened, as Mrs. Dickinson testified, on the evening of March 5. By then the picture had entirely changed. Moreover, the later date would fit perfectly with the course of battle on March 5, when Mexican fire did taper off around sunset.

All that's needed is to allow Rose the same leeway on dates as everyone else in the Alamo story. In the true frontier spirit, none of them cared very much—who ever saw a calendar? Ramón Caro said Santa Anna arrived on February 26; Seguin said February 22. Travis himself gave two different dates for the arrival of the Gonzales men.

So Rose was there and Rose fled—but still, did Travis draw the line? In her statement to the Adjutant General, Mrs. Dickinson didn't mention it. Now a recently uncovered Zuber letter casts further doubt on the story. He too was writing the Adjutant General about this time, apparently because his account had come under such heavy fire. In a letter dated September 14, 1877, Zuber acknowledged that he had made up Travis' speech completely, although it was based on information supplied by Rose. Moreover, Zuber admitted that he invented one paragraph which did not come from Rose at all: "I found a deficiency in the material of the speech, which from my knowledge of the man, I thought I could supply. I accordingly threw in one paragraph which I firmly believe to be characteristic of Travis, and without which the speech would have been incomplete."

Zuber never said what the passage was, but the omission itself is significant. The line was the crux of the whole speech

—the center of all the controversy. If his concoction ("without which the speech would have been incomplete") was not the line, it seems he would have said so, for this was the one thing everyone wanted to know.

Summing up his account of the speech, Zuber said all he was trying to do was show "That on the afternoon of the 3rd day of March 1836, Travis in a formal address explained to his command their real situation and offered to every man who might be disposed to accept it an opportunity to risk the chances of surrender or escape."

Again, no mention of the line. But perhaps it was just as well. If Zuber was hiding a gentle fabrication, he was also protecting a shining legend—and what harm in a legend that only serves to perpetuate the memory of valor and sacrifice? As matters stand, there's still room to speculate, and every good Texan can follow the advice of J. K. Beretta in the *Southwestern Historical Quarterly*: "Is there any proof that Travis didn't draw the line? If not, then let us believe it."

Who Was the Last Messenger from the Alamo?

John W. Smith gets all the glory and deserves much of it, for he carried Travis' last dispatch to the Convention on the night of March 3. But another messenger left later with a final appeal to Fannin. This man reached Goliad on March 8, and his arrival is noted in two different letters—Burr H. Duval to William P. Duval, March 9, 1836; and John Sowers Brooks to James Hagerty, same date.

The courier to Goliad evidently left the Alamo considerably after Smith, for his report is much more gloomy. On March 3 the walls were "generally proof against cannon balls"; now "every shot goes through, as the walls are weak." Clearly the later report was sent after the Mexicans erected their new battery on March 4 just to the north of the Alamo.

The evidence indicates that this last courier was 16-year-old James L. Allen and that he rode from the Alamo "after nightfall" on March 5. He left no written account, but through the years he told his story to others. At least three of these listeners have independently set down his story, and none seem to doubt his word. Allen himself was a responsible citizen— later tax assessor, justice of the peace, and Mayor of Indianola.

Did Travis Wear a Uniform?

No, despite all the portraits. He had ordered one from McKinney & Williams, but judging from his letter of January 21, 1836 to Captain W. G. Hill, it wasn't very far along. Since he left for the Alamo on the 23rd, there's little chance it caught up with him before the siege. Sergeant Felix Nuñez, who appropriated Travis' coat after the battle, said that it was of homemade Texas jeans.

Where Was Bowie Killed?

A wide variety of sources give six different places. The favorites: a small room on the north side of the church; the second-floor room in the southwest corner of the long barracks; a small room in the low barracks. Of these choices, the best evidence points to the low barracks. Authorities: Mrs. Alsbury, who was Bowie's sister-in-law; Captain Sánchez Navarro, Sergeant Loranca, and Sergeant Nuñez, all of the attacking force; Francisco Ruiz, who had the job of identifying Bowie's remains for Santa Anna. On Sánchez Navarro's plan of the Alamo, Bowie's room is clearly marked in the low barracks, just to the east of the main gate.

Did Travis Commit Suicide?

According to Antonio Pérez, one of the first friendly Mexicans to reach Gonzales after the massacre, Travis stabbed himself to avoid capture. Houston believed the story, and it was widely circulated. But later and more reliable evidence indicates that the Colonel was killed by enemy gunfire.

This certainly is the opinion of those who were there. Travis' slave Joe is emphatic on the point, and he was standing beside his master on the north battery. Captain Sánchez Navarro and Colonel José Enrique de la Peña, who wrote detailed firsthand accounts from the Mexican side, both agree that Travis fell fighting.

Much has been made of the report by Francisco Ruiz, who identified Travis' body for Santa Anna. In her celebrated thesis on the Alamo, Miss Amelia Williams pointed out that Ruiz said Travis' only wound was "a pistol shot through the forehead." But Ruiz never mentioned a pistol, and to one observer at least, there seems nothing remarkable about a soldier being shot in the head during battle.

Did David Crockett Surrender?

It's just possible that he did. A surprising number of contemporary sources suggest that Crockett was one of the six Americans who gave up at the end, only to be executed on Santa Anna's orders.

Colonel Peña flatly said so in his *Diario*, first published in September, 1836. Colonel Almonte told a similar story, according to a letter from Sergeant George M. Dolson in the Detroit *Democratic Free Press* of September 7, 1836. So did an unidentified Mexican officer (who sounds suspiciously like Ramón Caro), according to a letter appearing in the Frankfort, Kentucky, *Commonwealth* of July 27, 1836. A similar account also came from Captain Fernando Urizza after San Jacinto, according to Dr. N. D. Labadie. Urizza said the prisoner's name was "Cocket," but Labadie had no doubts whom he meant.

Nor are all the sources Mexican. Passengers on the schooner *Comanche*, arriving in New Orleans on March 27 with first details of the massacre, also reported how Crockett and others had tried to surrender "but were told there was no mercy for them." The New Orleans *Post-Union* picked up the story, and it quickly spread to the *Arkansas Gazette* and elsewhere. Even Mary Austin Holley, that most loyal of Texans, finally included it in her 1836 guidebook.

But it must be stressed that most early Texan accounts declared that Crockett fell in battle. "Fighting like a tiger," to use Andrew Briscoe's words. Both Joe and Mrs. Dickinson also believed he was killed in action, although neither saw him till after he was dead.

So there's a good chance Crockett lived up to his legend, and in some circles it remains dangerous even to question the matter. A few years ago when *The Columbia Encyclopedia* ventured the opinion that Crockett surrendered, an angry retort in the *Southwestern Historical Quarterly* declared that Texas would need better authority than "a New York publication." Next edition, the New York editors meekly changed their copy.

How Many Survivors?

At least fourteen people in the Alamo lived through the siege. Three were Americans: Mrs. Dickinson, her daughter Angelina, and Travis' slave Joe. Some early sources also listed a slave belonging to Bowie (variously called "Sam" and

"Ben"), but this was actually Almonte's cook Ben, detailed to escort the others to Gonzales. Mrs. Dickinson, Joe and Houston are all firm that only three Americans came out alive.

A minimum of ten Mexican women and children also survived: Mrs. Alsbury and her baby, her sister Gertrudis Navarro, Mrs. Gregorio Esparza and her four children, Trinidad Saucedo, and Petra Gonzales. There were probably others, but the evidence is conflicting. On the other hand, Madam Candelaria—one of the better-known claimants—definitely was not in the Alamo.

One member of the garrison almost certainly survived— Brigido Guerrero, who talked himself free by claiming to have been a prisoner of the Texans. Both Almonte and Gregorio Esparza mention him, and he later made a good enough case to get a pension from Bexar County in 1878.

There is also evidence that Henry Warnell lived through the assault but soon died from his wounds. A sworn statement in a land claim filed in 1858 declares Warnell "at the massacre of the Alamo . . . that he was wounded at the said massacre but made his escape to Port Lavacca, where he died in less than three months from the effects of said wound." (General Land Office, Court of Claims Application No. 1579, File W to Z, July 30, 1858.) This document seems stronger than an unsupported story that Warnell was fatally wounded while serving as a courier to Houston.

Finally, there is the bare possibility of two other survivors. The *Arkansas Gazette* of March 29, 1836—when it was still generally believed that the Alamo was safe—carried an intriguing item about two men (one badly wounded) turning up in Nacogdoches, "who said San Antonio had been retaken by the Mexicans, the garrison put to the sword—that if any others escaped the general massacre besides themselves, they were not aware of it." The item appeared a week before the *Gazette* carried Houston's "express" reporting the defeat. In the thirty-one other newspapers examined, the General's announcement was invariably the first word received.

None of these possibilities seem strong enough to detract from the Alamo as a genuine example of a group of men who knowingly sacrificed their lives rather than yield to their enemy.

How Many Texans Fell in the Alamo?

Figures range from 180 to Santa Anna's ludicrous 600. Best estimate seems to be 183. This is the final figure given by Ramón Caro, the Mexican general's secretary. Also by Jesse Badgett, one of the first Texans to supply details to the U.S. press (*Arkansas Gazette*, April 12, 1836). Francisco Ruiz, in charge of burning the bodies, listed 182—but he missed Gregorio Esparza, the only defender Santa Anna allowed to be buried.

How Many Mexican Casualties?

Nineteen different sources give nineteen different answers —ranging from 65 killed and 223 wounded (Colonel Almonte) to 2,000 killed and 300 wounded (Sergeant Francisco Becerra). Most Texan sources claimed a thousand Mexicans killed and wounded, while General Andrade's official report acknowledged 311 casualties. Both probably reflect wishful thinking, and the problem is complicated by the Mexicans' tendency after San Jacinto to say absolutely anything that might please a Texan—until they got back south of the border.

Best estimate seems about 600 killed and wounded. This is in line with figures worked out by Captain Reuben M. Potter, a contemporary Texan authority with firsthand knowledge of

Santa Anna's army; also with a Mexican study made in 1849, when enough time had passed for a little perspective. In addition, it fits figures reported by Dr. Joseph H. Barnard, a Texan physician captured by the Mexicans and sent to San Antonio to tend their injured. He was told that 400 men were wounded in the assault; an additional 200 killed would be about right, or 600 casualties altogether.

The estimate goes with what is known of the Mexican Army. Judging from Filisola's battle order figures and Santa Anna's attack order of March 5, there were no more than 2,400 Mexicans in San Antonio, or 1,800 in the actual assault. A casualty rate of 33 per cent is a stiff price, even if 600 seems a modest figure. No Texan need feel cheated.

What Was the Alamo Flag?

Traditionally the Alamo flew a modified Mexican flag, but the best evidence indicates that this was not the case.

The early Texan sources mention no specific flag, but in 1860 Captain R. M. Potter remedied the omission. In the first of several accounts he did on the subject, Captain Potter declared that the Alamo flag was the regular Mexican tricolor, but with the date 1824 substituted for the usual golden eagle. This was based on no evidence but on Potter's theory that the Texans were fighting for the Mexican Constitution of 1824, until the Declaration of Independence was formally passed on March 2, 1836. Since the Alamo defenders knew nothing of this event, the theory ran, they went down still fighting for a liberal Mexico. The irony of Potter's theory was appealing; others backed it up and it lingers on.

But the theory does not jibe with the facts. Actually, Texas had stopped fighting for the Constitution of 1824 long before the Alamo. The old Constitution had been a good enough goal for many during the fall and December, but early in 1836 popular opinion swung violently and overwhelmingly for independence. In the elections to the Convention, the independence candidate won a smashing victory in every Texas municipality.

As loyalty to Mexico ceased, so did the trappings. Down came the old 1824 flags; up went new, strange banners—each designed according to the maker's whim, but all proclaiming the idea of independence. There was the flag with the azure blue star raised at Velasco . . . another based on the stars and stripes at Victoria . . . a hodgepodge of red, white, blue and green at San Felipe. There was no time to wait—events had outstripped such formalities as conventions, declarations and official flags.

The men in the Alamo were no different. By February only Seguin's handful of local Mexicans seemed hesitant; the rest wanted no part of 1824. "All in favor of independence," Colonel Neill assured Governor Smith on January 23. The men's letters bore him out. "Every man here is for independence," wrote Private M. Hawkins. "God grant that we may create an independent government," prayed Amos Pollard.

These men, like the rest of Texas, had their improvised flags. The New Orleans Greys carried their azure blue. Travis' regulars had the five-dollar flag he bought en route to San Antonio (no description remains). Seguin's nine men might well have carried a Mexican tricolor with two stars standing for Coahuila and Texas as separate states—one was seen in Bexar as the Mexicans approached—but the Anglo-Americans remained all for independence.

Santa Anna's arrival only strengthened the men's resolve. Writing Jesse Grimes on March 3, Travis stated, "If independence is not declared, I shall lay down my arms and so will the men under my command. But under the flag of independence we are ready to peril our lives a hundred times a day. . . ."

Such a man was not likely to be flying any kind of Mexican flag three days later. Judging from Colonel Almonte's diary, only one Texan banner was taken on March 6; and judging from the Mexican archives, this was the azure emblem of the New Orleans Greys. Full details on its capture were uncovered in 1934 by Dr. Luis Castrillo Ledon, Director of the Mexican National Museum of Archaeology, and there's no reason to doubt his findings. So the Greys' flag was the one Santa Anna sent home, complete with its boast of New Orleans help. As he pointed out, it clearly showed the designs of "abettors, who came from the ports of the United States of the North."

The flag remains in Mexico City today, still with Santa Anna's faded victory message attached to it. Kept at Chapultepec, it is not on exhibit but buried in the files . . . crumbling to pieces in brown wrapping paper. Thanks to the courtesy of the Mexican government, it was recently brought out once again, and enough of it pieced together to identify it beyond any doubt.

The Men Who Fell
at the Alamo

As the years pass, new light is constantly thrown on the Alamo defenders. Descendants write in, correcting ages, home towns and spelling of names. A yellowed land grant shows that some new man should be added to the list; a long-forgotten file shows that some other "hero" wasn't there at all.

It is now clear, for instance, that Sherod Dover was never in the Alamo. His murder in December, 1835—and the hanging of his killer—is fully described in the land application filed by his heirs. (General Land Office, Court of Claims Application 211, File C to D.)

It appears that several other names should be removed from the list. José María Guerrero, known as "Brigido," survived by claiming he was a prisoner of the Texans. Toribio Domingo Losoya was in Seguin's company at the storming of Bexar, but not in the Alamo. He was honorably discharged October 25, 1836. (General Land Office, Court of Claims Voucher 271, File H-L; Bounty Warrant 196.)

John G. King of Gonzales was probably another absentee. There were both a father and son of that name in Gonzales, but the father lived until 1856 and the son was married in 1848, according to the family Bible. Finally, John Gaston and

John Davis of Gonzales are probably the same person. Gaston's widowed mother married G. W. Davis, and the boy was often known by his stepfather's name. The point is stressed in the application for land ultimately awarded Davis' heirs. (General Land Office, Bounty Warrant No. 886.)

At the same time, M. B. Clark should be added to the list. The land application filed by his heirs was one of six supported by Louis Rose's testimony and accepted by the Nacogdoches County Land Office. (Application 203, granted February 6, 1838.)

This process of addition and subtraction will go on. Meanwhile, it seems time to take stock. Here, then, is a revised list of the men who fell at the Alamo, together with their birthplaces and homes before coming to Texas (in that order). In the case of some early colonists, origin is unknown, and home in Texas is given instead.

> Juan Abamillo—San Antonio
> R. Allen
> Miles DeForest Andross—San Patricio, Texas
> Micajah Autry—North Carolina, Tennessee
> Juan A. Badillo—San Antonio
> Peter James Bailey—Kentucky, Arkansas
> Isaac G. Baker—Gonzales, Texas
> William Charles M. Baker—Missouri, Mississippi
> John J. Ballentine—Bastrop, Texas
> Richard W. Ballentine—Alabama
> John J. Baugh—Virginia
> Joseph Bayliss—Tennessee
> John Blair—Tennessee
> Samuel B. Blair—Tennessee
> William Blazeby—England, New York
> James Butler Bonham—South Carolina, Alabama
> Daniel Bourne—England

James Bowie—Tennessee, Louisiana
Jesse B. Bowman—Red River, Texas
George Brown—England
James Brown—Pennsylvania
Robert Brown
James Buchanan—Alabama
Samuel E. Burns—Ireland, Louisiana
George D. Butler—Missouri
Robert Campbell—Tennessee
John Cane—Pennsylvania
William R. Carey—Maryland
Charles Henry Clark—Missouri
M. B. Clark—Nacogdoches, Texas
Daniel William Cloud—Kentucky, Arkansas
Robert E. Cochran—New Jersey
George Washington Cottle—Missouri
Henry Courtman—Germany
Lemuel Crawford—South Carolina
David Crockett—Tennessee
Robert Crossman—Massachusetts, Louisiana
David P. Cummings—Pennsylvania
Robert Cunningham—New York, Indiana
Jacob C. Darst—Kentucky, Missouri
Freeman H. K. Day—Gonzales, Texas
Jerry C. Day—Missouri
Squire Daymon—Tennessee
William Dearduff—Tennessee
Stephen Denison—Ireland, Kentucky
Charles Despallier—Louisiana
Almeron Dickinson—Pennsylvania, Tennessee
John H. Dillard—Tennessee
James R. Dimpkins—England
Lewis Duel—New York
Andrew Duvalt—Ireland

Carlos Espalier—San Antonio
Gregorio Esparza—San Antonio
Robert Evans—Ireland, New York
Samuel B. Evans—Kentucky
James L. Ewing—Tennessee
William Fishbaugh—Gonzales, Texas
John Flanders—Massachusetts
Dolphin Ward Floyd—North Carolina
John Hubbard Forsyth—New York
Antonio Fuentes—San Antonio
Galba Fuqua—Gonzales, Texas
William H. Furtleroy—Kentucky, Arkansas
William Garnett—Virginia
James W. Garrand—Louisiana
James Girard Garrett—Tennessee
John E. Garvin—Gonzales, Texas
John E. Gaston—Kentucky
James George—Gonzales, Texas
John Camp Goodrich—Tennessee
Albert Calvin Grimes—Georgia
James C. Gwynne—England, Mississippi
James Hannum—Refugio, Texas
John Harris—Kentucky
Andrew Jackson Harrison
William B. Harrison—Ohio
Joseph M. Hawkins—Ireland, Louisiana
John M. Hays—Tennessee
Charles M. Heiskell—Tennessee
Thomas Hendricks
Patrick Henry Herndon—Virginia
William D. Hersee—New York
Tapley Holland—Grimes County, Texas
Samuel Holloway—Pennsylvania
William D. Howell—Massachusetts

William Daniel Jackson—Ireland, Kentucky
Thomas Jackson—Kentucky
Green B. Jameson—Kentucky
Gordon C. Jennings—Missouri
Lewis Johnson—Wales
William Johnson—Pennsylvania
John Jones—New York
Johnnie Kellog—Gonzales, Texas
James Kenny—Virginia
Andrew Kent—Kentucky
Joseph Kerr—Louisiana
George C. Kimball—New York
William P. King—Gonzales, Texas
William Irvine Lewis—Pennsylvania
William J. Lightfoot—Virginia
Jonathan L. Lindley—Illinois
William Linn—Massachusetts
George Washington Main—Virginia
William T. Malone—Georgia
William Marshall—Tennessee, Arkansas
Albert Martin—Tennessee
Edward McCafferty—San Patricio, Texas
Jesse McCoy—Gonzales, Texas
William McDowell—Pennsylvania
James McGee—Ireland
John McGregor—Scotland
Robert McKinney—Ireland
Eliel Melton—South Carolina
Thomas R. Miller—Virginia
William Mills—Tennessee, Arkansas
Isaac Millsaps—Mississippi
Edward F. Mitchusson—Kentucky
Edwin T. Mitchell—Georgia
Napoleon B. Mitchell

Robert B. Moore—Virginia
Willis Moore—Mississippi, Arkansas
Robert Musselman—Ohio
Andres Nava—San Antonio
George Neggan—South Carolina
Andrew M. Nelson—Tennessee
Edward Nelson—South Carolina
George Nelson—South Carolina
James Northcross—Virginia
James Nowlin—Ireland
George Pagan—Mississippi
Christopher Parker—Mississippi
William Parks—San Patricio, Texas
Richardson Perry
Amos Pollard—Massachusetts, New York
John Purdy Reynolds—Pennsylvania
Thomas H. Roberts
James Robertson—Tennessee
Isaac Robinson—Scotland
James M. Rose—Virginia, Tennessee
Jackson J. Rusk—Ireland
Joseph Rutherford—Kentucky
Isaac Ryan—Louisiana
Mial Scurlock—Louisiana
Marcus L. Sewell—England
Manson Shied—Georgia
Cleland Kinloch Simmons—South Carolina
Andrew H. Smith—Tennessee
Charles S. Smith—Maryland
Joshua G. Smith—North Carolina, Tennessee
William H. Smith—Nacogdoches, Texas
Richard Starr—England
James E. Stewart—England
Richard L. Stockton—Virginia

A. Spain Summerlin—Tennessee, Arkansas
William E. Summers—Tennessee
William D. Sutherland—Alabama
Edward Taylor—Liberty, Texas
George Taylor—Liberty, Texas
James Taylor—Liberty, Texas
William Taylor—Tennessee
B. Archer M. Thomas—Kentucky
Henry Thomas—Germany
Jesse G. Thompson—Arkansas
John W. Thomson—North Carolina, Tennessee
John M. Thurston—Pennsylvania, Kentucky
Burke Trammel—Ireland, Tennessee
William Barret Travis—South Carolina, Alabama
George W. Tumlinson—Missouri
Asa Walker—Tennessee
Jacob Walker—Nacogdoches, Texas
William B. Ward—Ireland
Henry Warnell—Arkansas
Joseph G. Washington—Tennessee
Thomas Waters—England
William Wells—Georgia
Isaac White—Kentucky
Robert White—Gonzales, Texas
Hiram J. Williamson—Pennsylvania
David L. Wilson—Scotland
John Wilson—Pennsylvania
Antony Wolfe—England
Claiborne Wright—North Carolina
Charles Zanco—Denmark

Acknowledgments

It was anything but a day for work. The blinding glare, the blast-furnace heat, the heavy silence of Austin in August made the New Yorker understand why nearly everyone seemed to have left town. Yet Dr. Carlos E. Castañeda worked on, oblivious to the heat, poring over Captain Sánchez Navarro's faded manuscript, translating and interpreting page after page, looking up points from a stack of obscure Mexican books beside him, muttering Spanish phrases to himself . . . always meticulous, always thorough.

Dr. Castañeda was giving up his summer to help me. He was the outstanding authority on the Mexican side of the Texas Revolution (his own book remains a classic), and his contribution was naturally priceless. But there was so much more to it than that. For he was in poor health—far worse than his friends realized—and every day must have been a struggle. Yet he gave himself to the task as though he had all the time in the world, generously pouring out his knowledge for another to use. I only wish he were still here, to see how much I owe him.

So many people have been so generous: John B. Shackford of Cornell, Iowa, who edited his late brother James' fine biography of David Crockett and filled me in on important points . . . Mrs. James T. Anderson of Garrison-on-Hudson, New

York, who made available a fascinating, never-published letter from one of Fannin's men . . . B. W. Crouch, a spry 90-year-old from Saluda, South Carolina, who helped me in fixing Travis' and Bonham's exact birthplaces . . . and many, many more. In all, useful information was received from over a hundred people in twenty-three states—illustrating once again that the Alamo is truly a national story.

I'm especially grateful to the many descendants of defenders who came forward with fresh material on their gallant ancestors. L. C. Sparks of St. Louis supplied valuable details on Robert Cunningham's background; Mrs. Clifford Lewis of Media, Pennsylvania, contributed a fine vignette of William Irvine Lewis; Mrs. Ernest W. King of Charleston, South Carolina, sent in wonderful data on Cleland K. Simmons. Other helpful descendants included Roberts H. Brown, Mrs. James E. Darst, Mrs. A. Ray Oliver, Mrs. I. O. Miller, Mrs. Louis A. Klein, Mrs. Edward B. Richards. Here again, aid came from all over the country.

Not that Texas was eclipsed. On the contrary, Mrs. Cordelia McFall of Abilene gave fresh information on her great-grandfather Thomas Jackson; Rufus Floyd of Gonzales did the same for his great-grandfather Dolphin Floyd, and in addition supplied a fascinating 1855 letter from the Floyd family in North Carolina, re-establishing contact with Dolphin's wife and son. In fact, nothing seemed too much trouble to these Texas descendants, and I'm equally grateful to R. H. Nowlin, Albert C. McDavid, Clarence W. Roberson, Jr., and R. D. Johnson.

No less helpful were the descendants of several men who were not defenders, but who nevertheless played a key part in the Alamo's story. Mrs. Sue Hardeman lent me some records of Dr. J. H. Barnard, who tended the Mexican wounded. Mrs. Frank C. Gillespie gave up a whole afternoon to answer questions about John W. Smith. Mrs. Annie D. Ayers (who jetted into New York at 86 years of age) confirmed that Travis' last hasty note about his son Charles had indeed been sent to her grandfather David Ayers.

As a rewarding by-product of mountainous correspondence with these helpful people, it was occasionally possible to bring together distant members of the same family. For instance, Stanley Horn of Nashville and Mrs. Louis A. Klein of Philadelphia both wrote in regarding their mutual ancestor John Camp Goodrich. Their addresses were soon forwarded on to one another, in the hope that a family reunion-by-mail might result.

Along with the descendants, many authorities have rallied around, generously contributing their *expertise*. Ben Palmer supplied marvelous material on Jim Bowie's knife. James Presley and Colonel E. J. Stolle gave me the benefit of their immense research on Santa Anna's march north. Needless to say, where I differ from their conclusions, the responsibility for any errors lies at my door.

Other authorities have supplied a great deal of data on particular individuals. Jack Butterfield writes glowingly of Juan Seguin. Dr. Pat Nixon roots for Amos Pollard and the Alamo surgeons. S. J. Folmsbee relentlessly pursues David Crockett. Ruby Mixon is matchless on Travis. Llerena Friend can answer anything about Sam Houston. I'm grateful to them all.

And in this connection, I'm especially grateful to Mrs. Jack Shelton, who has practically adopted the entire thirty-two-man contingent from Gonzales. This has been a greatly neglected part of the Alamo saga, and if any new light has been thrown on it in these pages, it is largely due to Mrs. Shelton and the corps of assistants she recruited to the cause—Miss Lenore Bright, Miss Eleonore Jandt and others.

The libraries and historical societies have played their usual selfless role. I owe so much to the Tennessee, Kentucky, Missouri, Maryland and Mifflin County (Pennsylvania) societies—just to name a few. Also, the Texas State Library and Archives, the Library of Congress, the Yale University and New York Public Libraries. But of them all, it would be unfair not to single out the superb library staff of the University of Texas. Whether "upstairs" with Llerena Friend or "downstairs" with Dorman Winfrey and Winnie Allen, no request was ever too small to get the closest attention at the Barker History Center. In this connection, a special vote of thanks goes to Dr. Walter Prescott Webb, who put me on the track of at least six unpublished theses in the library, covering important parts of the story.

Most librarians have perhaps grown used to a researcher's whims, but Mrs. Nellie Carroll had no reason to expect such harassment the day I first invaded her files at the Texas General Land Office in Austin. Yet for over a week she tolerated the raid with her rare mixture of patience, good humor and fortitude. More than that, she pulled countless file boxes, giving access to fresh, interesting information on many Alamo defenders.

The Mexican archives played their part too. I'm especially grateful to the staff at Chapultepec Castle for unearthing once more the remnants of the New Orleans Greys' flag, carefully piecing it together, and making available the documents that accompanied it. General Gustavo A. Angulo Chamorro also went far out of his way to provide me with material at the Military Archives. This Mexican co-operation was won largely through the tact of my friend and guide Agustin Espinosa Sierra.

In addition to all these sources, certain friends seemed to bear an extra-heavy share of the burden on this book. Charles Ramsdell, who is Mrs. Dickinson's great-grandson and has "lived with" the Alamo all his life, gave me many days of his time, generously sharing all he knew. His only reward was to be dragged from bed one dawn and driven five hundred miles in a single day, to confirm the records on Louis Rose at the Nacogdoches Courthouse. I only hope he felt the thrill I did when we finally found that green steel cabinet and pulled out the ancient record book. There, sure enough, were the entries for Rose.

Maury Maverick, Jr., who has Texas in his blood, was another of those unselfish souls who gave me days of their time. He was bullied into driving me to Goliad, Gonzales and the Rio Grande. But he did have a measure of revenge when, carried away by a passion for realism, he persuaded me to eat some of the bitter mesquite nuts that so often were the staple diet of Santa Anna's troops.

My friend Jess McNeel also contributed an immense amount of time. Forgetting the operation of his ranch for a day, we bounced cross-country in a jeep, trying to follow Santa Anna's line of march. I can't imagine a better way to grasp the country or the hardships of the advancing Mexicans.

Everett DeGolyer, Jr. was another shepherd who herded me along . . . only in his case it was not over the prairies but through the magnificent library collected by his late father in Dallas. Needless to say, the material was marvelous. Other valued guides included Gerald Ashford and Kay Hart in San Antonio, Doris Connerly and Frank Wardlaw in Austin.

Finally, nothing could have been done without the all-out co-operation of the Daughters of the Republic of Texas, who are the custodians of the Alamo and handle their responsibility with immense care and taste. Mrs. R. G. Halter and Miss Marg-Riette Montgomery, the Alamo librarian, have been of invaluable assistance.

Apart from all these sources, there are those close to the actual production of the book. In moments of self-pity, it is not unknown for a writer to feel that he struggles through this vale of tears alone. When that happens around here, a host of apparitions arise to confront the author with the truth:

James V. Reese, who at the last moment checked a handful of names for me in Austin . . . Jack Crooks, who helped so much on the index . . . Barbara Thacher, who turned a thousand scraps of paper into an orderly bibliography . . . Evan Thomas, who edited as skillfully as ever . . . and Florence Cassedy, who once again worked through reams of penciled foolscap, to turn out a superbly typed manuscript.

Sources

The Alamo has intrigued writers for more than 125 years, but the contradictions and gaps in the story remain as exasperating as ever. In the end, the only solution was to go back to the original sources and start all over again. . . .

Accounts by Participants

Almonte, Colonel Juan Nepomuceno. Private Journal, recovered after San Jacinto. First carried in New York *Herald* in June, 1836, reprinted in *Southwestern Historical Quarterly*, Vol. XLVIII, pp. 10-32. Description purportedly by Almonte of executions after the battle is contained in letter dated Galveston Island, July 19, 1836, from George Dolson to Detroit *Democratic Free Press* and reprinted in *Journal of Southern History*, August, 1960, pp. 373-374.

Alsbury, Mrs. Horace A. John S. Ford Papers, pp. 122-124, Texas University Archives. Although Mrs. Dickinson denied Mrs. Alsbury remained till the end, Enrique Esparza and Travis' slave Joe both remembered her there; her story was also accepted by such contemporaries as Mrs. Sam Maverick, John Sutherland and Dr. J. H. Barnard.

Becerra, Sergeant Francisco. John S. Ford Papers, pp. 16-23, Texas University Archives. Probably the least reliable of all the Mexican accounts.

"Ben," Colonel Almonte's orderly. Newell, C., *History of the Revolution in Texas* (1838), pp. 88-89.

Caro, Ramón Martinez. Account as translated by Castañeda, C. E., *The Mexican Side of the Texan Revolution* (1928), pp. 101-104. This and all other Mexican accounts are highly flavored, yet essential to the story.

Dickinson, Susannah. Mrs. Dickinson gave five different interviews describing her experiences: Morphis, J. M., *History of Texas* (1874), pp. 174-177; "Testimony of Mrs. Hannig touching the Alamo Massacre, September 23, 1876," *Adjutant General's Letters Concerning the Alamo, 1875-78*, Texas State Archives; interview given in 1878 to unknown Ohio newspaper, reprinted San Antonio *Express*, February 24, 1929; interview, San Antonio *Express*, April 28, 1881; talk with the Rev. Walter Raleigh Richardson in 1881, included in Green, R. M., *Memoirs of Mary A. Maverick* (1921) pp. 135-136. Also valuable are Mrs. Dickinson's depositions supporting following land claims, all on file at General Land Office: David Cummings, Court of Claims Vouchers 4271, File A-C; James M. Rose, Court of Claims Application 22, File M-R, also Petition 201; Henry Warnell, Court of Claims Vouchers 400, 1579, File S to Z. But the account by Mrs. Dickinson in A. J. Sowell's *Rangers and Pioneers of Texas* was lifted from Morphis; and the highly dramatized piece in Rufus C. Burleson's *Life and Writings* is too much at variance with her, other accounts to carry any weight.

Esparza, Enrique. Interview with Charles Meritt Barnes, San Antonio *Express*, May 12 and 19, 1907.

Filisola, General Vicente. *Memorias Para la Historia de la Guerra de Tejas*, published by R. Rafael (1849), Part II, pp. 347-390; also a somewhat different account, bearing same title and date but published by Ignacio Cumplido, pp. 3-17; *Representación Dirigida al Supremo Gobierno*, as translated by Castañeda (*supra*), pp. 163-203.

"Joe," Travis' Negro slave. Joe was examined by the Texas cabinet on March 20, 1836, and his story was written up by a number of those present. Most detailed account was a letter by William F. Gray to the Fredericksburg *Arena*, reprinted in the Frankfort, Kentucky, *Commonwealth*, May 25, 1836. (A much-condensed version is included in Gray's *From Virginia to Texas*, pp. 136-138.) Other accounts of Joe's examination, each giving a different slant, appear in the Columbia, Tennessee, *Observer*, April 14, 1836; *National Intelligencer*, April 30, 1836; New Orleans *Commercial Bulletin*, April 11, 1836.

Loranca, Sergeant Manuel. Interview in San Antonio *Express*, June 23, 1878.

Menchaca, Antonio. *Memoirs*, Yanaguana Society Publications II, 1937.

Nuñez, Sergeant Felix. Interview in Fort Worth *Gazette*, July 12, 1889.

Peña, José Enrique de la. Account originally published in Matamoros, September 1836, but suppressed by authorities. Republished as follows: Sánchez Garza, J., *La Rebelion de Texas Manuscrito Inédito de 1836 por un oficial de Santa Anna* (1955).

Rodríguez, J. M. *Memoirs of Early Texas* (1913), pp. 7-10.

Ruiz, Francisco. *Texas Almanac*, 1860, pp. 80-81, as reprinted in Frederick C. Chabot's *The Alamo, Mission, Fortress, Shrine*.

Sánchez Navarro, Captain José Juan. Account contained in Carlos Sánchez Navarro's *La Guerra de Tejos* (1938), pp. 127-151. A second account, in the form of a handwritten daily journal, can be found in two ledger books kept by the Captain, entitled *Ayudentia de Inspección de Nuevo Leon y Tamaulipas*, University of Texas Archives. Volume II of these ledgers also contains a plan of the storming of the fort; this plan is reproduced in the University of Texas *Library Journal*, Summer 1951, pp. 71-74. Finally, the account usually attributed to "An Unknown Mexican Soldier" in *El Mosquito Mexicano*, April 5, 1836, also appears to have been written by Sánchez Navarro. It seems much too similar to the foregoing to come from a different hand.

Santa Anna, General Antonio López de. Reports addressed to Minister of War and Marine, dated February 27 and March 6, 1836; Letter addressed to the Senate and House of Representatives of Texas, October 12, 1836; *Manifesto* (1837), as translated by Castañeda, pp. 5-89; *Mi Historia Militar y Politica, Memorias Inéditas* (1874), as translated by Willye Ward Watkins, M.A. Thesis, University of Texas (1922), pp. 91-92.

Seguin, Juan N. *Personal Memoirs of Juan Seguin* (1858); Testimony given in land claim filed for Andres Nava, General Land Office, Court of Claims Application 416, File M-R; letter to W. W. Fontaine, June 7, 1890, contained in W. W. Fontaine Papers, University of Texas Archives.

Soldana, Captain Rafael. Account in DeShields, James T., *Tall Men with Long Rifles* (1935), pp. 162-164.

Sutherland, John. Narrative edited by Annie B. Sutherland, *The Fall of the Alamo* (1936). This is the most authoritative, least embellished of several versions of the same account. For others, see DeShields, pp. 134-150; the same author's feature article in the Dallas *News*, February 5 and 12, 1911; and John S. Ford's *Memoirs*, University of Texas Archives.

Urizza, Capt. Fernando. Experiences described in Labadie, N.D., "Urizza's Account of the Alamo Massacre," *Texas Almanac*, 1859, pp. 61-62.

Unknown Mexican Officer. Detailed account of the execution of six Texans at the battle's end, as related to correspondent of the New York *Courier and Enquirer*. Letter dated Galveston Bay, June 9, 1836, and reprinted by Frankfort, Kentucky, *Commonwealth*, July 27, 1836. The narrator sounds suspiciously like Ramón Caro, but certain identification impossible.

Purposely omitted from the above is "*Col. Crockett's Exploits and Adventures in Texas*, Written by Himself." James Shackford's biography of Crockett offers far too convincing evidence that this account is spurious. Also missing are all accounts by Madam Candelaria. None of the other participants remember her in the fort; her stories violently contradict one another; and too many of her details clash with the known facts.

Contemporary Letters

Next to accounts by participants, contemporary letters form the most important source material on the Alamo. Taken in order, they give perhaps the best picture of all. Here, then, is a chronological list of those most important to the story, covering the period December, 1835–March, 1836. Occasionally this list may duplicate other parts of the bibliography, but as a useful tool for anyone interested in the Alamo, it seems worth the risk:

December 7, 1835: Micajah Autry to wife. *Southwestern Historical Quarterly*, XIV, 317-318.

December 13. Autry to wife. *SWHQ*, XIV, 318-319.

December 25 c. Daniel Cloud to friend. Jackson *Mississippian*, May 6, 1836.

December 26.   Cloud to brother.   San Antonio *Express*, November 24, 1901.

December 31.   James Bonham to Sam Houston.   Texas State Archives.

January 2, 1836.   Samuel Williams to D. C. Barret.   Binkley, William C., *Official Correspondence of the Texas Revolution*, I, 266-267.

January 6.   James C. Neill to the Governor and Council.   Binkley I, 273-275.

January 9.   David Crockett to son and daughter.   Shackford, James, *David Crockett, the Man and the Legend*, pp. 214-216.

January 11.   Houston to J. W. Robinson.   Binkley I, 294.

January 12.   John Forbes to Robinson.   Texas State Library, *Papers of Mirabeau Buonaparte Lamar*, I, 296.

January 12.   William R. Carey to sister.   *SWHQ*, LXII, 513.

January 13.   Micajah Autry to wife.   *SWHQ*, XIV, 319-320.

January 13.   J. H. Forsyth to Council.   Binkley I, 291-292.

January 14.   J. C. Neill to Governor and Council.   Lamar I, 297-298.

January 14.   Neill to Houston.   Army Papers, Texas State Archives.

January 16.   Amos Pollard to Henry Smith.   *Ibid.*

January 17.   William Barret Travis to Houston.   Yoakum, H., *History of Texas*, II, 59.

January 17.   Houston to Smith.   Yoakum, II, 458-459.

January 18.   Green B. Jameson to Houston.   De Zavala, Adina, *The Alamo and Other Missions* (1917), 23-30.

January 20.   David Cummings to father.   General Land Office, Court of Claims Vouchers, 4271, File A-C.

January 21.   Travis to W. G. Hill.   Mixon, Ruby, *William Barret Travis*, M.A. Thesis, University of Texas, 1930.

January 23.   Neill to Governor and Council.   Binkley I, 328.

January 23.   Neill to Smith.   Binkley I, 329.

January 24.   M. Hawkins to Robinson.   Lamar I, 307-308.

January 27.   Neill to Smith.   Binkley I, 344.

January 27.   Neill to Council.   Binkley I, 345.

January 27.   Amos Pollard to Smith.   Binkley I, 345-346.

January 28.   Neill to Provisional Government.   Binkley I, 349-351.

January 28. Travis to Smith. Binkley I, 352-353.

January 29. Travis to Smith. Binkley I, 362-363.

January 30. Houston to Smith. Yoakum II, 460-470.

February 2. James Bowie to Smith. Army Papers, Texas State Archives.

February 8. James Walker Fannin to Robinson. Foote, Henry Stuart, *Texas and the Texans*, II, 202.

February 11. Jameson to Smith. Army Papers, Texas State Archives.

February 12. Travis to Smith. *SWHQ*, XXXVII, 280-281.

February 13. Travis to Smith. Army Papers, Texas State Archives.

February 13. John J. Baugh to Smith. *Ibid*.

February 13. Pollard to Smith. Nixon, Pat Ireland, *A Century of Medicine in San Antonio*, 55-56.

February 14. Travis and Bowie to Smith, Archives of the State Department, Book 3, p. 250, Texas State Archives.

February 14. Fannin to Robinson. Foote II, 206.

February 14. David Cummings to father. Court of Claims Vouchers, 4271, File A-C.

February 16. Jameson to Smith. Army Papers, Texas State Archives.

February 16. Travis to Smith. Binkley I, 439-440.

February 16. Fannin to Council. Lamar I, 332-334.

February 16. Santa Anna to Filisola. Filizola, Umberto Daniel, *Correspondence of Santa Anna during the Texas Campaign, 1835-36*, M.A. Thesis, University of Texas (1939), 68-69.

February 16. Santa Anna to Minister of War Tornel. Castañeda, Carlos E., *The Mexican Side of the Texas Revolution*, 64-70.

February 21. Fannin to Robinson. Foote II, 213.

February 22. Fannin to Robinson. Foote II, 214.

February 23. Travis to Andrew Ponton. Yale University Library.

February 23. Travis and Bowie to Fannin. Foote II, 224.

February 23. Bowie to Santa Anna. Yale University Library.

February 23. José Batres to Bowie. *SWHQ*, XXXVII, 16.

February 24. Travis to "the People of Texas & All Americans in the World." Texas State Archives.

February 24. Launcelot Smithers to "All the Inhabitants of Texas." *SWHQ*, XXXVII, 305.

February 25. Travis to Houston. *Arkansas Gazette*, April 19, 1836.

February 25. Fannin to Robinson. Lamar I, 338-339.

February 25. John Sowers Brooks to Mary Ann Brooks. *SWHQ*, IX, 178-182.

February 25. J. S. Brooks to A. H. Brooks. *Ibid.*

February 27. Santa Anna to Minister of War Tornel. Filizola, 70-73.

February 27 (misdated the 29th). Fannin to Robinson. Foote II, 225-226.

February 28. Fannin to Robinson. Lamar I, 341-342.

February 28. Fannin to Joseph Mims. W. W. Fontaine Papers, University of Texas Archives.

March 1. Fannin to Francis De Sauque and John Chenoworth. Binkley I, 474-476.

March 2. J. S. Brooks to mother. *SWHQ*, IX, 182-184.

March 3. Travis to Convention. Army Papers, Texas State Archives.

March 3. Travis to Jesse Grimes. *Telegraph and Texas Register*, March 24, 1836.

March 3. Travis to David Ayers. Mixon, 72.

March 4. J. S. Brooks to Mary Ann Brooks. *SWHQ*, IX, 185.

March 5. Santa Anna to certain officers. *Texas Almanac*, 1870, 37-38.

March 5. George Childress to friend. Nashville *Republican*, April 9, 1836.

March 6. Santa Anna to Tornel. *Texas Almanac*, 1870, 39-40.

March 6. Unidentified Mexican soldier to "Brothers of My Heart." *El Mosquito Mexicano*, April 5, 1836.

March 9. Burr H. Duval to William P. Duval. *SWHQ*, I, 49.

March 9. J. S. Brooks to James Hagerty. *SWHQ*, IX, 190-192.

March 10. Brooks to A. H. Brooks. *SWHQ*, IX, 192-194.

March 10. W. P. M. Wood to the New Orleans *Bee*. Richmond *Enquirer*, May 6, 1836.

March 11. Houston to Fannin. Yoakum II, 471-472.

March 13. Houston to James Collinsworth. Yoakum II, 473.

March 13. Houston to Henry Raguet. Williams and Barker, ed., *The Writings of Sam Houston*, IV, 17-18.

March 14. Fannin to A. C. Haton. *United States Magazine and Democratic Review*, October, 1838.

March 15. Houston to Collinsworth. Yoakum II, 475-477.

March 15. Benjamin Goodrich to Edmond Goodrich. University of Texas Archives.

March 15. George Childress to friend. Columbia, Tennessee, *Observer*, April 14, 1836.

March 16. C. B. Stewart to Ira R. Lewis. *National Intelligencer*, April 16, 1836.

March 16. Calvin Henderson to Joseph W. Chalmers. *New-Yorker*, April 30, 1836.

March 16 c. A. Briscoe to *Red River Herald*, reprinted in the *New-Yorker*, April 16, 1836.

March 17. Houston to Collinsworth. Yoakum II, 477-479.

Land Office Records

Heirs of Alamo victims, claiming the land granted to the defenders by the Texas government, supported their applications with as convincing evidence as possible. This supporting evidence often throws great light on the defenders themselves—where they came from, what they looked like, why and how they came to Texas. Here is a list of the applications which seemed most useful; all are from the General Land Office in Austin, unless otherwise indicated. Names and spelling, not necessarily accurate, are given as they appear on the original files:

Andros, Miles de Forrest, C/C Applications, 1427, File (A-B).
Ballentine, Richard W., C/C Vouchers, 314, File (A-C).
Bayliss, Joseph, Sp. Acts. Vouchers, 1323.
Blair, John, Nacogdoches County, Board of Land Commissioners, 254, Feb. 7, 1838.
Bonham, James Butler, C/C Vouchers, 161, File (A-C).
Clark, M. B., Nacogdoches County, 203, Feb. 6, 1838.
Courtman, Henry, C/C Applications, 1965, File (C-D).
Cummings, David P., C/C Vouchers, 4271, File (A-C).
Day, F. H. K., Nacogdoches County, 125, Jan. 25, 1838.
Denison, Stephen, C/C Applications, 1114, File (D-G); C/C Vouchers 209, 1257; File (C-G).
Dover, Sherod J., C/C Applications, 211, File (C-D).
Esparza, Gregorio, C/C Applications, 572, File (D-G).
Garnett, William, C/C Applications, 1824, File (E-G).

George, William, C/C Applications, 195, File (E-G).
Harris, John, C/C Vouchers, 2627, File (H-L).
Harrison, Andrew Jackson, C/C Vouchers, 579, File (H-L).
Haskel, Charles, Nacogdoches County, 269, Feb. 8, 1838.
Hendricks, Thomas, C/C Vouchers, 474, File (H-L).
Hersee, William, C/C Vouchers, 384, File (H-L).
Holland, Tapley, C/C Vouchers, 16, File (H-L).
Holloway, Samuel, C/C Vouchers, 4/38, File (H-L).
Losoya, Domingo, C/C Vouchers, 271, File (H-L).
Marshall, William, C/C Vouchers, 2, 1454, File (M-R).
McKinney, Robert, C/C Vouchers, 160, File (M-S).
Mills, Willie, C/C Vouchers, 351, 426, File (M-R).
Moore, Willis A., C/C Vouchers, 3/54, File (M-S).
Nava, Andres, C/C Applications, 416, File (M-R); C/C Applications, 80, File (M-R).
Neggan, George, C/C Vouchers, 790, File (M-R).
Nelson, Andrew M., C/C Vouchers, 275, File (M-S).
Northcross, James, C/C Applications, 1029, File (M-R).
Reynolds, John Purdy, Vouchers, Sp. Acts. Certifs.
Rose, James M., C/C Vouchers, 3/100, File (M-S); C/C Applications, 22, File (M-R); Sp. Application, Adjutant General, No. 201.
Rose, Louis, Nacogdoches County, 244, Feb. 12, 1838; C/C Vouchers, A.S.R. 1525, File (M-R).
Scurlock, Mial, C/C Applications, 134, File (S-Z).
Sewell, Marcus, Nacogdoches County, 579, March 19, 1838—April 13, 1838.
Simmons, Clelland K., C/C Vouchers, 390, File (S-Z).
Thomas, Henry, C/C Applications, 1972, File (S-Z).
Thomson, John W., Vouchers, Sp. Acts. Certifs., Nos. 14/63, 14/64, 14/65, 14/66.
Warnell, Henry C/C Vouchers, 869, File (S-Z); C/C Vouchers, A.S. & R., 400, File (S-Z); C/C Applications, 1579, File (S-Z).
Wells, William, C/C Applications, [no number], File (W-Z; C/C Applications, 2006, File (W-Z).
White, Isaac, C/C Vouchers, 869, File (S-Z).
White, Robert, C/C Vouchers, 1215, File (S-Z).
Wilson, David, Nacogdoches County, 427, Feb. 22, 1838.
Zanco, Charles, C/C Vouchers, 37, File (S-Z).

Other Official Records

Adjutant General's Letters concerning the Alamo, 1875-78. "Testimony of Mrs. Hannig (i.e., Dickinson) Touching the Alamo Massacre," September 23, 1876; W. P. Zuber to General William Steele, September 14, 1877. Texas State Archives.

Adjutant General's Miscellaneous Papers; Texas State Archives.

Army Papers; Texas State Archives.

Comptroller's Military Service Records. No. 5926, claim submitted by Travis' administrator for $143, detailing out-of-pocket expenditures for various military supplies. Texas State Archives.

Deed Records of Guadalupe County, Texas. Vol. 51, pp. 294-295.

Labastida, Ygnacio de, Plat of the Alamo drafted by Labastida as Chief Engineer of the Mexican Army for General Filisola, about March 10, 1836. University of Texas Archives.

Muster Rolls. Gonzales Ranging Co. of Mounted Volunteers, Roll book, p. 1; List of names of those who fell in the Alamo, Roll book, pp. 2-4; Neill's Roll, February 11, 1836 (probably misdated); Breece's Men Who Fell at the Alamo, Roll book, p. 25; Group enlistment in Texas Volunteer Auxiliary Corps, January 14, 1836. General Land Office.

U.S. Senate, Report to the Secretary of War, Texas and Adjacent Mexican States on the Rio Grande. 31st Congress, 1st Session, Senate, Executive Document 32.

Manuscript Material

Asbury, Samuel E., Papers. University of Texas Archives.

Blake, R. B., *Rose and His Escape from the Alamo.* University of Texas Archives.

Bonham, Milledge Lipscomb, Letter to Z. T. Fullmore, November 18, 1913; Letter to Dorah McConnico Wade, June 26, 1929. Alamo Library.

Bowie, Lucy (compiler), Collection of letters and miscellaneous papers regarding James Bowie. Courtesy of Ben Palmer, Baltimore.

Crockett, David, Letter to Messrs. Carey and Hart, August 11, 1835. Maryland Historical Society.

Davenport, Harbert, Notes from an unfinished story of Fannin and his men. Texas State Archives.

Filizola, Umberto Daniel, *Correspondence of Santa Anna during the Texas Campaign, 1835-1836*. Translated, with Introductions and Notes. M.A. Thesis, University of Texas, 1939.

Fontaine, W. W., Papers. University of Texas Archives.

Ford, John S., *Memoirs*. University of Texas Archives.

Forsyth, George A., Letter to Adjutant General re John Hubbard Forsyth, July 12, 1909. Texas State Library.

Franklin Papers. Letter, Robert Wilson to W. B. Travis, June 9, 1835. University of Texas Archives.

Goodrich, Benjamin Briggs, Letter to Edwin Goodrich, March 15, 1836. University of Texas Archives.

Harris, Helen Willits, *The Public Life of Juan Nepomuceno Almonte*. Ph.D. Thesis, University of Texas, 1935.

Hockley, George Washington, Report of examination of Andres Barsena and Anselmo Bergara, who brought first word of the Alamo massacre to Gonzales, March 11, 1836. Courtesy of Louis Lenz, Houston.

Jenkins, John H., *Reminiscences from Texas History*. University of Texas Archives.

McArdle, Ruskin (compiler), "The Alamo Book," consisting of research collected by Henry Arthur McArdle for his painting *Dawn at the Alamo*. Texas State Archives.

Miller, Thomas, *Bounty Land Grants of Texas*, 1835-1888. Ph.D. Thesis, University of Texas, 1956.

Mixon, Ruby, *William Barret Travis, His Life and Letters*. M.A. Thesis, University of Texas, 1930.

Santa Anna, Antonio López de, Letter to the Honorable Gentlemen of the Senate and the House of Representatives (of the Republic of Texas), Orazimba, October 12, 1836. Yale University Library.

Shelby, Charmion, *Notes on the Mexican Army of Operations in Texas, 1835-1836*. University of Texas Archives.

Sutherland, Mrs. George, Letter to Sally Menefee, June 5, 1836. University of Texas Archives.

Travis, William Barret, Diary, August 30, 1833 to June 26, 1834. University of Texas Archives.

Walker, Asa, Petition for letters of Administration re Walker's estate, filed by William W. Gant, together with supporting documents. Courtesy of Louis Lenz, Houston.

Williams, Amelia W., *A Critical Study of the Siege of the Alamo and of the Personnel of Its Defenders*. Ph.D. Thesis, University of Texas, 1931. (In condensed form, *Southwestern Historical Quarterly*, Vols. XXXVI-XXXVII, 1933-1934).

Contemporary Newspapers, 1835–1836

Boston *Daily Evening Transcript.*
Boston *Independent Chronicle and Boston Patriot.*
Boston *Morning Post.*
Charleston *Courier*
Charleston *Observer.*
Charleston *Southern Patriot.*
Cincinnati *Daily Whig and Commercial Intelligencer.*
Columbia, Tennessee, *Observer.*
Frankfort, Kentucky, *Argus.*
Frankfort, Kentucky, *Commonwealth.*
Fredericksburg *Virginia Herald.*
Hartford *Connecticut Courant.*
Hartford *Northern Courier.*
Huntsville, Alabama, *Southern Advocate.*
Jackson *Mississippian.*
Little Rock *Arkansas Advocate.*
Little Rock *Arkansas Gazette.*
London *Times.*
Louisville *Journal.*
Mexico City *El Mosquito Mexicano.*
Mobile *Daily Commercial Register and Patriot.*
Nashville *Republican.*
Natchez *Free Trader.*
New Orleans *Commercial Bulletin.*
New Orleans *Louisiana Courier.*
New Orleans *Price Current and Commercial Intelligencer.*
New York *American.*
New York *Commercial Advertiser.*
New York *Evening Post.*
New York *Evening Star.*
New-Yorker.
Philadelphia *American Saturday Courier.*
Portland, Maine, *Eastern Argus.*
Richmond *Enquirer.*
San Felipe *Texas Gazette.*

Telegraph and Texas Register.
Washington *National Intelligencer.*

Pamphlets, Magazines, Etc.

Ashford, Gerald, "Jacksonian Liberalism and Spanish Law in Early Texas," *Southwestern Historical Quarterly*, Vol. LVII, 1953.

Baker, Karle Wilson, "Trailing the New Orleans Greys," *Southwest Review*, Vol. XXII, April, 1937.

Barker, E. C., "Difficulties of a Mexican Revenue Office in Texas," *Texas Historical Association Quarterly*, Vol. IV, 1901.

Barker, E. C., "Land Speculation as a Cause of the Texas Revolution," *Southwestern Historical Quarterly*, Vol. X, 1906.

Barker, E. C., "The Firearms of the Texan Revolution," *Political Science Quarterly*, Vol. XIX.

Barker, E. C., "The San Jacinto Campaign," *Southwestern Historical Quarterly*, Vol. IV, 1901.

Barker, E. C., "The Texan Revolutionary Army," *Texas Historical Association Quarterly*, Vol. IX, 1906.

Barnard, J. H., *Dr. J. H. Barnard's Journal from December, 1835, to March 27, 1836, Giving an Account of Fannin Massacre*, 1912.

Beazley, Julia, "William Barret Travis," *Southwest Review*, Vol. IX.

Bennett, Miles S., "The Battle of Gonzales," *Texas Historical Association Quarterly*, Vol. II, 1899.

Bonham, Milledge L., Jr., "James Butler Bonham, A Consistent Rebel," *Southwestern Historical Quarterly*, Vol. XXXV, 1931.

Bradford, A. L., and Campbell, T. N. [eds.], "Journal of Lincecum's Travels in Texas, 1835," *Southwestern Historical Quarterly*, Vol. LIII, 1949.

Brown, John Henry, *Texas Farm and Ranch*, May 15, 1889.

Brown, R. R., "Expedition under Johnson and Grant," *Texas Almanac*, 1859.

Burke, Jackson, "The Secret of the Alamo," *Man's Illustrated*, Aug., 1956.

Butterfield, Jack C., *Men of the Alamo, Goliad, and San Jacinto*, c. 1936.

Caplain Sylvester's description of Santa Anna, *Southwestern Historical Quarterly*, Vol. L, 1947.

Chabot, Frederick C., *The Alamo, Mission, Fortress, and Shrine*, 1936.

Connelly, Thomas Lawrence [ed.], "Did David Crockett Surrender at the Alamo?" *The Journal of Southern History*, Aug., 1960.

Corner, William, "John Crittenden Duval: the Last Survivor of the Goliad Massacre," *Texas Historical Association Quarterly*, Vol. I, 1898.

Crimmins, M. L., "American Powder's Part in Winning Texas Independence," *Southwestern Historical Quarterly*, Vol. LII, 1948.

Crimmins, M. L., "The Alamo and Its History," *Frontier Times*, Vol. XVIII, 1940.

Davenport, Harbert, Note on the Angel of Goliad, *Southwestern Historical Quarterly*, Vol. LIV, 1951.

Davenport, Harbert, "The Men of Goliad," *Southwestern Historical Quarterly*, Vol. XLIII, 1939.

"Deaf" Smith, biographical note on, *Texas Almanac*, 1857.

Delgado, Pedro, *Mexican Account of the Battle of San Jacinto*, 1919.

Dobie, J. Frank, "The Alamo's Immortalization of Words," *Southwest Review*, Vol. XXVII, 1942.

Dobie, J. Frank, "James Bowie, Big Dealer," *Southwestern Historical Quarterly*, Vol. LX, 1957.

Elfer, Maurice, *Madam Candelaria—Unsung Heroine of the Alamo*, c. 1933.

Elliott, Claude, "Alabama and the Texas Revolution," *Southwestern Historical Quarterly*, Vol. L, 1947.

Folmsbee, S. J. and Catron, A. G., "David Crockett in Texas," *East Tennessee Historical Society's Publications*, No. 30, 1958.

Ford, John S., *Origin and Fall of the Alamo*, 1895.

G. A. Giddings to parents, letter dated April 10, 1836, *Southwestern Historical Quarterly*, Vol. IX, 1905.

Garrison, George P., "Guy Morrison Bryan," *Southwestern Historical Quarterly*, Vol. V, 1901.

Gould, Stephen, *The Alamo City Guide*, San Antonio, 1882.

Greer, James K. [ed.], "Journal of Ammon Underwood, 1834-1838," *Southwestern Historical Quarterly*, Vol. XXXII, 1928.

Harris, Dilue, "Reminiscences," *Texas Historical Association Quarterly*, Vol. IV, 1901.

Henderson, H. M., "A Critical Analysis of the San Jacinto Campaign," *Southwestern Historical Quarterly*, Vol. LIX, 1956.

Hunnicutt, Helen, "A Mexican View of the Texas War," *The Library Chronicle of the University of Texas*, Summer, 1951.

Jones, R. L. [contrib.], "Folk Life in Early Texas: The Autobiography of Andrew Davis," *Southwestern Historical Quarterly*, Vol. XLIII, 1939.

Kuykendall, J. H., "Recollections of the Campaign," *Texas Historical Association Quarterly*, Vol. IV, 1901.

Kuykendall, J. H., "Reminiscences of Early Texans," *Southwestern Historical Quarterly*, Vols. VI-VII, 1903.

Kuykendall, J. H., *Sketches of Early Texans*, n.d.

Looscan, Adèle B., "Harris County, 1822-1845, II," *Southwestern Historical Quarterly*, Vol. XVIII, 1915.

Looscan, Adèle, "Micajah Autry," *Texas Historical Association Quarterly*, Vol. XIV, 1911.

McCall, G. A., "William T. Malone," *Texas Historical Association Quarterly*, Vol. XIV, 1911.

McLendon, James H., "John A. Quitman in the Texas Revolution," *Southwestern Historical Quarterly*, Vol. LII, 1948.

Mixon, Ruby, Notes on Travis, *Southwestern Historical Quarterly*, Vol. XLVI, 1942.

Muir, Andrew Forest, "The Destiny of Buffalo Bayou," *Southwestern Historical Quarterly*, Vol. XLVII, 1943.

Muir, Andrew Forest, "The Municipality of Harrisburg, 1835-1836," *Southwestern Historical Quarterly*, Vol. LVI, 1952.

Muir, Andrew Forest, "The Mystery of San Jacinto," *Southwest Review*, Vol. XXXVI, 1951.

Notes on David Crockett's rifle, *Southwestern Historical Quarterly*, Vol. XLVII, 1944.

Notes on Richard W. Ballentine, *Texas Historical Quarterly*, Vol. V, 1902.

Notes regarding question of whether Crockett surrendered at the Alamo, *Southwestern Historical Quarterly*, Vol. XLVII, 1943.

Potter, R. M., *The Fall of the Alamo*, 1860.

Potter, R. M., "The Fall of the Alamo," *Magazine of American History*, Jan., 1878.

Potter, R. M., "The Texas Revolution, Distinguished Mexicans Who Took Part in the Revolution of Texas," *Magazine of American History*, October, 1878.

Presley, James, "Santa Anna in Texas: A Mexican Viewpoint," *Southwestern Historical Quarterly*, Vol. LXII, 1959.

Ramsdell, Charles, "The Storming of the Alamo," *American Heritage*, February, 1961.

Rather, Ethel Ziveley, "DeWitt's Colony," *Texas Historical Association Quarterly*, Vol. VIII, 1905.

Roller, John E., "Captain John Sowers Brooks," *Southwestern Historical Quarterly*, Vol. IX, 1906.

Rourke, Constance, "Davy Crockett: Forgotten Facts and Legends," *Southwest Review*, Vol. XIX, 1934.

Ryan, W. M., *Shamrock and Cactus, the Story of the Catholic Heroes of Texas Independence*, 1936.

Santa Anna's general orders of March 5, 1836, translated, *Texas Almanac*, 1870.

Scarborough, Jewel Davis, "The Georgia Battalion in the Texas Revolution: A Critical Study," *Southwestern Historical Quarterly*, Vol. LXIII, 1960.

Shelton, Bertie C., Notes on Gonzales Defenders, *Southwestern Historical Quarterly*, Vol. LXIV, 1961.

Smith, Ruby Cumby, "James W. Fannin, Jr. in the Texas Revolution," *Southwestern Historical Quarterly*, Vol. XXIII, 1919.

"Some Fannin Correspondence," *Southwestern Historical Quarterly*, Vol. VII, 1904.

Steele, Alfonso, *Biography*, c. 1926.

Steen, Ralph W., "A Letter from San Antonio de Bexar," *Southwestern Historical Quarterly*, Vol. LXII, 1959.

Sutherland, John, *The Fall of the Alamo*, 1936.

Swisher, John M., *The Swisher Memoirs*, 1932.

Taylor, Maude Wallis, "Ben Franklin Highsmith," *Frontier Times*, April, 1938.

Terrell, A. W., "Recollections of General Sam Houston," *Southwestern Historical Quarterly*, Vol. XVI, 1912.

Thompson, Ernest T., *The Fabulous David Crockett*, 1956.

Wilcox, Seb. S., "Laredo During the Texas Republic," *Southwestern Historical Quarterly*, Vol. XLII, 1938.

Williams, Amelia, Notes on Alamo Survivors, *Southwestern Historical Quarterly*, Vol. XLIX, 1946.

Williams, Robert H., Jr., "Travis, a Potential Sam Houston," *Southwestern Historical Quarterly*, Vol. XL, 1936.

Winston, James E., "Kentucky and the Independence of Texas," *Southwestern Historical Quarterly*, Vol. XVI, 1912.

Winston, James E., "Mississippi and the Independence of Texas," *Southwestern Historical Quarterly*, Vol. XXI, 1917.

Winston, James E., "New York and the Independence of Texas," *Southwestern Historical Quarterly*, Vol. XVIII, 1915.

Winston, James E., "Pennsylvania and the Independence of Texas," *Southwestern Historical Quarterly*, Vol. XVII, 1914.

Winston, James E., "Virginia and the Independence of Texas," *Southwestern Historical Quarterly*, Vol. XVI, 1913.

de Zavala, Adina, *History and Legends of the Alamo and Other Missions*, 1917.

Zuber, W. P., "An Escape from the Alamo," *Texas Almanac*, 1873.

Zuber, W. P., "Escape of Rose from the Alamo," *Texas Historical Association Quarterly*, Vol. V, 1901.

Later Newspapers

Austin *City Gazette*, April 14, 1841.

Baltimore *Sun*, May 27, 1934: feature story by Meigs Frost on "The Baptism of the Bowie Knife."

Dallas *News*, March 9, 1930: feature story by Maurice Elfer on "Madam Candelaria"; March 8, 1931: "Why Bonham Chose to Die with Travis" by Jan Isbelle Fortune; March 20, 1954: description of Mrs. Dickinson by the Rev. J. H. Wells.

Fort Worth *Star-Telegram*, February 28, 1932: details on James L. Allen as last courier to Goliad.

Houston *Post*, April 9, 1911: Mary Autry Greer's reminiscence of Micajah Autry.

Jackson *State Times*, May 8, 1955: data on Isaac Millsaps.

Lewistown, Pennsylvania, *Sentinel*, May 23, 24, 26, 1960: feature articles on David Cummings and John Purdy Reynolds.

New Orleans *Times*, August 2, 1876: letter from Matilda E. B. Moore correcting misstatements made concerning her uncle James Bowie.

San Antonio *Express*, November 24, 1901: letter from Daniel W. Cloud to his mother; January 24, 1915: documents recovered on Bowie's will and administration of his estate.

San Antonio *Light*, August 13, 1911, November 5, 1916: background data on Andrew Kent; May 13, 1955: details on Travis giving ring to Angelina Dickinson.

Seguin, Texas, *Enterprise*, October 15, 1937: data by Willie Mae Weinert on George Kimball and Gonzales; August 4, 11, 25, 1960: data by Ella Jandt on Thomas R. Miller.

Telegraph and Texas Register, October 21, 1840: Alamo keepsake sent mother of William Irvine Lewis.

Texas National Register, January 18, 1845: Obituary of John W. Smith.

Books

Adair, A. G. and Crockett, M. H. [eds.], *Heroes of the Alamo*, 1956.

Archivo Historico Militar Mexicano, Num. 4, *Guía del Archivo Histórico Militar de México*, 1949.

Baker, D. W. C., *A Texas Scrapbook, Made up of the History, Biography, and miscellany of Texas and Its People*, 1875.

Bancroft, Hubert Howe, *The Works of Hubert Howe Bancroft*, Vol. XVI, *History of the North Mexican States and Texas*, 1889.

Barker, E. C. and Williams, A. W. [eds.], *The Writings of Sam Houston*, Vol. IV, 1941.

Binkley, William C. [ed.], *Official Correspondence of the Texas Revolution, 1835-1836*, I, 1936.

Binkley, William C., *The Texas Revolution*, 1952.

Brown, John Henry, *Indian Wars and Pioneers of Texas*, 1904.

Burleson, Georgia J. [compiler], *The Life and Writings of Rufus C. Burleson*, 1901.

Callcott, Wilfrid Hardy, *Santa Anna, the Story of an Enigma Who Once Was Mexico*, 1936.

Castañeda, Carlos E., *The Mexican Side of the Texan Revolution*, 1928.

Castañeda, Carlos E., *Our Catholic Heritage in Texas, 1519-1936*. Vol. VI, *The Fight for Freedom*, 1950.

Chabot, Frederick C., *With the Makers of San Antonio*, 1937.

Chapman, John A., *History of Edgefield County*, 1897.

Corner, William, *San Antonio de Bexar*, 1890.

Cox, Mamie Wynne, *The Romantic Flags of Texas*, 1936.

Crockett, David, *Col. Crockett's Exploits and Adventures in Texas*, 1836.

Delaney, Caldwell, *Deep South*, 1942.

DeShields, James T., *Tall Men with Long Rifles*, 1935.

Dewees, W. B., *Letters of an Early Settler in Texas*, 1858.

Dixon, Sam Houston, and Kemp, Louis Wiltz, *The Heroes of San Jacinto*, 1932.

Douglas, Claude Leroy, *James Bowie: The Life of a Bravo*, 1944.

Duval, J. C., *Early Times in Texas*, 1892.

Edward, David B., *The Emigrant's, Farmer's, and Politician's Guide*, 1836.

Ehrenberg, Herman, *With Milam and Fannin*, 1935.

Field, Joseph E., *Three Years in Texas Including a View of the Texan Revolution*, 1836.

Foote, Henry Stuart, *Texas and the Texans*, 1841.

Foreman, Grant, *Pioneer Days in the Early Southwest*, 1926.

Friend, Llerena, *Sam Houston, the Great Designer*, 1954.

Gray, William F., *From Virginia to Texas*, 1909.

Green, Rena Maverick [ed.], *Memoirs of Mary A. Maverick*, 1921.

Green, Rena Maverick [ed.], *Samuel Maverick, Texan: 1803-1870*, 1952.

Hanighen, Frank Cleary, *Santa Anna; the Napoleon of the West*, 1934.

History of Alabama and Dictionary of Alabama Biography.

Holley, Mary Austin, *Texas*, 1836.

Horgan, Paul, *Great River—the Rio Grande in North American History*, 1954.

Houston, Andrew Jackson, *Texas Independence*, 1938.

Houstoun, M. C., *Texas and the Gulf of Mexico, or Yachting in the New World*, 1844.

James, Marquis, *The Raven*, 1929.

Jenkins, John Holmes III [ed.], *Recollections of Early Texas*, 1958.

Johnson, Francis White [ed. Eugene C. Barker and E. W. Winkler], *A History of Texas and Texans*, 1914.

Kennedy, William, *Texas, Its Rise, Progress, and Prospects*, 1840.

Lane, Walter P., *Adventures and Recollections*, 1887.

LeClerc, Frédéric, *Le Texas et Sa Révolution*, 1840.

Linn, John J., *Reminiscences of Fifty Years in Texas*, 1883.

Lundy, Benjamin, *The Life, Travels, and Opinions of Benjamin Lundy*, 1847.

Lundy, Benjamin, *The War in Texas*, 1836.

Menchaca, Antonio, *Memoirs*, 1937.

Morphis, J. M., *History of Texas*, 1874.

Morrell, Z. N., *Flowers and Fruits in the Wilderness*, c. 1872.

Muir, Andrew Forest, *Texas in 1837*, 1958.

Myers, John Meyers, *The Alamo*, 1948.

Newell, Rev. C., *History of the Revolution in Texas*, 1838.

Nieto, Angelina; Hefter, J.; and Brown, Mrs. John Nicholas, *El Soldado Mexicano, 1837-1847*, 1958.

Niles, John M., *South America and Mexico with a Complete View of Texas*, 1838.

Nixon, Pat Ireland, *A Century of Medicine in San Antonio*, 1936.

Olmsted, Frederick Law, *A Journey Through Texas, or a Saddle-Trip on the Southwestern Frontier*, c. 1857.

Ramsdell, Charles, *San Antonio, a Historical and Pictorial Guide*, 1959.

Riley, B. F., *History of Conecuh County, Alabama*, 1881.

Robles, Vito Alessis, *Coahuila y Texas* [n.d.].

Rourke, Constance M., *Davy Crockett*, 1934.

Shackford, James, *David Crockett, the Man and the Legend*, 1956.

Siegel, Stanley, *A Political History of the Texas Republic, 1836-1845*, 1956.

Smithwick, Noah, *Evolution of a State*, 1900.

Sowell, Andrew Jackson, *Early Settlers and Indian Fighters of Southwest Texas*, 1890.

Sowell, Andrew Jackson, *Rangers and Pioneers of Texas*, 1884.

Stiff, Edward, *The Texan Emigrant*, 1840.

Texas Folklore Publications No. XV, *In the Shadow of History*, 1939.

Texas State Library, *Papers of Mirabeau Buonaparte Lamar*, 1920.

Thrall, Homer S., *A Pictorial History of Texas*, 1879.

Tinkle, Lon, *Thirteen Days to Glory*, 1958.

Tolbert, Frank X., *The Day of San Jacinto*, 1959.

Tornel y Mendivil, José María, *Tejas y Los Estados-Unidas de América en sus Relaciones con la República Mexicana*, 1837 (trans. C. E. Castañeda).

Urrea, José, *Diario*, 1838 (trans. by C. E. Castañeda).

Valades, José C., *Santa Anna y la Guerra de Tejas*, 1936.

Webb, Walker Prescott [ed.], *The Handbook of Texas*, 1952.

Willson, Marcius, *American History Comprising History of the United States, History of Mexico, and History of Texas*, 1847.

Winkler, Ernest William, *Manuscripts, Letters and Documents of Early Texas, 1821–1845*, 1937.

Woodman, David, *Guide to Texas Emigrants*, 1835.

Wooten, Dudley Goodall, *A Comprehensive History of Texas*, 1898.

Yanaguana Society, *Texas Letters*, 1940.

Yoakum, Henderson, *History of Texas from Its First Settlement in 1685 to Its Annexation to the United States in 1846*, 1856.

Index

Abolitionists, 45, 169
Agua Dulce Creek, 139
Alabama, 32, 172
Alamán, Lucas, 31
Alamo (see also guns, flags, etc.)
    arrangement of, 59-60, 77
    decision to hold, 60-61, 78, 79, 85
    nature of garrison, 83, 86
    orders to abandon, 75, 200-201
    preparations at, 77 ff.
    shortages at, 59, 60, 76, 85
    warnings received by, 77, 78-79,
        87-88
    why named, 40
Alavez, Capt., 66
Alazan Creek, 100
Aldama battalion, 138, 150, 156, 159
Alexandria Gazette, 21
Allen, James L., 152, 205
Allende battalion, 124
Almonte, Col. Juan, 118, 178, 208,
    209
    at Alamo, 139, 158, 175
    and Crockett, 175, 206
    and San Jacinto, 187, 188, 189, 196
    Santa Anna and, 66, 104, 147, 150-
        151
Alsbury, Dr. Horace, 95, 130, 133
Alsbury, Juana, 95, 106, 164-165, 176,
    205, 208
Amador, Gen. Juan V., 159, 163
Amat, Col. Agustin, 148, 158
Ampudia, Gen. Pedro, 72, 129
Anáhuac, Tex., 32, 33, 34, 36, 37
Andrade, Gen. Juan José, 65, 68, 71,
    209
Arcadia Coffee House, 45
Archer, B. T., 171
Arch Street Theater (Phila.), 171
Arkansas, 21, 23, 26

Arkansas Gazette, 172, 190, 207, 208,
    209
Artillery, Mexican, 70, 72
    at Alamo, 106, 108, 114, 138, 143-
        146
    at San Jacinto, 193, 194, 195
Athens, Ga., 23
Augustin I, Emperor of Mexico, 63
Austin, Stephen F., 22, 27, 29, 34, 35,
    36, 38, 40, 64
Autry, Martha, 24, 49, 54-55
Autry, Mary, 167-168
Autry, Micajah, 24, 43-44, 49, 54-55,
    132
Avon, N. Y., 19, 81
Ayers, David, 142

Badgett, Jesse, 81, 209
Baker, Mrs. Isaac, 29
Baker, Capt. Moseley, 129
Baker, William Charles M., 144
Ballentine, Richard W., 55, 82
Baltimore, Md., 57
Baltimore American, 20
Baltimore Chronicle, 45
Barcena, Andres, 181
Bardstown, Ky., 171
Barnard, Dr. Joseph Henry, 55, 140,
    210
Barragan, Capt., 189, 193
Barrymore, W., 17
Basquez, Juan, 66
Bateman farm, 15, 127
Batres, Col. José, 102
Battle of Medina, 63
Baugh, Capt. John J., 47, 77, 153, 154-
    155, 162
Becerra, Francisco, 119, 209
Ben (orderly), 150-151, 178, 179, 180,
    182-183, 208
Bennett, Col. Joseph, 195

Beretta, J. K., 204
Bexar, *see* San Antonio de Bexar
Biddle, Nicholas, 51
Blair, John, 202
Blair, Samuel B., 85
Blake, R. R., 202
Bonham, James Butler, 75, 78
  at Alamo, 101, 136-137, 146, 165
  death of, 165, 168
  early life of, 134-136
  and Fannin, 91, 98, 133
  as leader, 132-134
  and Mobile Greys, 47, 135-136
  and Texas Revolution, 44
  and Travis, 135, 136
Borden, Gail, 183
Borgara, Anselmo, 181
Boston, Mass., 17, 20, 42, 43, 44, 47, 48, 168, 173
Boston *Morning Post*, 42
Bowie, James, 83, 136, 170
  at Alamo, 75 ff., 96, 102, 144, 164, 200
  death of, 165, 177, 178, 205
  early life of, 26-28
  and Fuentes, 85, 153
  and Houston, 27, 75, 76, 200
  illness of, 78, 84-85, 106, 123, 144, 199-200
  as leader, 27, 56, 77, 78-79, 84-85, 86, 102, 144
  marriage of, 27
  and Rose, 75, 147
  and Sand Bar fight, 26
  and San Saba mine, 27
  and 1835 siege of Bexar, 56
  and Travis, 84-85, 98, 102, 104, 105-106, 144
Bowie, Ursula, 27, 28, 95
Bradburn, Col. John, 34-35, 36, 37
Brazoria, Tex., 16, 29, 36, 38, 136, 137, 211
Brazos Guards, 90
Brazos River, 186, 187, 188, 199
Breece, Capt. Thomas H., 47
Bringas, Col. Juan, 108, 110
Briscoe, Andrew, 207
Brooks, Capt. John Sowers, 49, 91, 113, 131, 139-140, 152, 204
Brown, Robert, 109
Bryan, Guy, 16
Buffalo, N. Y., 172
Buffalo Bayou, 188, 189, 192, 193
Burgin, Abner, 52
Burleson, Gen. Edward, 56, 57, 58
Burnet, David G., 184, 187

Bustamente, Presidente Anastacio, 35
Bustillo, Domingo, 89
Byron, George Gordon, 42, 134, 174

Cairo, Ill., 21
Candelaria, Madam, 208
Carey, Capt. William R., 57, 86, 107, 108, 162
Caro, Ramón, 66, 67, 149, 158, 177, 196, 198, 203, 206, 209
Cassiano, José, 74, 78
Castañeda, Lt., 38-39
Castrillón, Gen. Manuel Fernández, 65, 124, 148, 161, 174-175, 196
Cato, Rosanna, 32
"centralism," 32, 64
Chapultepec, Mex., 212
Charleston, S. C., 17, 43, 56, 168, 173
Charleston *Courier*, 168
Chenoworth, Capt., 130
Childress, George, 44, 171
cholera, 28
church of the Alamo, 60, 76, 93, 97, 107, 152, 156, 175, 205
Cibolo Creek, 86, 127, 130, 136, 182
Cincinnati, 172, 193
Claiborne, Ala., 32
Clark, Isabelle, 53
Clark, M. B., 214
Clarksville, Ark., 53
Cloud, Daniel William, 21, 41, 43, 54, 173
Coahuila, Mex., 35, 70, 100, 211
Coleman's Company, 56
Collinsworth, Capt. James, 39-40, 200
colonization of Texas, under Mexico
  attempts to encourage, 22-23, 30
  empresarios, 22, 35
  Law of 1825, 22, 31
  misgivings, 31
  repressive measures, 31-32, 34, 36-37
Colorado River, 80, 184, 186, 187
Columbia, 17
Columbia, Tex., 16, 29
Columbia Encyclopedia, 207
Columbus, 45, 55
Comanche, 207
Comanches, 29, 181
Committee of Twenty, 44
Committees of Safety, 38, 39
Concepción, Battle of, 56, 90
Connell, Sampson, 182
Constitution of *1824* (Mexican), 32, 49, 100, 210-211

Convention, to establish Texas govt., 81, 129, 141, 142, 204, 211
Conway, M., 56
Copano, Tex., 38, 75, 200
Cós, Gen. Martin Perfecto de, 135
    at Alamo, 60, 148, 149, 151, 154, 158, 159-160
    at Copano, 38
    as leader, 37
    at San Antonio, 40, 56, 57, 73
    at San Jacinto, 194
    and Santa Anna, 37, 67, 138
Cottle, George Washington, 29
couriers from Alamo
    Allen, 152, 204-205
    Bonham, 91, 98, 117, 132 ff.
    Highsmith, 133-134
    Johnson, 96, 98
    Martin, 15, 107, 126
    Seguin, 111-112
    Smith, 97-98, 125, 141-143, 204
    Smithers, 15-16
    Sutherland, 97-98, 125
Courtman, Henry, 47, 48
Crockett, Col. David, 106, 137, 147
    at Alamo, 83, 96-97, 107, 109, 115-116, 117, 128, 144, 160, 161-162
    death of, 175, 176, 178, 198, 206-207
    description of, 52, 115-116
    early life of, 49 ff.
    at Nacogdoches, 53-54
    political career of, 50-53, 169-170
    and Tennessee Mounted Volunteers, 54-55, 81-82, 160, 161-162
    trip to Texas, 52-55
Cruz, Antonio, 112
Cummings, David P., 46, 82, 83, 86, 88, 127
Cummings, John, 33
Cummings, Rebecca, 33, 34, 142, 145, 186
Cunningham, Robert, 22
customs duties, 35, 36, 65

Damon & Pythias, 44
Darst, Jacob C., 24, 29, 38-39, 126
Davis, G. W., 214
Davis, John, 214
Declaration of Independence of Texas, 129, 133, 142, 210
Dedrick, George, 42
Degüello, 159
Delgado, Col., 195, 196
Denison, Stephen, 47-48
De Sauque, Capt., 130
Despallier, Charles, 109

Detroit *Democratic Free Press,* 206
Dewees, William, 24, 25
Díaz, Juan, 101
Dickinson, Capt. Almeron, 38-39, 199
    at Alamo, 77, 85, 107, 108, 123, 128, 165
    background of, 23, 29-30
    death of, 165
    and family, 95, 115, 160
Dickinson, Angelina, 95, 153, 156, 166, 175, 179, 180, 207
Dickinson, Susannah, 200, 207
    at Alamo, 95, 146, 156, 160, 166, 175-176
    and husband, 95, 115, 160
    and Santa Anna, 179
    and Travis' speech, 146, 201, 202-203
    and trip to Gonzales, 179, 180-182
Dimitt, Capt., 96
Dimitt's Landing, 121
Dolores cavalry, 124, 133, 161
Dolson, Sgt. George M., 206
Donohoe farm, 186
Dover, Sherod, 56-57, 213
Dromundo, Col. Ricardo, 66, 177
Duel, Lewis, 23
Du Pont, M., 51
Duque, Col. Francisco, 148, 149, 156, 161
Durango, Tex., 66
Duval, Burr H., 204
Duval, William P., 204
Duval's Kentucky Mustangs, 47
Duvalt, Andrew, 215

earthworks, Mexican, 104, 106, 108, 110, 117, 124, 133, 144, 146
Edward, David, 24-25
El Mosquito Mexicano, 71, 72
empresarios, 22, 35
Esparza, Gregorio, 105, 132, 165, 178, 208, 209
Esparza, Mrs. Gregorio, 175, 176, 208
Esparza, Enrique, 105, 155, 166, 201
Evans, Robert, 165-166
Exchange Hotel (Cincinnati), 172

Fall of the Alamo . . . , 171
Falmouth, Mass., 26
fandango, 83, 89, 90, 92
Fannin, Col. James Walker, 113, 118, 126, 129, 137, 148, 181
    and Alamo, 119-121, 122, 124, 130-131, 132, 139, 152, 199, 204
    early life of, 90-91

at Goliad, 90, 98, 99, 112, 117, 119-120, 124, 133, 136, 139-140, 184
as leader, 90-91, 99, 120-121, 122, 140
surrender and death of, 184, 186
Ferguson, Joseph G., 140
Filisola, Gen. Vicente, 70, 72
and Alamo, 210
and San Jacinto, 188, 189, 194
and Santa Anna, 64, 65, 71, 118, 186
firearms
Mexican, 67, 68, 116
Texan, 68, 115
flags
at Alamo, 210-212
blue star, Velasco, 211
"Come and Take It," Gonzales, 40
lone star and stripes, Victoria, 211
Moseley Baker's, 129
New Orleans Greys', 48, 163, 178, 211, 212
Red, flown from San Fernando, 13, 101, 117, 139
red, white, blue and green, San Felipe, 211
Travis', purchased for $5, 80, 211
tricolor, Centralist govt., 101, 163
tricolor, two-star, 100-101, 211
tricolor, *1824*, 210
Flaherty, Capt., 17
Flanders, John, 20, 21, 125
Flórez *rancho*, 119
Floyd, Dolphin Ward, 20-21, 23, 125, 153
Floyd, Ester, 125
Fontaine, W. W., 198
Foote, Henry Stuart, 199
Forbes, John, 54
Forsyth, John Hubbard, 19, 20, 81
Fort Defiance, 99, 121
Frankfort (Ky.) *Argus*, 169
Frankfort (Ky.) *Commonwealth*, 206-207
Fuentes, Antonio, 85, 95, 153
Fulton, Ark., 53
Fuqua, Galba, 126, 156

Galveston, Tex., 17, 36-37, 188
Galveston Bay, 189
Gaona, Gen. Antonio, 118, 148, 167, 186
and Alamo, 138
and graft, 65-66
on the march, 68, 71, 110, 124, 129, 189
García, Margarito, 108

Garnett, William, 81, 86
Gaston, John E., 39, 126, 213-214
Gaston, Sydney, 126
General Consultation, 38, 56
Georgia, 90, 216, 217, 218, 219
Georgia battalion, 47
German volunteers, 47, 48
Giddings, G. A., 191
Goliad, Texas, 39, 75
couriers to, 91, 96, 98, 117, 132 ff., 152, 204
efforts to relieve Alamo, 112-113, 119-122, 131
preparations to defend, 90-91, 99, 121, 130, 139-140
surrender and massacre, 184, 186, 190
Gonzales, José María, 152, 154
Gonzales, Petra, 95, 208
Gonzales, Texas, 29-30
couriers to, 15, 97-98, 107
relief force, 123 ff., 132, 156
revolution starts at, 38-40
survivors sent to, 179, 180-182
withdrawal from, 182 ff.
Gonzales Mounted Volunteers, 126
Goodrich, Benjamin, 168, 191
Goodrich, Edmund, 168
Goodrich, John Camp, 168
Gorostiza, Manuel Eduardo de, 17
Grant, Dr. James, 58, 139
Gray, William, 191
Greeley, Horace, 190, 191
Greensborough, Ala., 172
Grimes, Jesse, 142, 143, 211
Guadalupe River, 15, 39, 125, 127, 129, 130, 182
Guerrero, José María ("Brigido"), 166, 208, 213
Guide to Texas Immigrants, 30
guns of Alamo, 13, 76, 77, 98, 101, 106, 108-109, 114-115, 123, 128, 143, 155

Hagerty, James, 204
"Hail, the Conquering Hero Comes," 53
Hamilton, Gov., 135
Hamm, Mrs., 33
Harrisburg, Tex., 184, 187, 188, 189, 190, 194
Hawkins, M., 211
Herrera, Blas, 87
Hewlitt's Coffee House (New Orleans), 17
Highsmith, Ben, 133-134

Hill, Henry, 44
Hill, Capt. W. G., 205
Holley, Mary Austin, 25, 172, 207
Hondo River, 89
House, Ester, 125
Houston, Sam, 46, 59, 104, 198
  and Alamo, 75-76, 79, 181, 182, 200-201, 208-209
  and appeal for American aid, 41, 43
  and Bonham, 132-133, 135-136
  and Bowie, 27, 75-76, 84
  as congressman, 42
  early life of, 24
  and Goliad, 186
  as governor of Tenn., 24
  and Lamar, 194
  as leader, 111, 182, 183
  and Mrs. Millsaps, 184
  and retreat from Gonzales, 182-186
  and San Jacinto, 187, 188, 189, 190, 192, 194, 195, 196
  and Santa Anna, 196
  and Swarthout, 29

Illinois, 21, 23
Indalencio, Juan, 101
independence, sentiment in Texas for, 35, 48-49, 78, 210-212
Indiana, 21
Iturbi, Augustin, 63

Jack, Patrick, 34-35
Jackson, Andrew, 17, 51, 169-170
Jackson, Tenn., 24, 167
Jackson, William Daniel, 23, 86
Jameson, Green B., 23
  and Alamo, 76, 77, 86, 102, 114, 115, 116, 137, 144, 159
  as lawyer, 29, 59
Jenkins, John, 182
Jiménez battalion, 101, 149, 150, 163, 165
Joe (slave), 153, 155, 156, 176-177, 179, 180-181, 207, 208
Johnson (courier), 96, 98
Johnson, Col. Frank, 58, 101, 122, 133, 139
Jones, Isaac, 53

Karnes, Henry, 181
Kellogg, Johnnie, 126, 153
Kellogg, Sydney, 126, 182, 184
Kent, Andrew, 23, 153

Kent, Elizabeth, 23
Kentucky, 21, 23, 95
Kentucky Mustangs, 47
Kerr, Nathaniel, 83
Kimball, George C., 125, 126, 127, 130, 133, 153, 162
Kimball, Prudence, 125
King, John G., 126, 127, 213
King, William P., 127

Labadie, Dr. N. D., 207
Lafitte, Jean, 26
Lamar, Mirabeau Buonaparte, 194
La Peña, see Peña
Laredo, Tex., 73, 87, 100
La Villita, San Antonio, 109, 110, 111, 115, 144, 145
Ledon, Dr. Luis Castrillo, 212
Lentner, Capt., 55
Leona River, 79
Leon Creek, 93
Lewis, Nat, 26, 93, 94, 95, 96, 97-98
Lewis, William Irvine, 46
Lewiston, Pa., 46
Lexington, Ky., 172
"Lexington of Texas," 125
Liberty, Tex., 32, 82
Lindley, Jonathan L., 23, 126
"Line Speech" by Travis, 146, 201-204
Linn, John J., 30
Linn, William, 48
Lion Theatre (Boston), 17
Little Goodie Two Shoes, 17
Little Rock, Ark., 53
long barracks, 59, 96, 163, 205
Loranca, Sgt., 205
Losoya, Toribio Domingo, 213
Lost Prairie, Ark., 53
Louisiana, 26
Louisville, Ky., 21
Louisville *Journal,* 170
low barracks, 59-60, 97, 106, 116, 205
Lundy, Benjamin, 169
Lynch's Ferry, 188, 189, 192, 193

McCardle, Henry Arthur, 199
McCoy, Jesse, 29-30, 126
McDonald & Arnold's, 45
McDowell, William, 46-47, 54
McGregor, John, 29, 86, 115, 117, 128
McKean's bookstore, 23
McKinney & Williams, 205
McMullen house, 108
Macon, Ga., 44
Madison, James, 46, 201

Main Plaza, 26, 81, 85, 93, 101, 105, 128, 150, 176
mal de lengua, 72
Malone, William T., 23, 86
maps: Mexican plan for assault, 157
 San Antonio during siege, 103
 Santa Anna's route to San Antonio, 69
 Santa Anna's route to San Jacinto, 185
Marengo County, Ala., 55
Martha, 36-37
Martin, Albert, 15, 38-39, 102, 104, 107, 126
Martinez, Lt. Damasco, 163
Masonic Hall (N. Y.), 171
Massachusetts, 20, 21
Matagorda, Tex., 189
Matamoros, Mex., 58
Matamoros expedition, 58, 76, 90, 91, 110, 122, 136, 148, 149, 150, 165
Matawamkeag, 47
Maverick, Sam, 57, 81
Mayan Indians, 66, 71
Medina, Battle of, 63
Medina River, 87, 90
Melton, Eliel, 132, 161
Memphis, Tenn., 44, 52
Memphis *Enquirer,* 169, 170, 173
Menchaca, Manuel, 90, 98, 119
Menefee, Sally, 168
Mexican army, organization of, 69-70
 finances, 65, 73
 graft, 65-66, 177
 medical service, 72, 148, 177
 supplies, 67, 73, 119
 transport, 70
 uniforms, 68
 weapons, 67, 68
Mexicans in the Alamo, 87, 95, 111, 141, 145, 155
Mexico, 22, 31-32
Mexico City, 64, 119, 177, 178
Mifflin County, Pa., 46
Milam, Ben, 57
Military Plaza, 26, 93, 97, 101
Mill Creek, Tex., 33, 186
Miller, Thomas R., 126, 153
Millsaps, Isaac, 126
Millsaps, Mrs. Isaac, 184
Mims, Joseph, 121
Mississippi, 190
Missouri, 21, 23, 24, 26
Mobile, Ala., 17, 44, 135, 171
Mobile Greys, 47, 135
Monclova, Mex., 36, 70, 73

Monterey Cathedral, 65
Montgomery, Ala., 135
Moore, Robert B., 48
Moore, Willis, 141
Morales, Col., 110, 149, 160, 163, 165, 186
"Muldoon Catholics," 31
Musquiz, Gov., 89
Musquiz house, 95, 176
Musselman, Robert, 46, 48

Nacogdoches, Tex., 16, 29, 41, 45-46, 48, 49, 53, 54, 75, 86, 147, 186, 208
Nacogdoches County Courthouse, 202
Nacogdoches County Land Office, 214
Nash, Prudence, 125
Nashville, Tenn., 44, 168
Natchez, Miss., 44, 171-172, 173
Natchez *Courier,* 170
Natchitoches, La., 41, 43
Natchitoches (La.) *Red River Herald,* 41
National Intelligencer, 17-18
Nava, Andres, 198
Navarro, Gertrudis, 95, 164-165, 176, 208
Navarro, Juana, *see* Alsbury
Navarro, Louisiano, 178-179
Navarro, Capt. José Juan Sánchez, *see* Sánchez
Navarro family, 77
Navarro home, 176
Neill, Col. James C., 58-59, 61, 75-76, 77, 79, 83-84, 211
New Orleans, La., 17, 21, 22-23, 45-46, 47, 55, 168, 207
New Orleans *Bee,* 18, 21
New Orleans *Commercial Bulletin,* 45, 167, 168-169, 170-171
New Orleans Greys, 46, 47-49, 55, 59, 76, 140, 178, 211, 212
New Orleans *Post-Union,* 207
New Washington, Tex., 188, 189
New York, N. Y., 17, 20, 45, 47, 168, 171
New York *American,* 18
New York *Commercial Advertiser,* 20, 42, 45
New York *Evening Post,* 17
New York *Post,* 169
Nixon house, 104
Nobles, Lt., 96
North Carolina, 20, 24, 46

Nueces River, 79, 88, 89
Nuevo León, Mex., 73
Nullification crisis, 134
Nuñez, Sgt. Felix, 161, 165, 205

Ohio, 46, 48
Ontario, 172
Othella, 171

Pacheco, Estaban, 108
Patton, William, 52
"Peace party," 36
Peña, Col. José de la: and Alamo,
  162, 164, 165, 175
  as leader, 66
  and Santa Anna, 150
  thoughts of, 150, 151, 162
  and Travis, 206
Pendleton, S. C., 134, 135
Pennsylvania, 42, 83
Pensacola, Fla., 17
Pérez, Antonio, 181, 206
Pérez, Manuel, 176
Philadelphia, Pa., 20, 23, 44, 171, 190
Philadelphia *Courier*, 45
Philadelphia *Gazette*, 41
Pittsburgh, Pa., 47
Pollard, Dr. Amos, 20, 21, 23, 78, 85,
  211
Ponton, Andrew, 97
Portland, Me., 168
Port Lavacca, 208
Potrero Street, 87, 95, 96, 139
Potter, Capt. Ruben M., 198, 199,
  209-210
powder house, 15, 110, 124, 137, 144
Powder House Hill, 133, 136, 139
Presidio de Rio Grande, Mex., 73
Provisional Council, 77-78, 200
Provisional Government of Texas,
  38, 56, 77-78

Quachita, 55
Quitman, John A., 172
"Quitman Fencibles," 172

railroads, 20, 22
Ramirez y Sesma, *see* Sesma
Raymond, Miss., 141
Ream, Lt. S. Y., 83
Red Bank, S.C., 32, 134
Red River Exchange, 41
Red River Valley, Ark., 21, 53
Red Rovers of Alabama, 47
Refugio, Tex., 216
Reyes, N., 67
Reynolds, John Purdy, 33, 46-47, 54

Richardson's Hotel, 45
Richmond, Tex., 199
Richmond, Va., 171
Rio Frio, 78, 89
Rio Grande, 62, 73, 74, 78, 87, 88,
  110, 118
Rivas, cousin of Mrs. Rodríguez, 87,
  92
Robinson, Lt. Gov., 91, 99, 113, 122,
  127, 130, 136
Rodríguez, Ambrosio, 87, 92
Rodríguez, Mrs. Ambrosio, 87, 92
Rodríguez, José, 92
Rodríguez, Pablo, 92
Romero, Col., 148, 149, 158, 161
Rose, James M., 46, 54, 109, 114, 201
Rose, Louis, 75, 147, 201, 202, 203,
  214
Rose (P. W.) family, 16, 152, 183
Ross, John, 172
Rubio, Señor, 73
Rubio & Errazu, 65
Ruiz, Francisco, 105, 178, 205, 206
"Runaway Scrape," 184, 190
Rusk, Sec'y of War, 190
Russelville, Ky., 173

Sabinas River, 73
Sabine River, 24, 46, 48, 53
St. Augustine, Fla., 48, 54
St. Louis, Mo., 21
Salado Creek, 15, 98, 180
Salisbury, Mass., 20
Saltillo, Mex., 66-67, 70
San Antonio, Texas, 13, 28-29, 62,
  75 ff.
  citizens in Alamo, 87, 95, 111, 141,
  145
  description of, 25-26, 109
  siege of 1835, 40, 56-57, 65
  sympathies of populace, 38, 74, 77,
  89, 90, 105, 145, 178-179
San Antonio River, 26, 59, 87
Sánchez, Capt. José Juan (Navarro),
  57, 58, 67, 138, 177, 205, 206
Sand Bar Fight, 26
San Felipe, Tex., 15-16, 29, 33, 37, 39,
  56, 59, 77, 78, 79, 86, 91, 129, 137,
  183, 186, 187, 211
San Jacinto, Battle of, 193-196, 197,
  207, 209
San Jacinto River, 188, 189, 192, 193,
  194
San Juan, Mex., 73
San Luis battalion, 148, 150
San Luis Potosí, 66, 119

San Miguel de Allende, Mex., 73
San Patricio, Tex., 122, 133, 139
San Pedro Creek, 101
San Saba mine, 27
Santa Anna, Gen. Antonio Lopez de, 77, 79, 92, 133, 182
  and Alamo, 91, 93, 102, 107-108, 110, 111, 116-117, 119, 121, 129, 145, 147 ff., 154, 156, 158, 167, 174-175, 177-179, 205, 206, 209, 210, 211-212
  attitude toward Americans, 62, 88, 89, 101
  background of, 62-63
  description of, 63, 64-65, 67, 90, 114
  and Mrs. Dickinson, 179
  as dictator, 35, 36, 37, 38, 63-64
  and finance, 65
  generals of, 65-66
  as leader, 67-68, 72, 73-74, 88-89, 100, 107-108, 110, 111, 119, 124, 148-149
  and march to Texas, 68-73, 88-90, 100-101
  and preparations for campaign, 65-69
  and San Antonio, 62, 65, 105
  and San Jacinto, 186 ff.
  sentiment against, 44, 169, 170-172
  sentiment for, 95
  and Tornel, 67
  troops of, 14, 66, 70-74, 87, 88, 89, 97, 100 ff., 138, 143 ff., 159, 188-189
  at Veracruz, 90
Santiago, 55-56
Saucedo, Trinidad, 95, 208
Scott, Sir Walter, 42-43, 134
Scott, Gen. Winfield, 169
Seguin, Capt. Juan, 92, 130, 133, 181, 213
  at Alamo, 102, 108, 111-112, 198
  and company of local Mexicans, 87, 100, 105, 155, 211
  as courier, 111-112
Seguin *rancho*, 119, 121
Seminole Indians, 46, 169
Serpent, 47
Sesma, Gen. Ramírez y, 78, 124
  and Fannin, 129
  as leader, 70, 73-74, 100
  and San Jacinto, 186, 188, 189
  and Santa Anna, 138, 147
  troops of, 88-90, 109, 110, 111, 114, 116, 136, 137, 144, 149, 186

Sevier County, Ark., 24
Sewell, Marcus L., 23, 126
Shackleford's Red Rovers, 47
Shakespeare Theater (Mobile), 44, 135
sharpshooting, 115-116
Sherman, Col. Sydney, 182, 193-194
Simmons, Cleland Kinloch, 55-56, 82, 109, 162
slavery, 31, 32, 90
smallpox, 55
Smith, Andrew H., 80
Smith, "Deaf," 181, 192, 193, 195
Smith, Gov. Henry, 77-78, 79, 80-81, 85, 86, 136, 200, 211
Smith, John W., 88, 104
  as courier, 97-98, 125, 141-143, 204
  discovers the Mexican army, 94-95
  as early settler, 26
  as guide, 126-128
  at siege of 1835, 57
Smithers, Launcelot, 15-16
Smithwick, Noah, 30
smuggling, 31, 32, 33, 36
soldaderas, 70-71, 196
Soldana, Capt. Rafael, 115
Soledad Street, 28, 89
South Carolina, 168
Southwestern Historical Quarterly, 204, 207
speculation, land, 26, 29, 33
Stafford's Point, 16, 183
Stanley, Col. E. H., 47
Starr, Franklin J., 86
steamboats, 20, 21
Steele, Alfonso, 195
Sterne, Adolphus, 45-46, 48-59
Stoneall's Tavern, 45
survivors of Alamo, 207-209
Sutherland, Dr. John, 78, 101, 125, 133
  as courier, 96-98
  discovers the Mexicans, 93-95
  and Lewis, 93
  and Seguin, 198
Sutherland, Fanny, 168
Sutherland, William D., 168
sutlers, Mexican, 71
Swarthout, Samuel, 29
Swiss Boy, 172

Tamaulipas *Gazette*, 62
Tammany Hall, 45
taxes, 30, 31
Taylor, Creed, 58
Taylor, Edward, 82

Taylor, George, 82
Taylor, James, 82
Telegraph and Texas Register, 38, 86, 174, 183, 188
telele, 72
Tennessee, 23, 24, 44, 50, 82, 83, 168, 190
"Tennessee Mounted Volunteers," 54, 81, 107, 108-109, 160, 161, 162
Tenorio, Capt. Antonio, 36, 37
Teran, Gen. Manuel Mier y, 32
"Texas fever," 23
"Texas Loan," 171
"Texas meetings," 44
Texas Republican, 37
"Thompsonian System," 78
Thompson's Ferry, 187, 189, 199
Tinaja, Tex., 129
Tinkle, Lindsy K., 52
Tolsa, Gen. Eugenio, 68, 167, 186
Toluca battalion, 138, 150, 156, 158
Tontine (Phila.), 171
Tornel, Minister of War, 67, 68, 88, 177
Torres, Lt. José María, 163
Tragedy of Venice Preserved, The, 45
Travis, Charles, 36, 80, 142-143, 152
Travis, Rosanna, 32, 36, 143
Travis, William Barret
  at Alamo, 84-88, 93, 109, 111-113, 114, 116, 117, 118, 125, 128, 137, 141-146, 152-153, 155-156, 191, 211-212
  appeals for aid, 13-14, 85, 91, 97, 98-99, 107, 111-112, 117, 129, 132, 141-143, 152
  arrival in Texas, 33
  and Bonham, 117, 134, 135
  and Bowie, 84-85, 98, 102, 104, 105-106, 144
  death of, 155-156, 162, 177, 178, 206
  description of, 32, 33, 34
  drawing the line, 146, 201-204
  early life, 32-33
  as leader, 34, 79-81, 83, 84-88, 93, 116
  and marriage, 32, 36
  ordered to Alamo, 79-81
  and Rebecca Cummings, 33, 142
  and Texas Revolution, 32, 34-37, 39, 56
  uniform of, 205
Tremont House (Boston), 17
True American, 17

"Twin Sisters," 193
Tyler, Gen. John S., 44

Ugartechea, Col., 38
United States Bank, 51
Urizza, Capt. Fernando, 158, 167, 207
Urrea, Gen. José, 66, 68, 122, 139, 167, 184, 189

Velasco, Tex., 16, 86, 211
Veracruz, Mex., 90
Veramendi, Juan Martín, 28
Veramendi, María Ursula de, 27
Veramendi family, 28
Veramendi house, 28, 95, 104
Victoria, Tex., 129, 211
Vince's Bayou, 189, 192
Vince's bridge, 189, 192, 193, 195, 196
Virginia, 48, 49

Wales, 217
Walker, Asa, 82-83
Walker, Jacob, 137, 166
Ward, Sgt. William B., 96, 132, 160
Ward's Georgia Battalion, 47
"War Party," 35
Warnell, Henry, 121, 144
  at Alamo, 86, 115, 118, 137
  death of, 208
  early life of, 23-24
Washington, D.C., 17, 50, 52
Washington-on-the-Brazos, 16, 82, 129, 133, 141, 183
Webster, Daniel, 51
Wharton, Col., 129, 130
Whigs, 18, 45, 51-52, 169
Wheelock, Lt., 47
Wheelock's Dragoons, 47
Williamson, Hiram J., 23, 77
Wolfe, Antony, 166
Woll, Adrian, 65
Woodman, M., 30
Wright, Maj. Morris, 26

Ximenes family, 92

Yellow Stone, 186, 187
Yturri house, 105, 150
Yucatán battalion, 66, 71

Zapadores battalion, 66, 138, 149, 150, 158, 162, 163
Zuber, William, 201-204